# LONG-TERM CARE

## 3RD EDITION

DEARBORN™
A **Kaplan Professional** Company

©1993, 1997, 1999, 2001 by Dearborn Financial Publishing, Inc.®
Published by Dearborn Financial Institute, Inc.®

Printed in the United States of America.

First printing, March 2001

**Library of Congress Cataloging-in-Publication Data**

Goetze, Jason G.
    Long-term care / [ Jason G. Goetze]. – – 3rd ed., Revised
      p.    cm.
    ISBN 0–7931–4797-2 (paper)
     1. Insurance, Long-term care– –United States.   2. Long-term care
facilities– –United States.   3. Medicare.   I. Dearborn Financial
Institute.  II. Title.
HG9396.G63   2001
362.1'6– –dc21                          99–22817
                                       CIP

# ·····  Table of Contents

# ····· Acknowledgment

T he publisher wishes to acknowledge and thank Jason G. Goetze as the principal author of this text. Mr. Goetze is Northwestern Mutual Life's Assistant Director of Long-Term Care Compliance and Marketing. He received a degree in finance from the University of Oregon and in 1998 he chaired the Health Insurance Committee at the Life Insurance Marketing and Research Association (LIMRA).

# ..... Introduction

Of what value is long-term care insurance? Let me tell you a personal story that answered this question for me in a powerful way. Several years ago, I was in Omaha, Nebraska, making a training film for the insurance company I was working for at the time. An elderly woman I'll call Mrs. Baines had volunteered to help me. Mrs. Baines had recently entered a nursing home, where she had made many new friends and become involved in the many activities that took place in the home. She seemed very happy and content with her new home. During one of our filming sessions, I asked Mrs. Baines where she would be if she didn't have long-term care insurance. She replied, "Up a creek without a paddle!" I remember smiling and thinking how cute that sounded coming from this delightful 78-year-old lady.

I didn't understand how serious and profound her comment was until several years later when I was back in Omaha and had the opportunity to talk with the agent who had introduced us. He told me that a nephew who handled Mrs. Baines's finances had told him that after Mrs. Baines's three-year benefit maximum had run out and her insurance benefit checks stopped coming, she had lost her will to live and had died a few months later. Mrs. Baines's plight has had a lasting influence on my life and work. It showed me how valuable long-term care insurance is when it's needed.

When you sell a policy that results in a claim that saves someone from destitution or dependence on others, you too will become a believer in long-term care insurance. This product does much more than just enhance your income. It enhances the quality of life of a person who depends on others for assistance with activities healthy people take for granted. When a person is no longer physically independent, long-term care insurance benefits ease the financial and emotional strain. These benefits may even keep the person alive longer.

Without long-term care insurance, will your clients need to sell the life insurance you sold them in order to pay for nursing home care? What will happen to the annuities and mutual funds you placed to be sure their retirement years would be financially independent? Will your own family and friends have to spend their retirement savings on long-term care? Will they be forced to depend on the government to pay for their care? Or will they be able to keep their pride and dignity by using long-term care insurance benefits to protect their assets and pay for their long-term care needs?

In 1992, I wrote the first edition of this course for Dearborn because I couldn't find training materials that gave agents the tools to be successful selling long-term care insurance. This third edition has even more information about long-term care providers and the payers of care, as well as questions to ask prospects and concepts to help them understand why they should consider purchasing long-term care insurance.

Learning and applying the information in this book will help you use long-term care insurance to protect people you know and people you'll meet. You'll benefit financially; they'll benefit before a claim from enhanced peace-of-mind and during a claim from the financial resources they need to pay for their care and maintain their pride and dignity.

Jason Goetze

# 1

# The Challenge of Long-Term Care

**A** mericans are living longer and many can expect to live a substantial portion of their lives in retirement. That's the good news. The bad news is, although statistics regarding longevity for older Americans may be improving, many individuals over age 65 still have to deal with poor health during their retirement years. As people age, they consume a larger proportion of health-care services because of chronic illnesses such as Alzheimer's disease, heart disease and stroke. Poor health means increased medical bills for services, medicine and equipment that may be only partially covered by health insurance. Furthermore, an extended nursing home stay or around-the-clock nursing care can quickly deplete a lifetime of savings.

The challenge of long-term care for the elderly is an opportunity for an agent to offer clients both an education and a well-chosen insurance product. Your knowledge of what types of policies clients might currently have, and whether those policies are adequate to meet their long-term care needs, is vital.

In this chapter, we provide an overview of the demographics and the medical and social changes that created the challenge of long-term care. We'll also look at the projected costs of providing health care for this aging population and ways to fund the cost of long-term care.

■ ■ ■ ■ ■

## ■ THE GRAYING OF AMERICA

Rapid advances in medical care and in health care technology have eliminated many major causes of premature death and terminal illness. As a result, the older population in the United States is growing rapidly. Since 1900, the percentage of Americans 65 and over has more than tripled from 4.1 percent in 1900 to 12.7 percent in 1997, and the number has increased 11 times from 3.1 million to 34.1 million. Furthermore, the older population will burgeon between the years 2010 and 2030 when the baby boomers (those born between 1946 and 1964) reach age 65. By 2030, there will be about 70 million older persons in the United States, more than twice their number in 1997. People over 65 will represent 13 percent of the population in 2000 and 20 percent of the population of the United States in 2030.

As people age, they often become less active and begin to face increasing infirmity and illness. They are more likely to suffer from chronic diseases such as arthritis, senile dementia and Alzheimer's disease. (See Ill. 1.1.) Chronic diseases develop gradually over months and years and last a long time. They often leave residual disabilities and require a long period of supervision, observation or care. Because of medical advancements, the chronically ill can be kept alive longer—but often at tremendous financial and emotional costs. Older people often become dependent on others for their care. In many cases, they turn to loved ones who may not have the time, ability or desire to meet those needs. Frequently the adult child is also a senior citizen who finds it difficult or impossible to care for a much older parent.

## ■ THE CHANGING ROLE OF THE FAMILY

Most elderly people depend on their family and friends to take care of them as they grow old. At this time, only about one in five elderly Americans who needs special care currently lives in a nursing home. But the demand for care will rise as the elderly population increases. Although most families would prefer to take care of their parents or other elderly relatives, they will have a difficult time providing that care.

Why is it so difficult for families to provide needed care for their elderly parents? Primarily, because during the past three decades the United States has experienced tremendous social changes that have affected the traditional family structure. Some of the most significant changes include:

- women in the workforce

- lower birth rates

- divorce

- increased mobility

- increased longevity

In addition to having other social and political consequences, these changes have limited the number of family members available to care for elderly relatives.

## Women in the Workforce

Prior to World War II, women traditionally married, raised their children and then cared for their elderly parents and in-laws. Women were the primary care providers for the family, so few had the time or energy to work outside the home for wages. The first major movement of women into the workforce came about as a result of World War II. By 1944, almost 20 million women were working at jobs previously held by men who were now overseas fighting a war. Even after the war ended, many women continued to work and were no longer able to devote the same amount of time to care for those remaining at home.

A second factor that moved women into the workforce was the women's movement, which began to raise questions about women's roles in the family and in society. In the past 25 years, women have made enormous social, legal and political gains. Regardless of how people perceive the movement, it has fostered many changes—socially and legally—that give women a new freedom of choice both at home and at work.

The third factor affecting women's traditional roles as wives and mothers is inflation. Even at modest levels, inflation has a significant effect on the cost of living. In today's economy, it often takes two incomes simply to stay abreast of rising costs. The time demands and pressures on a family with both spouses working make it difficult if not impossible to care for an elderly parent. Many families simply cannot sacrifice one spouse's income so that he or she can stay home to provide needed care to an elderly parent.

## Lower Birth Rates

When the United States was predominantly an agrarian society, large families were necessary to operate farms. As populations moved to the cities, however, the importance of a large family lessened. Today, birth rates are down and large families are rare. Smaller families mean fewer children to care for aging parents.

Many Americans are also marrying later in life and having children later. Commonly called the "sandwich generation," these people struggle to meet the needs of two generations: their aging parents and growing children. In many cases, people in this situation will actually spend more time caring for their parents than raising their children. Other Americans choose a career over marriage, live with a partner rather than marrying or remain single after a divorce or a spouse's death. Whatever the reason for their lifestyle choice, more and more people are remaining single and childless. As they age those who remained single and childless cannot turn to children for needed care.

### Divorce

People once married for life; today, however, many marriages end in divorce. As a result of many social pressures and trends, the "traditional" American family—wage earner father, homemaker mother and two children—is harder to find.

Divorces have created many single-parent families. Half of the children born today will live with only one parent most of their lives. Single parenthood often means poverty—more than 50 percent of single-parent families live below the national poverty level. Limited funds will simply not permit many single parents to take on the added financial and emotional responsibilities of caring for an aging parent.

After a divorce, a person cannot be expected to care for his or her ex-spouse or the ex-spouse's parents. In addition, a divorced person likely will have fewer people to turn to when he or she needs care.

### Increased Mobility

Most individuals leave their childhood homes to marry, travel or pursue career opportunities. Once children moved only a few blocks from home, but now they often live hundreds or thousands of miles from their parents. Air travel and telephones give the illusion of proximity and make it easier to live further away. But the reality is that physical distance makes it more difficult for children to care for parents who have aged and lost their ability to remain independent.

### Increased Longevity

Finally, thanks to medical technology and better health care, people are living much longer after retirement. A child born in 1997 could expect to live 76.5 years, about 29 years longer than a child born in 1900. Because of increased longevity, retirees themselves often have to care for their own 80-year-old and 90-year-old parents. This puts the retiree in a caregiving role at a time when he or she may need medical assistance or may have other plans for retirement.

There are also financial considerations for the retiree who is asked to care for a parent or spouse. Contrary to what many people believe, the cost of living does not automatically decline at retirement. Even with an employer-sponsored retirement plan and Social Security benefits, an individual and his or her spouse may not have adequate funds to support both their parents and themselves. A retiree's limited income may be insufficient when a spouse or other loved one requires expensive medical treatment or has other special needs.

This increased longevity means that more and more people will live long enough to experience some disability or impairment that will require ongoing assistance from another person. Whether the disability is sudden and major, such as a stroke, or gradual, such as a loss of vision or hearing, the elderly person will require some assistance in the home, at an adult day center or in a nursing home. Increasingly, long-term care is becoming a predictable life event for a large part of the U.S. population.

## ■ WHAT IS LONG-TERM CARE?

You'll often see nursing home care referred to as "long-term care." However, *long-term care (LTC)* generally refers to a broad range of medical, personal and environmental services provided to chronically ill, aged or disabled persons in an institution or in their place of residence. These persons require convalescent, physical supportive or restorative services on a long-term basis. Although care may be provided for short periods of time while a patient is recuperating from an accident or illness, long-term care generally refers to care provided for an extended period of time, normally more than 90 days. People receiving long-term care are not in an acute phase of an illness.

Typically, the need for long-term care arises when physical or cognitive conditions impair a person's ability to perform the basic activities of everyday life—eating a meal, taking a bath, getting dressed or moving from a bed to a chair. Long-term care may be provided by family, friends or a number of health care professionals. There are three levels of long-term care:

1. *Skilled care*. Continuous around-the-clock care provided by licensed health care professionals under the direct supervision of a physician and designed to rehabilitate or restore the care recipient.

2. *Intermediate care*. Intermittent care (three to four days per week) provided by registered nurses (RNs), licensed practical nurses (LPNs) and nurse's aides under the supervision of a physician, and, like skilled care, designed to rehabilitate or restore the care recipient.

3. *Custodial care*. Assistance in performing activities of daily living is provided by a number of professional and nonprofessional caregivers. Such care need not be provided under the supervision of a physician and typically is designed to maintain the care recipient's health condition rather than rehabilitate or "cure" the recipient.

### Long-Term Care Services

Long-term care services may be provided by *informal caregivers* (immediate family, relatives or friends) as well as *formal* or *professional providers* (physicians, nurses and therapists) and community-based *service providers* (adult day centers). Care can range from chore types of services to around-the-clock skilled nursing care. Formal care becomes necessary when family caregiving is inadequate or inappropriate. (The roles of these caregivers are discussed in more detail in Chapter 2.)

**ILL. 1.1 ■ *Common Chronic Conditions of the Elderly***

Alzheimer's disease                Hypertension
Arteriosclerosis                   Orthopedic ailments
Arthritis                          Sinusitis
Diabetes                           Varicose veins
Hearing impairments                Visual impairments
Heart conditions

As individuals age, they are likely to suffer from acute and/or chronic illnesses or conditions. An *acute illness* is a serious condition, such as pneumonia or influenza, from which the body can fully recover with proper medical attention. The patient may also need some assistance with chores for short periods of time until recovery and rehabilitation from the illness are complete.

Some people will suffer from *chronic conditions,* such as arthritis, heart disease or hypertension, that are treatable but not curable illnesses. When chronic conditions such as diabetes or heart disease initially manifest, many people ignore the inconvenience or pain they cause. Over time, however, a chronic condition frequently goes beyond being a nuisance and begins to hinder a person's independence. Eventually he or she must look to others for help with various activities such as eating, bathing or dressing. Many people with chronic illnesses eventually become impaired and need long-term care.

Because of chronic conditions or illnesses, the elderly or disabled often suffer from limitations in performing activities that most people take for granted. As shown in Illustration. 1.2, these *activities of daily living (ADLs)* include eating, dressing, toileting, bathing, continence and transferring from one location to another. The elderly may also be limited in performing one or more *instrumental activities of daily living (IADLs),* such as completing housework, using the telephone, managing money or preparing meals.

The first sign of a loss of independence is normally with IADLs. Typically, difficulties with such ADLs as bathing and dressing occur next. During this period, care can be *scheduled.* For example, a family member can bathe and dress the individual in the morning, go to work, then come back at night to put on their sleepwear. However, once an individual requires assistance with toileting, everything changes. The assistance can no longer be scheduled—it must be performed *on demand.* Regular, full-time assistance will be needed. (Ill. 1.3 shows how physical impairment progresses over time.)

Once a person suffers physical or cognitive impairment, personal care is often provided by family members. Professionals can help with this care when the impaired

### ILL. 1.2 ■ *Activities of Daily Living (ADLs)*

**Bathing**
The ability to wash oneself by spongebath; or in either a tub or shower, including the tasks of getting into or out of the tub or shower.

**Dressing**
The ability to put on and take off all items of clothing and any necessary braces, fasteners or artificial limbs.

**Toileting**
The ability to get to and from the toilet, get on and off the toilet, and perform associated personal hygiene.

**Transferring**
The ability to move in and out of a bed, chair or wheelchair.

**Continence**
The ability to maintain control of bowel and bladder function or, when unable to maintain control of bowel or bladder function, the ability to perform associated personal hygiene (including caring for catheter or colostomy bag).

**Eating**
The ability to feed oneself by getting food into the body from a receptacle (such as a plate, cup or table), or by a feeding tube, or intravenously.

person has no family or when the family is no longer able to provide the care. Because of the increasing size of the older population, there will be an increasing need for people who can supply *medical, environmental* and *personal care* to the elderly.

### Medical Care

After surgery or as the result of an illness, an elderly person may need medical care. Such care can help maintain the elderly person's health status, slow the progress of the condition that restricts the individual's independence or promote recuperation from a hospital stay or surgery. This care may be provided by physicians, registered nurses (RNs), licensed practical nurses (LPNs) or a variety of other types of health care professionals.

Advances in health sciences have made the delivery of health and health-related services easier and more efficient. With the aid of rented hospital beds, walkers, wheelchairs or monitoring devices, many patients can be treated at home rather than in a hospital. Equipment once used only in hospitals, such as X-ray machines and electrocardiographs, are now often portable and easily transported to the patient's home. Oxygen therapy, intravenous feeding and drug therapy, chemotherapy, respiratory therapy, catheter therapy and nutritional services are also available in the patient's home.

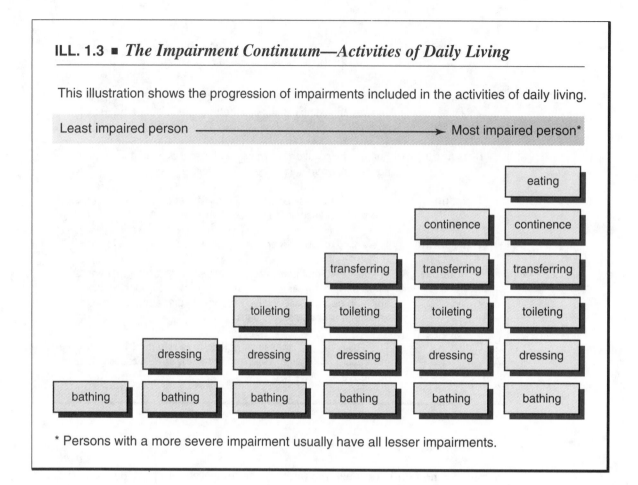

**ILL. 1.3 ■ *The Impairment Continuum—Activities of Daily Living***

This illustration shows the progression of impairments included in the activities of daily living.

Least impaired person ⟶ Most impaired person*

| | | | | | eating |
| | | | | continence | continence |
| | | | transferring | transferring | transferring |
| | | toileting | toileting | toileting | toileting |
| | dressing | dressing | dressing | dressing | dressing |
| bathing | bathing | bathing | bathing | bathing | bathing |

* Persons with a more severe impairment usually have all lesser impairments.

Typically, medical care is needed because of an acute condition that inhibits one's physical abilities. Individuals with these conditions will recover, be rehabilitated or die. The need for medical care lasts for shorter periods of time than either environmental or personal care.

### Environmental Care

When a person is elderly or disabled, the *environment* in which he or she lives can become threatening rather than comforting. Stairways, basements and long hallways become physical barriers. Labor saving devices, such as microwave ovens or remote controls, may be confusing to operate. Simple chores, such as preparing a meal or washing clothes, that once took only a few minutes now take hours to complete.

Activities that most people take for granted, such as grocery shopping, housecleaning and paying bills, can present huge difficulties for elderly or disabled persons. These IADLs, which range from basic housekeeping to balancing a checkbook, are daily tasks that ensure that the household environment operates smoothly.

In most cases, an elderly or a disabled person's family or friends are called on to provide environmental care. For example, an elderly person's son may provide yard maintenance and exterior repairs, such as painting and roof repair. In addition to cleaning the home, such a caregiver may adapt the interior with grab bars in the bathroom, wide doorways to accommodate a wheelchair and ramps to suit the elderly or disabled person's needs.

### Personal Care

Like environmental care, *personal care* is designed to help the elderly or disabled person throughout the day with tasks that other people take for granted. These tasks include bathing, dressing, toileting, transferring from a bed or chair, continence care and eating. The amount of assistance required varies by the level of disability or impairment that exists. Some people need to have the task completed for them; others need only minor assistance; some simply need a reminder to complete a task.

In some cases, IADLs, such as using a telephone, driving an automobile or using public transportation or handling money, can also be considered personal care. Again, the assistance required will depend on the degree of the person's disability. In addition to family assistance, some communities offer supportive or social services such as senior centers, telephone reassurance programs, church activities and Meals-on-Wheels programs. (These programs are discussed in more detail in Chapter 2.)

### How the Three Types of Care Come Together

Ideally, the three types of care—medical, environmental and personal—all work together to ensure that the needs of the care recipient are being met. Let's look at an example. Dave Smith is an elderly gentleman who suffers from several chronic conditions that have impaired his ability to live independently. Dave's children, Sara and Bill, help provide environmental care by managing Dave's finances, cooking meals, doing the laundry, shopping for groceries and mowing the lawn. A nurse's aide stops by daily to help Dave with his personal care, like bathing and dressing. A nurse also visits regularly to provide medical care by administering medications, changing bandages or adjusting IVs. The lines between the types of care and the providers are not always clearly drawn. For example, Sara and Bill often perform the personal care tasks on weekends. Individuals needing long-term care require different types of care and, quite often, different caregivers. However, there may come a time when, even with numerous caregivers, at-home care is no longer feasible.

## ▪ THE NEED FOR NURSING HOME CARE

A large percentage of the elderly population will spend some time in a nursing home. In fact, the Department for Health and Human Services estimates that in 1996 about 2.2 million elderly or disabled people received services in nursing homes at a cost of

---

### ILL. 1.4 ■ *Elderly People Using Nursing Homes*

| Age | Number of Persons | Percent Distribution |
|-----|-------------------|----------------------|
| 65–74 | 242,000 | 17.5% |
| 75–84 | 586,000 | 42.3% |
| 85 + | 557,000 | 40.2% |
| TOTAL | 1,385,000 | 100% |

*Source: Based on the 1995 National Nursing Home Survey conducted by the National Center for Health Statistics, Centers for Disease Control and Prevention.*

---

more than $78 billion. An additional 5.2 million elderly or disabled people remained at home but required some type of home care at a cost of about $30 billion.

Note the figures in Ill 1.4. They exclude all but the elderly. Based on the 1995 National Nursing Home Survey conducted by the National Center for Health Statistics, these figures most accurately reflect the number of elderly people using nursing homes. The nursing homes included in the survey routinely provided nursing and personal care services.

### Funding Long-Term Care

The cost of health care has been increasing at double-digit inflationary rates during the early 1990s. The national expenditure for long-term nursing home care is the fastest growing element of health care costs. Currently, the average cost of a nursing home stay is more than $45,000 per year—with the average stay being 2.5 years. In some urban areas, the costs already exceed $50,000 annually. With such staggering costs, approximately 75 percent of the elderly cannot now afford to finance even one year in a nursing home. Even worse, the cost of an annual nursing home stay is projected to be $97,000 by 2030.

Who pays for the cost of nursing home care? Most of the cost of nursing home care is paid by the nursing home resident or by his or her family. In addition, individual taxpayers absorb rising health care costs for the poor, the disabled and the elderly by funding Medicare and Medicaid programs with their taxes, even though the federal budget deficit has increased pressure to reduce benefits in both programs over the past several years. As shown in Ill. 1.5, about 12 percent of nursing home costs were paid by Medicare while another 48 percent were paid for by Medicaid.

Many elderly people feel their health care needs are adequately met by Medicare and Medigap policies. However, these policies will be of little use should the elderly person develop a chronic illness and need nursing home care. Currently,

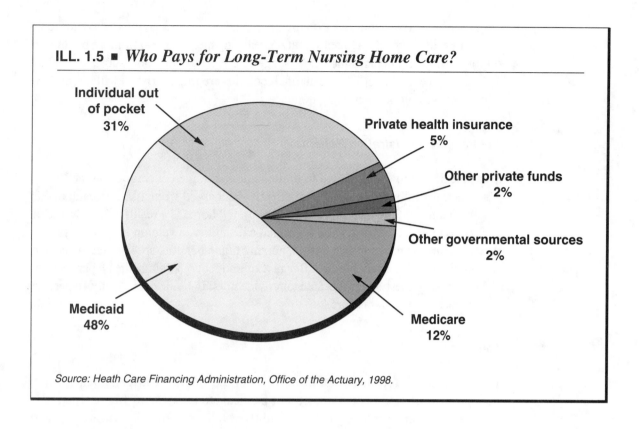

**ILL. 1.5 ■ *Who Pays for Long-Term Nursing Home Care?***

Individual out of pocket 31%

Private health insurance 5%

Other private funds 2%

Other governmental sources 2%

Medicaid 48%

Medicare 12%

*Source: Heath Care Financing Administration, Office of the Actuary, 1998.*

there are six sources of funds that most people use to meet their long-term care expenses:

1. personal assets and savings

2. Veterans' Administration benefits

3. Medicare

4. Medigap insurance

5. Medicaid

6. long-term care insurance

We'll briefly look at each of these sources now, though Medicare, Medicaid, Medigap and long-term care insurance are discussed in more detail in later chapters.

### Personal Assets and Savings

For the purpose of this text, *assets* are defined as cash or other near-cash items or any real or personal property that an individual owns and could convert to cash. These items will usually include savings accounts, certificates of deposit, mutual funds and so on. Those who depend solely on their personal assets and savings to pay for long-term care will be shocked to learn that it is easy to spend $3,000 or more per month for long-term care. In fact, since the average cost of a nursing home stay is more than $45,000 per year, almost 50 percent of all couples are impoverished within one year of one spouse entering a nursing home.

### Veterans' Administration Benefits

Some elderly people are entitled to limited nursing home coverage from the Veterans' Administration (VA) if they are directly discharged from a VA hospital into a nursing home or if the patient's need for a nursing home is a result of a service-connected disability. However, even with such a disability, a veteran is not always entitled to nursing home care. In addition, nursing home benefits are very restricted and seldom last more than six months. Because of budget constraints, the Department of Veterans' Affairs estimates it is able to provide nursing home care to only 16 percent of veterans who need this care.

### Medicare

Who pays the bill for the cost of health care for the elderly? Currently, federal and state programs cover much of the cost of medical attention. *Medicare,* a federal insurance program, was designed to provide benefits for hospitalization, surgery and physician care for more than 39 million Americans. The program acts as a way to control the costs for these medical services through its system of regulations and procedures. In other words, Medicare attempts to hold down the cost of medical care by limiting the scope of its coverage and benefit amounts, thus making the consumer and service provider more cost conscious and less likely to "overuse" the program.

One of the most dangerous myths about Medicare is that it pays for nursing home costs. In fact, Medicare pays only limited benefits for the cost of long-term nursing care. Medicare covers nursing home care *only* if skilled care is received in a Medicare-approved facility after a hospital stay of at least 3 consecutive days (measured as 72 consecutive hours in the hospital) within 30 days before entering the nursing home. The care must be designed to make the patient well rather than to help with personal needs or custodial care on a long-term basis. Even if the patient meets all the requirements, Medicare pays only the first 20 days of nursing home care in full. The patient pays a copayment ($96 per day in 1999) for the next 80 days. After that, Medicare pays nothing. This means that after 100 days, the patient and his or her family are on their own. As stated earlier, because the average stay in a nursing home is 2.5 years, Medicare is simply not the answer to long-term care costs.

### Medigap Insurance

Unfortunately, Medicare leaves many "gaps" in its coverage. With its structure of limited benefit periods, deductibles, copayments and exclusions, the coverage it provides is limited. To help fill these gaps, private insurance companies have developed *Medicare supplement (Medigap) insurance policies,* designed to supplement

Medicare's coverage to some extent. There are 10 Medicare supplement policies, ranging from a basic "core" policy to those with more comprehensive coverage.

These policies complement Medicare's coverage rather than cover types of services excluded by Medicare. Their purpose is to reduce some of the cost of care. For example, a basic Medigap policy will assist the policyowner by covering such charges as the Medicare Part A coinsurance amounts. However, neither Medicare nor Medigap insurance pay for custodial nursing home care.

### Medicaid

In addition to Medicare, the government offers Medicaid coverage through local health and human services departments. *Medicaid* is a joint federal and state health program that provides medical assistance to certain low-income individuals and families. Medicaid is by far the largest payor of nursing home care in the United States. Typically, Medicaid will cover inpatient and outpatient services, certain prescription drugs and medical supplies. However, because each state designs its own Medicaid program within federal guidelines, the extent of coverage and the quality of services vary widely from state to state.

Unlike Medicare, Medicaid will pay for custodial nursing home care designed to assist those who need help with activities of daily living. However, Medicaid is a "means-tested" program, and, in order to qualify for benefits, one must essentially be impoverished. In other words, a person must have virtually no income and no assets. In an attempt to qualify for Medicaid, many people transfer ownership of their resources. However, legislation now restricts the elderly Medicaid applicant from "giving away" most of his or her assets in order to qualify for Medicaid. In addition, as we'll see in Chapter 4, anyone who advises an individual to transfer assets for the purpose of qualifying for Medicaid will be subject to *criminal* penalties.

Medicaid—not the applicant or the family—chooses the patient's nursing home. A patient goes to the nearest available bed in a nursing home that may be far from family and friends. (All of these options—Medicare, Medigap and Medicaid—will be discussed in detail later in this text.)

### Long-Term Care Insurance

As beneficial as Medicare benefits and Medicare supplement policies are to the elderly in protecting them against the costs of medical care, there still exists a critical risk that neither of these covers: long-term custodial or nursing home care. How can these costs be paid? The solution may be *long-term care (LTC) insurance,* an insurance product that many insurance companies are now beginning to offer as the need for it grows. It is similar to most insurance plans: the insured pays a premium for specified benefits in the event that he or she suffers a financial loss. With LTC insurance, this loss occurs when the insured has to pay for long-term care, as defined by the policy. Most long-term care policies sold today are reimbursement plans. This means that they reimburse an insured for expenses incurred each day he or she receives the kind of care the policy covers.

Most long-term care policies are individual policies, but group coverage is also available. In general, benefits under long-term care policies cover the level of care specified in the policy up to a specified dollar amount per day. Insurers offer a wide range of daily maximum amounts, ranging from, for example, $40 a day to $200 a day or more for nursing home care. The daily benefit amount for at-home care is selected at the time of application and can be less than the benefit amount selected for nursing home care.

Many policies include an inflation rider or an option to purchase additional coverage, enabling the policies to keep pace with increases in long-term care costs. Benefits vary for different levels of care. Most policies offer a waiting period to reduce the cost of coverage. Generally, these policies exclude (among other things) war or acts of war, treatment for drug or alcohol abuse and attempted suicide.

## ■ THE ROLE OF THE PROFESSIONAL

You are probably already aware of the vital role you play in your clients' lives. You know that life, health, property and casualty insurance provide a practical solution to the economic losses associated with death, sickness and accidents. But, have you considered how important it is to counsel clients about their long-term care needs?

At the present time, long-term care insurance is the only form of coverage available to elderly people that is designed especially to shield families and their assets against what has been called the "cruel" cost of long-term care. Although this coverage is still evolving, 117 insurers, including Blue Cross and Blue Shield companies, now offer coverage for long-term care in either a nursing home or the patient's home.

As a professional, you must be able to assess whether a client's health insurance needs are adequately addressed by his or her current programs. If additional coverage is needed, you should be able to compare products honestly and intelligently to show how one policy differs from another in coverage, benefits and overall treatment of claims. Throughout this text, we will discuss the challenges of long-term care and how you can help your clients meet their needs for long-term care insurance.

## ■ SUMMARY

Studies show that, as the American population lives longer, it will place unprecedented pressure on the health care system. Medical costs are rising and the need for medical services increases with age. Although government programs provide some coverage, most elderly or impaired people will have to pay for much of their own long-term care costs.

Long-term care refers to a wide range of medical, environmental and personal care services for individuals who have lost their ability to remain completely independent. In Chapter 2, we'll discuss how these services may be provided by a number of informal and formal caregivers in a variety of settings.

## ■ CHAPTER 1 QUESTIONS FOR REVIEW

1. What percentage of the population will people over 65 represent in the year 2000?

   A. 9 percent
   B. 13 percent
   C. 21 percent
   D. 30 percent

2. Which of the following is defined as continuous around-the-clock care provided by licensed health care professionals under a physician's supervision?

   A. Custodial care
   B. Intermediate care
   C. Skilled care
   D. Long-term care

3. All of the following are factors that reduce the number of family members available to care for the elderly EXCEPT

   A. lower birth rates
   B. divorce
   C. decreased longevity
   D. increased mobility

4. Generally, long-term care is needed when an elderly person loses the ability to remain independent because he or she has

   A. limited financial resources
   B. few family members to care for him or her
   C. physical or cognitive impairments
   D. diminished social skills

5. According to recent figures, about how many people in the United States receive nursing home care in a year?

   A. 1 million
   B. 2.2 million
   C. 5.5 million
   D. 10 million

6. Each of the following is a level of long-term care EXCEPT

    A. chronic care
    B. skilled care
    C. intermediate care
    D. custodial care

7. The largest payor of nursing home care is

    A. insurance companies
    B. Medicare
    C. Medicaid
    D. individuals out of pocket

8. A professional insurance agent

    A. makes sure all of his or her clients qualify for Medicaid
    B. counsels clients about their long-term care needs
    C. tries to replace a client's Medicare Part B
    D. coordinates the medical care a client needs

# 2

## Providers of Care

I t is important that both you and your clients understand the options individuals face when they lose their independence and need help with the activities of daily living. There is no single solution to every individual's needs. While there are a variety of health-care options available, these options will not work the same way for everyone. A helpful way to consider these options is to visualize a continuum of care that moves from the least intensive care to the most intensive care or from the setting in which one has the most independence to the setting in which one is most dependent on others. On one end of that continuum is the home and on the other end is the hospital. In between are community centers for seniors, homemaker services, home health care, adult day care services, board-and-care homes, assisted-living facilities and nursing homes. Where someone resides along this continuum often depends on his or her ability to finance care and his or her social support system. For example, there are many elderly people receiving the same health-care services in their homes as others are receiving in assisted-living or board and care facilities as well as in nursing homes. However, those at home have the financing or social support system or both necessary to remain in the home.

Emotions run high when people recognize that they or their loved ones may need care. Initially, most people experience denial—no one expects or wants to need care as they age. Then they feel inadequate when they realize that finding care for themselves or providing care for someone else is difficult. They may then look for help. But after searching for some professional assistance, individuals often are shocked at how much care from qualified professionals will cost. In this chapter, we discuss various long-term care resources and support services to help you better understand available long-term care options.The development of a care plan provides a useful guide to the provision of services to the elderly and to the evaluation of those services. It also serves as an invaluable tool to improving the quality of services provided to the elderly.

■ ■ ■ ■ ■

## ■ THE CARE CONTINUUM

Long-term care is delivered along a continuum as shown in Illustration 2.1. As an individual ages and their chronic condition worsens, he or she will need more care moving from left to right along the continuum. As an individual recovers from an acute condition, he or she will need less care while moving from right to left. No two care recipients move along the continuum in the same manner—some move more quickly in their decline or recovery while others may remain at a particular point along the continuum for a long time. Also, care recipients may not receive care from each of the care providers. The providers have a range within which they can deliver care. And care can be received from more than one type of care provider, especially while receiving care at home.

This care continuum is constantly evolving as people's needs for care change. Just 10 years ago, adult day centers and assisted living facilities were rare. Today, they have gained acceptance and are an integral part of most networks of care providers and are recognized by long-term care insurers. How care is delivered will continue to change. For example, in Finland a new type of care called *day hospital care* has been developed and tested. People in rural settings go to a hospital during the day for various therapies, social interaction and nutrition. Initial results show people using these services in this setting need less care and for shorter periods of time. Once such experiments prove successful, they often are adopted in the United States and then further adapted to meet the needs of our particular circumstances. Such developments encompass care providers as well as care settings. In this manner, the continuum of care continues to evolve.

## ■ LONG-TERM CARE PROVIDERS

At some point in their lives, most people will provide care for an elderly spouse, parent, in-law or relative. This care may be as simple as driving a favorite uncle to the doctor once a month or as complex as providing around-the-clock care to a terminally ill spouse. Regardless of the degree of care provided, those providing the care are called *caregivers* or *providers.* The majority of caregiving responsibilities will fall on a *primary caregiver,* such as a spouse or child, with additional responsibilities falling on *secondary caregivers,* such as home care agencies. An individual who receives assistance with daily activities is called a *care recipient.*

Long-term care providers fall into one of two categories: informal caregivers and formal caregivers. *Informal caregivers,* such as a spouse, children, friends or neighbors, provide care in addition to their regular professional and personal responsibilities. They are seldom trained to give care and receive no monetary compensation for their work. On the other hand, *formal caregivers,* such as social workers, home care aides and nurses, make their living providing care—it is their chosen profession. Both types of caregivers are crucial to the caregiving process.

## ILL. 2.1  ■  *The Care Continuum*

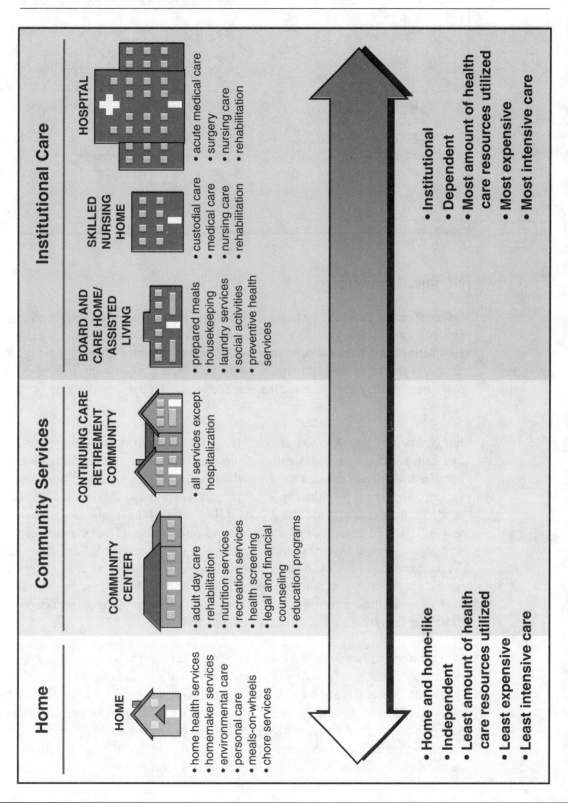

**Home**

HOME
- home health services
- homemaker services
- environmental care
- personal care
- meals-on-wheels
- chore services

**Community Services**

COMMUNITY CENTER
- adult day care
- rehabilitation
- nutrition services
- recreation services
- health screening
- legal and financial counseling
- education programs

CONTINUING CARE RETIREMENT COMMUNITY
- all services except hospitalization

**Institutional Care**

BOARD AND CARE HOME/ ASSISTED LIVING
- prepared meals
- housekeeping
- laundry services
- social activities
- preventive health services

SKILLED NURSING HOME
- custodial care
- medical care
- nursing care
- rehabilitation

HOSPITAL
- acute medical care
- surgery
- nursing care
- rehabilitation

- Home and home-like
- Independent
- Least amount of health care resources utilized
- Least expensive
- Least intensive care

- Institutional
- Dependent
- Most amount of health care resources utilized
- Most expensive
- Most intensive care

---

### ILL. 2.2 ■ *Long-Term Care Providers*

| Informal | Formal |
|---|---|
| Children | Adult day centers |
| Community services | Adult foster-care homes |
| Friends | Assisted-living facilities |
| Neighbors | Continuing care retirement communities |
| Parents |    (CCRCs) |
| Siblings/other relatives | Home care aides |
| Spouse | Home health care agencies |
| Volunteers | Nurses/physicians/therapists |
| | Nursing homes |
| | Social workers |

---

## Informal Caregivers

Informal care is provided by family, friends, volunteers and community services. *Informal care* includes assistance with daily activities, such as preparing meals, completing some housework or yard work, grocery shopping, driving, paying bills or simply providing companionship. As a care recipient's needs increase, the informal caregiver may have to assist the care recipient with bathing, dressing or eating.

For generations, people who were elderly, disabled or terminally ill were attended by family and friends at home. Although the traditional family structure has changed, families still provide the vast majority of long-term care in America. Most people feel an obligation to give their spouses, parents, siblings and children the assistance needed to protect their pride and dignity if they can no longer take care of themselves. Today, 65 percent of seniors who need care receive it from unpaid, informal caregivers. Women have been and still are the primary providers of long-term care. As indicated in Ill. 2.3, over 70 percent of the caregivers are female: daughters, wives, daughters-in-law, siblings, grandchildren, other relatives and friends. The average age of these informal caregivers is 57, with about one-third over age 65. But today, families have a more difficult time providing care.

When looking to family (and friends) to provide care, the two most difficult questions to ask are: *Are they willing to provide care?* and *Are they able to provide care?* In order to answer these two questions, the caregiver must consider a number of other questions. The list of questions in Ill. 2.4 indicates the breadth and scope of the issues a caregiver may face. Questions such as these must be answered honestly and completely before the informal caregiver undertakes the enormous responsibilities that lie ahead.

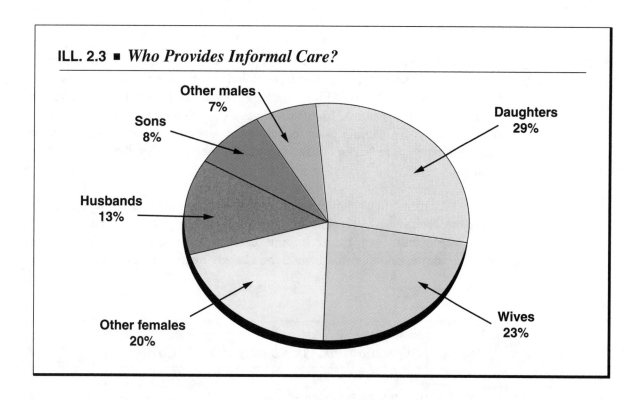

**ILL. 2.3 ■ *Who Provides Informal Care?***

Other males 7%
Sons 8%
Husbands 13%
Other females 20%
Daughters 29%
Wives 23%

However, even when an informal caregiver is willing and able, providing care can create emotional, physical and financial stress. It is difficult to help someone for long periods of time. The caregiver must be able to balance his or her personal needs with those of the care recipient, who may demand almost constant attention. If the caregiving role goes on too long, it can result in emotional, physical or financial exhaustion.

*Emotional Stress*

Some caregivers see the care they are providing as the only thing left in the care recipient's life; they gain strength from providing the care. Other caregivers try to remove themselves from the situation, hoping that someone else will step in, that the caregiving chore will become less demanding or that the situation will just resolve itself. Still other caregivers continue to provide care until they push themselves to the point of emotional exhaustion, which results in their own need for care.

Caring for the elderly or disabled people can be disheartening and frustrating. After months of care, the caregiver can be emotionally exhausted. Everyone reacts differently in these caregiving situations. People should be conscious of one simple fact: not everyone is emotionally able to provide care for a loved one until he or she gets better or dies. No one should be criticized for trying to provide care and later recognizing they are emotionally unable to continue.

*Physical Stress*

The caregiving role will test even the most physically fit person's abilities. Assume that the average small person is five feet tall and weighs 100 pounds. Now, assume that this person is unable to lift himself or herself from a bed; thus, the caregiver must lift and replace the person 5, 10 or more times a day. Although proper training and physical fitness are helpful, caring for a disabled person, even with these relatively small dimensions, can be physically demanding, especially when the caregiver is an elderly spouse.

The care recipient often needs care all day long and several times during the night. Therefore, caregiving will require adjustments to the caregiver's own personal needs, responsibilities and career. Informal caregivers also tend to avoid taking time during the day to do things for themselves. Caregiving can be a 24-hour,

---

### ILL. 2.4 ■ *Questions to Ask About Informal Caregiving*

**Are the informal caregivers *willing?***

- Are they willing to live with the care recipient?
- Are they willing to have the care recipient move in with them?
- Are they willing to adapt their home to provide the necessary care?
- Are they willing to stay at home 24 hours a day, 7 days a week to provide the necessary care?
- Are the care recipient's children working?
- Are they raising their own family?
- Are they willing to sacrifice their careers to provide the necessary care?
- Can they quit work or work part time to provide the necessary care?
- Did they quit work to raise their own children?
- Have they cared for others too many times?
- Will someone be pressured into providing the necessary care?

**Are the informal caregivers *able?***

- Do they live nearby?
- Are they healthy enough to provide the care?
- Are they financially able to take time from work?
- Is one family member able to move in with another family member?
- Can their home be adapted to provide the necessary care?
- Are they trained, physically and emotionally, to care for a loved one?
- Can they lift the care recipient?
- Can they bend over and lift the care recipient out of bed?
- Have they experienced seeing a loved one's body deteriorate?

7-days-a-week job that does not leave much time to address personal desires and responsibilities.

When the caregiving role is physically or emotionally exhausting, a caregiver needs a break from the daily routine. In many cases, a relative, friend or health-care professional can provide what is called *respite care* to relieve the caregiver for a few hours a day or a few days a month. While the substitute provides the caregiving responsibilities, the primary caregiver has an opportunity to do things he or she wants or needs to do. He or she could go to a movie, fish, play golf, have lunch with a friend, go for a drive or simply sit on a park bench and read a book. For some, it takes several days or a week to recharge their battery to regain the physical and emotional strength to continue the caregiving role.

### Financial Stress

In addition to the emotional and physical stress that caregivers experience, they also face the cost of providing appropriate care for the recipient. This can be expensive. Let's look at an example. First, assume that the services of an inexpensive home health aide cost $10 per hour. If the aide works a four-hour shift on a daily basis, the cost of care would amount to $1,200 per month. Now, if the recipient needs 24-hour-a-day care, the cost of care rises to about $7,200 per month.

Surprisingly, the cost of providing care in a nursing home is a bargain compared to around-the-clock care at home. Nursing home costs vary by location and quality of care. Costs in metropolitan areas are higher than rural areas and costs on the coasts are higher than in the middle of the country. In addition, "better" nursing homes charge more for their higher quality of care. Generally, however, an average nursing home will charge more than $3,500 per month, or about $45,000 per year.

Family members who provide care themselves rather than asking for professional assistance find that this is expensive as well. Providing care to an elderly parent likely will require the caregiver to quit his or her job or find part-time rather than full-time work.

Friends or family members cannot do the entire job of caregiving themselves. Sooner or later informal caregivers need professional help providing care. This help comes from services provided by formal caregivers.

## Formal Caregivers

As the population of the United States continues to age, more people will be needed to care for our elderly population. Formal caregivers, such as social workers, home care aides and nurses, provide needed professional care when informal caregivers are unavailable, unable or unwilling to care for elderly or disabled people.

### Social Workers

Both the family and the care recipient have important decisions to make and personal issues to consider when a person becomes disabled or ill. Unfortunately, the family is often unaware of the available health-care options. They are confused about what steps to take and are worried about the care recipient. Social workers can be a valuable resource to families at this time.

*Social workers* are trained to provide care consultation, counseling, information, referrals and case management. If the family has not established a plan prior to the loved one's illness, social workers are available to assist and support individuals in devising a plan. In addition to helping meet medical and emotional needs, social workers often assist the family with managing finances. They also have access to support and educational groups.

### Home Care

Many people are reluctant to give up their homes even though they are unable to perform household chores or personal activities of daily living (ADLs). Most individuals want to remain in their own home as long as possible. Home care from trained professionals is a way to delay the need for institutional care. But home care is expensive. The best use of home care is to complement, not replace, a family member or other primary caregiver.

As explained in Chapter 1, home care can be grouped into three categories: medical, personal or environmental care. (See Ill. 2.5.) The type of care needed will determine the type of professional to be hired.

**Medical Care.**   When a care recipient is recovering from major surgery or suffering from a chronic illness, he or she may need the services of a variety of health-care professionals. The patient may require visits from registered nurses, licensed practical nurses, speech-language pathologists and physical and occupational therapists. In some cases, pharmacists and laboratory technicians who draw blood will also make home visits. Typically, these health-care professionals will administer the patient's medication, monitor his or her progress, change bandages, give injections and so on.

Advances in health sciences have made it easier to deliver health care and health-related services in the home. Smaller, portable equipment permits respiratory therapy, drug therapy and chemotherapy to be performed in the home rather than in the hospital. In addition, hospital beds, power lift chairs, walkers, wheelchairs and monitoring devices can be rented so that most people can return home sooner and remain home longer.

Health care delivered at home is designed to make sure the care recipient gets the health-care services he or she needs. However, depending on the recipient's condition, such care may not be able to restore good health. Sometimes the care is not designed to restore the recipient's health but simply to help maintain his or her health status or slow the progress of the condition that restricts independence.

**Personal Care.** Personal care is assistance with activities of daily living (ADLs), such as bathing, dressing and eating. Personal care is designed to help a person throughout the day. The amount of personal care needed varies according to the recipient's level of impairment. Some people need to have tasks completed for them while others need only some help to complete the task themselves. Still others need only the reassurance that someone is there to be sure the task gets completed. The care recipient with a mental impairment may be physically able to complete the ADL but may need someone there to remind them when and how to do it.

*Home health aides* and *homemaker-health care aides* may be hired if patients need personal care and home management services. Home health aides are nursing assistants who work under the supervision of a physician or nurse. The aide's primary job is to care for the patient's personal needs but he or she is also there to help the family. Many of these aides are trained in geriatric care and are certified to provide some basic medical services. Aides may check the patient's temperature, blood pressure and pulse and respiration rates. Generally, aides do not administer medication.

**Environmental Care.** The third category of home care—environmental care—provides care for the home or environment rather than the care recipient. Environmental care encompasses such household tasks as cleaning, laundry, meal preparation, yard work, grocery shopping and paying bills. Home care aides can provide all these services, or some of the care can be provided by *chore services* based in the community. Chore services groups offer home repair and maintenance assistance at reduced cost to older adults who are disabled or ill or have a low income. Services often include yard work, minor household repairs and general maintenance, such as cleaning gutters or installing storm windows.

## ■ COMMUNITY SERVICES

Caregivers are not always available on a 24-hour basis. For example, an adult child may need to be at work while a parent or other care recipient needs assistance during the day. However, with the range of services now available in many communities, the care recipient may still be able to remain at home.

*Community services* consist of a wide variety of options from nutrition services to assisted living. Each service is designed to assist—not replace—a primary caregiver, and is provided either free of charge or at a nominal cost. These services are normally provided by volunteers or individuals receiving a small wage. A few of the most common programs are outlined here.

### Meals-on-Wheels

People with arthritis, impaired eyesight or other disabilities may find meal preparation difficult. Those who are homebound may be reluctant or unable to prepare a nutritious meal for themselves. Without basic nutrition, these people often become ill, lose their independence and may be forced to enter a nursing home.

The *Meals-on-Wheels* program seeks to provide a well-balanced meal to the homes of those who are unable to prepare meals. Generally, the meals are delivered five days a week, usually around midday. Some communities also provide an additional evening snack.

Volunteers usually deliver the meals and may spend time chatting with each recipient. Although some communities charge a modest fee for the meals, most communities rely on the federal government, the United Way and private donations for their funding.

### Telephone Reassurance

Caregivers who live far from their parents or who travel a great deal because of their work may be unable to telephone as often as they would like. Many communities offer *telephone reassurance programs* that provide regularly scheduled telephone calls by volunteers to elderly care recipients. These calls check on the elderly person's health and safety; depending on the program, the calls are made daily, weekly or monthly. Some programs are even designed to call several times during the course of the day to remind the care recipient to take his or her medication. Not only do these calls provide an important link to emergency services or medical care, they also help reduce the social isolation that so many homebound elderly experience.

### Personal Emergency Response Systems

Many elderly people who live alone fear that no one will be there to assist them if they have an accident or become ill. These people may be interested in small, wireless devices worn around the neck or wrist called *personal emergency response systems.* When activated, the devices alert the emergency room of a nearby hospital via the user's telephone. An emergency team, or a prearranged neighbor or relative, will then call the care recipient. These emergency systems can provide the elderly with a vital link to the outside world in difficult situations.

### Senior Centers

Even healthy seniors may lack the opportunities for social interaction that they previously enjoyed. Many communities now have *senior centers* where older people may gather for planned social activities, health screening, educational programs, communal meals or legal and financial counseling.

Senior centers usually charge a small fee for classes or activities; however, no one is denied participation in an event because of his or her inability to pay. Most communities offset costs through donations.

## Transportation

Seniors who must give up driving are often reluctant to ask others to drive them to doctor's appointments, shopping centers or senior activities. Their loss of independence is a source of embarrassment and frustration. When a community offers subsidized transportation, however, the senior may be more willing and able to get to the places he or she needs or wants to go.

## Adult Day Centers

About one-third of informal caregivers continue to work. This creates a challenge for those working during the day: how can they continue their caregiving role while maintaining their source of income? *Adult day centers* offer a way for these caregivers to continue to work while ensuring that their loved ones receive needed care.

Adult day centers usually provide an elderly person with social interaction, therapeutic activities, opportunities for learning, preventive health services and well-balanced meals. The care is offered in specially designed buildings, community halls, storefronts or in a separate area of a nursing home. Typically, centers are open Monday through Friday from the early morning through early evening; costs can range from $30 to over $100 per day. A typical adult day care recipient is a female in her mid-70s who lives with a spouse, adult child or other family and friends. About half of them have a cognitive impairment and the majority need assistance with multiple activities of daily living.

Some adult day centers have addressed the needs of caregivers who are providing for both young children and elderly parents. *Intergenerational day-care centers* offer structured programs for both young children and seniors. In many cases, these centers present the only opportunity for young children to interact with older people. Seniors have the opportunity to share their experience and nurturing skills with these young children.

Although caregivers may be reluctant to use these centers, they do provide the caregiver with some needed respite care. While the care recipient is at a center, the caregiver can take care of personal needs. And once the care recipient realizes that he or she is not being abandoned, the recipient often looks forward to time spent away from home and in the company of peers.

Adult day services demonstrate how the needs of the caregiver and care recipient have evolved over the past decade. While these facilities were extremely rare in the early 1980s, there are now over 3,000 such centers.

### Working Together

Regardless of the type or number of caregivers involved in a person's care, it is imperative that informal and formal caregivers attempt to keep an individual in his or her home as long as possible. Encouraging an older person to be independent

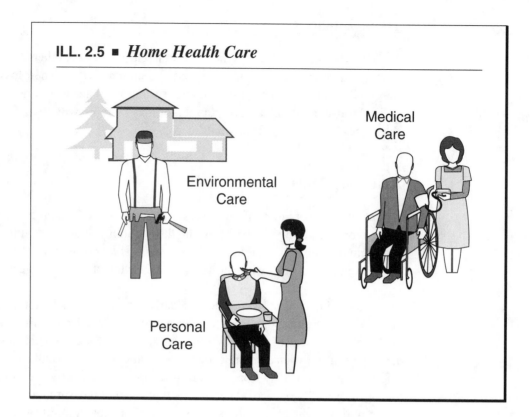

**ILL. 2.5 ■ *Home Health Care***

Environmental Care

Medical Care

Personal Care

helps guard against a premature need for institutional care. With the range of home care services available, it is no longer always necessary for an ill or disabled person to enter a nursing home. As represented in Illustration 2.6, a variety of arrangements—family and friends, community support services and home and adult day centers—provide the elderly with needed care.

An excellent source for the services available in your community is the local *Area Agency on Aging (AAA),* an organization that was established in 1973 as part of the federal Older Americans Act. Usually AAAs are funded by state and local governments and private contributions. Their role is to plan and coordinate community services, provide information and referrals, distribute educational materials and advocate for the elderly.

## ■ CARE PLANS

A care plan lists activities to be performed by providers of care on behalf of care recipients. Such plans are used to guide the provision of services and to evaluate the care recipients' needs and progress. A care plan is also invaluable in improving the quality of care and services provided to care recipients. Today, most insurers offering long-term care policies require the development of a care plan for insureds.

Care plans are usually developed by care managers who meet with the care recipient and his or her family to assess the recipient's health-care needs, including psychological concerns, the family history, the support system, financial resources and timing. The plan of care will be developed from such meetings. The plan takes into consideration the continuum of care and the providers of care available in the community as well as the recipient's financial resources, including Medicare and insurance. The care plan is evaluated periodically and updated.

Care managers can be found by contacting doctors, nurses, hospital discharge planners, staff of the local senior center or other individuals knowledgeable about health-care services in the community. Insurers may use a network of care managers to develop care plans for their insureds. A helpful criterion to select care managers is membership in the National Association of Professional Geriatric Care Managers.

Once developed, the plan of care can be managed by the primary caregiver or a professional care manager. Professional care managers are experienced in the assessment, coordination, monitoring and delivery of geriatric care services. Reports on the plan are regularly provided to the family. The cost for the services of a care manager can range from $50 to $170 an hour depending on location and the experience of the care manager.

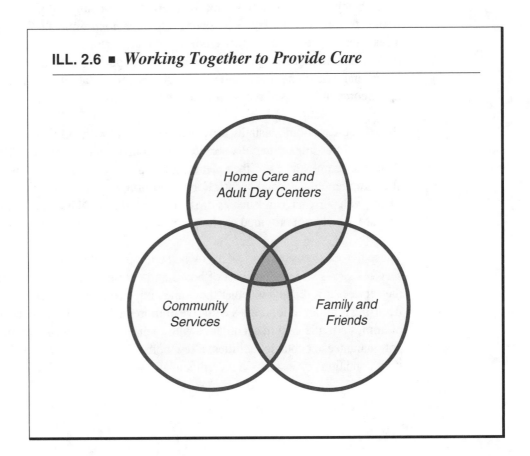

**ILL. 2.6 ■ *Working Together to Provide Care***

Home Care and Adult Day Centers

Community Services

Family and Friends

## ■ LONG-TERM CARE SETTINGS

At some point, it's likely a care recipient will need care 24 hours a day. When this happens, the family caregiver becomes a "project manager" at home who coordinates nursing care, family visits, personal care, feeding and so on. It is at this point that most care recipients will be best served in a long-term care setting by professional caregivers.

Not all retired or elderly people wish to remain in the family home. Although their health may be excellent, they may be less interested in yard work or housekeeping than they once were. Or, they may have some health problems, which are not yet severe enough to require medical assistance. While they may not be interested in maintaining the family home, most seniors do enjoy their independence and prefer to remain on their own as long as possible. There are several viable options for these elderly people.

### Board-and-Care Homes

As people age, it often becomes difficult for them to maintain a home or an apartment. Though they are fairly healthy and able to maintain a high degree of independence, they need some assistance with daily functions and activities. Individuals who enjoy being independent may look for alternative housing that gives them an "at-home" feeling. For these people, *board-and-care homes* may be the logical choice. These homes provide a friendly environment and custodial care (housekeeping and meals), as well as some personal care under the supervision of trained individuals. A board-and-care home is also called an adult foster care facility, residential care facility or community-based residential facility.

Board-and-care homes usually provide the residents with individual rooms and bathroom facilities, meals, laundry services and housekeeping services. Although residents may come and go as they please, the home often provides transportation to shopping centers or social events. For an additional fee, staff members can assist residents with personal care such as dressing and bathing. Nursing and medical attention are usually not provided on the premises.

These homes are usually privately-owned and operated and the quality of care and services varies widely. The cost of board-and-care homes also varies depending on the services offered and whether the home is licensed by the state. In many states, licensing is required for homes with five or more residents. Though the vast majority of homes provide care in accordance with their license, licensing requirements do not guarantee acceptable facilities; a few homes fail to comply with fire codes, sanitary conditions or inspection recommendations.

## Assisted-Living Facilities

*Assisted-living facilities* provide residents with their own individual apartments. These facilities are most appropriate for those who desire privacy but who also wish to take advantage of the support services that a community setting can provide. Most of these facilities offer prepared meals in a central dining room, housekeeping and laundry services, transportation for shopping, planned social activities and preventive health services (such as blood pressure checks and assistance with medications). A nurse is usually on call for residents who need limited amounts of health care.

Assisted-living facilities vary greatly in size, from those able to house five individuals to those that have adequate space for 250 people or more. Most states license these facilities. The costs for assisted-living facilities, like the costs for board-and-care homes, vary widely depending on the size of the facility and the amenities offered. Costs tend to average between half to three-quarters of nursing home costs in an area. Some facilities are more expensive because they offer many amenities to attract wealthy residents.

## Continuing Care Retirement Community

A *continuing care retirement community (CCRC)* or *life care community* is a community that provides services and housing options to meet the needs of the elderly. It provides independent and congregate living and personal, immediate and skilled nursing care. It also attempts to create an environment that allows each resident to participate in the community's life to whatever degree he or she wants. Continuing care communities often encompass the entire continuum of care, with the single exception of hospitalization.

Residents may live in a continuing care retirement community for a definite or indefinite period of time. But, because the facility is prepared to meet residents' needs if they become more disabled and need skilled nursing care, the residents are afforded peace of mind. They know they will be appropriately cared for in the same community as they age.

All continuing care retirement communities will offer both an area for "independent living" for residents still able to care for themselves and a nursing facility area for residents in need of assistance. As residents lose their ability to remain independent, they can move from the independent area to the assisted living area, or they can receive home care in their living unit. Meanwhile, the on-site nursing home is available as conditions worsen. In addition, CCRCs guarantee access to quality care as an individual's needs change.

The financial arrangements vary by facility. The basic design is an initial lump-sum payment followed by a monthly maintenance charge. This upfront payment can be as much as $100,000 or more for an individual. In most cases, residents pay for additional health care and nursing home services they may need in one of three ways:

1. Charges for home, assisted-living or nursing home care are included in the regular monthly bill, even if the services are not used.

2. The regular monthly bill subsidizes needed care, but residents must pay the balance of the charges.

3. The full cost of the care is billed separately from monthly maintenance charges.

### Nursing Homes

Individuals who require professional medical care around the clock will usually enter a *nursing home*. In fact, one out of every five elderly persons who has lost the ability to remain independent is currently residing in a nursing home; the others are receiving care from one of the other providers discussed earlier.

A "skilled" nursing home provides around-the-clock medical care, often to patients recently discharged from a hospital. They treat people with complex nursing and rehabilitative needs, such as intravenous therapy or physical therapy.

In theory, the goal of every skilled nursing facility is to rehabilitate the patient so that he or she can return home. In practice, however, a lack of care alternatives often

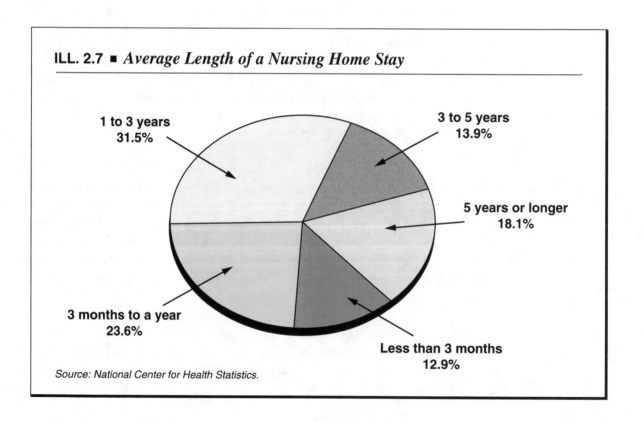

**ILL. 2.7 ■ *Average Length of a Nursing Home Stay***

1 to 3 years
31.5%

3 to 5 years
13.9%

5 years or longer
18.1%

3 months to a year
23.6%

Less than 3 months
12.9%

*Source: National Center for Health Statistics.*

means that the patient will be transferred to an intermediate or custodial care unit in the same facility.

Statistically, the majority of those entering nursing homes received care in either another nursing home or a hospital; just over one-third came from a residence. As shown in Ill. 2.7, although one-third of nursing home residents remain in the facility for one year or less, the average stay is 2.5 years. One-third have been there between one and three years and one-third have been in the facility three or more years. Considering that the average skilled nursing facility costs $45,000 per year, those in nursing homes for three years spend well over $100,000.

Of all the facilities we've discussed, nursing homes can provide the highest level of 24-hour care in the most cost-efficient manner. They have the staff, equipment, facilities and motivation to provide the kind of care that informal caregivers are unable to provide. It is important to remember, however, that skilled nursing facilities vary by the level and quality of care provided.

People enter nursing homes for a number of reasons. The most common reason is they need more care than a spouse or family member can provide. Other commonly cited reasons for entering a nursing home include:

- the caregiver has problems completing everyday activities

- there is no one at home to provide the care

- there is not enough money to purchase home care

- the patient is recuperating from surgery or illness

Generally speaking, nursing homes are more attractive and better run today than they were in the past. However, there are some basic guidelines that can help the caregiver or recipient select an appropriate nursing home.

- The facility should be state licensed.

- The facility should be a member of either the American Health Care Association or the American Association of Homes and Services for the Aging.

- The facility should be certified for Medicare or Medicaid reimbursement, as needed. (Keep in mind, however, that some nursing homes accept private pay residents only and may provide excellent care.)

- The grounds and the facility should be clean, comfortable and well maintained.

- Physicians and nurses should be on call 24 hours a day, assisted by a staff that is friendly and helpful.

- The lobby should be well decorated; the hallways should be wide and well-lit; and rooms should be clean and odor free.

As you will recall from Chapter 1, there are three levels of care that an individual may receive in a nursing home: skilled, intermediate or custodial. The care recipient's condition will determine the level of care that is provided. In turn, this will determine who provides the care. Let's look more closely at the three levels of care.

## Skilled Care

*Skilled care* is nursing and rehabilitative care that is prescribed by a physician and delivered on a daily basis by skilled health-care professionals, such as nurses or therapists.

People typically receive skilled care only for short periods of time; it often rehabilitates or restores their health quickly. Skilled care is usually delivered to complete the recovery process following a hospital stay for surgery or treatment of an acute condition. Some of the procedures and treatments included in skilled care are injections, administrations of medications, changing of dressings and observation and monitoring of a patient's condition, including taking vital signs.

## Intermediate Care

Unlike continuous skilled care, *intermediate care* is provided intermittently—two, three or four days a week. It is designed to aid the patient's recovery, and is delivered by a registered nurse, licensed practical nurse or therapist under the supervision of a physician. Generally, intermediate care is provided for patients who are still recovering from an accident or illness but who no longer need 24-hour care or daily rehabilitation services and therapies.

## Custodial Care

Custodial care in a nursing home is completely different from skilled or intermediate care. *Custodial care* provides assistance with the things healthy people take for granted—taking a bath or shower, getting dressed, using a toilet or eating a meal. While custodial care must be supervised by a physician, not all custodial care must be delivered by licensed health-care professionals. The care is normally provided by nurse's aides, volunteers and other caregivers. In nursing homes, custodial care is by far the most common type of care provided.

Custodial care is often needed due to a chronic condition that hinders the recipient's ability to remain independent. People struggling with Alzheimer's disease, arthritis, visual impairments and diabetes often need custodial care. Also, people may require custodial care as they complete their recovery from surgery. For example, a person with a broken arm set in a cast may need help taking a shower or dressing, or a person

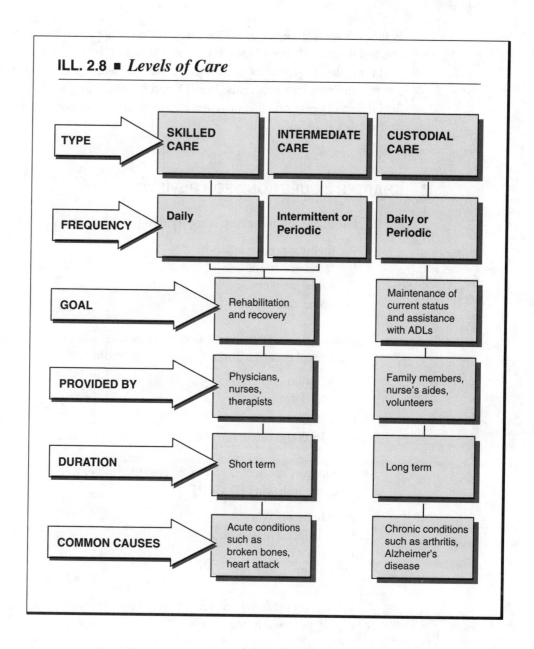

**ILL. 2.8 ■ *Levels of Care***

recovering from a heart attack may need someone to help with walking or transferring.

## ■ SUMMARY

Caring for a disabled or ill elderly person requires a commitment to provide quality care to the recipient and to preserve that person's dignity and health. It is not an easy task to become a caregiver; it takes great emotional and physical stamina. When people care for loved ones at home, there is little relief for the caregiver. Fortunately, many communities offer a variety of options that allow the caregiver to escape the worries and frustrations of long-term care for a few minutes or a few hours.

In this chapter, we've discussed the many different approaches to caring for a loved one and the many types of long-term care providers. How this kind of care can be paid for is the subject of the next four chapters, in which we'll discuss government and private insurance programs. We'll begin by discussing Medicare, a part of the Social Security program that provides health insurance to those receiving retirement or disability benefits.

## ■ CHAPTER 2 QUESTIONS FOR REVIEW

1. Informal long-term care is most often provided by

   A. medical professionals
   B. family or friends
   C. social workers
   D. home care workers

2. Although nursing home costs vary by location and services offered, the average annual cost of a nursing home is approximately

   A. $10,000
   B. $20,000
   C. $30,000
   D. $45,000

3. Community services that may be provided either free or at little cost include all of the following EXCEPT

   A. Meals-on-Wheels
   B. telephone reassurance
   C. senior centers
   D. nursing home care

4. Ideally, professional services provided by nurses or home health aides in an elderly person's home should

   A. be the primary care the recipient receives
   B. replace primary caregiver's services
   C. complement the primary caregiver's services
   D. be limited to medical, not personal, care

5. Which of the following best describes custodial care?

   A. Rehabilitative care provided after surgery
   B. Assistance with the activities of daily living
   C. Therapy provided at least four days a week
   D. Environmental care delivered in the home

6. Long-term care providers are categorized as

   A. formal and informal
   B. Medicare and Medicaid
   C. licensed and custodial
   D. educated and trained

7. Which of the following statements best describes a nursing home?

   A. It provides independent and congregate living as well as hospitalization.
   B. It provides a friendly environment, custodial care and some personal care.
   C. It provides professional health-care services around the clock in the most cost-efficient manner.
   D. It provides residents with their own apartment and on-call nursing services.

8. Which of the following statements best describes a board-and-care home?

   A. It provides independent and congregate living as well as personal, intermediate and skilled nursing care.
   B. It provides a friendly environment, custodial care and some personal care.
   C. It provides professional health services around the clock in the most cost-efficient manner.
   D. It provides residents with their own apartment and on-call nursing services.

9. Which of the following statements best describes an assisted-living facility?

   A. It provides residents with their own apartment and on-call nursing services.
   B. It provides professional health-care services around the clock in the most cost-efficient manner.
   C. It provides independent and congregate living as well as personal, intermediate and skilled nursing care.
   D. It provides a friendly environment, custodial care and some personal care.

10. Which of the following statements best describes a continuing care retirement community?

   A. It provides residents with their own apartment and on-call nursing services.
   B. It provides professional health-care services around the clock in the most cost-efficient manner.
   C. It provides independent and congregate living as well as personal, intermediate and skilled nursing care.
   D. It provides a friendly environment, custodial care and some personal care.

# 3

# Medicare and Medicare Supplements

I n the previous chapter, we looked at a number of health care and assisted-living care options available to the elderly. In this chapter and those that follow, we'll discuss different programs and plans—government and private— that are designed to help pay for this care. Professionals who work the senior health market should have a basic understanding of these plans, notably their benefits and limitations. This knowledge will enable the agent or advisor to evaluate a client's situation, including any potential need for additional coverage, and to provide advice and counsel.

Our discussion will begin with the *Original Medicare Plan*. Following that, we'll discuss *Medicare supplement insurance,* which is a plan of private insurance designed to cover the gaps the Original Medicare Plan leaves. We'll conclude with a discussion of Medicare+Choice, a new program created by the Balanced Budget Act of 1997. Under Medicare+Choice, beneficiaries can opt out of the Original Medicare Plan and choose from a variety of alternatives. However, each alternative must cover at least the services covered in the original plan.

## ■ A BRIEF HISTORY OF MEDICARE

The federal government's role of providing the nation's elderly with some degree of financial security was established by the Social Security Act of 1935. In its original form, Social Security was designed to provide a retirement benefit for a worker, to be drawn upon when he or she reached age 65. Subsequently, benefits for unemployment compensation, for workers' compensation due to injuries sustained on the job, for personal disability and for survivor benefits for a deceased worker's family were added to the program.

Health insurance was considered in the original Social Security Act, but it was not included. It was not until 1965 that the Medicare Act was signed into law, with an anticipated expenditure for that year of $2 billion. Its purpose was to provide afford-able health care for elderly Americans and to prevent the impoverishment of senior citizens due to their health-care costs.

Since its enactment, Medicare has undergone numerous changes affecting its financ-ing, its method of operation, its benefits and its methods of cost control. Despite these changes, the basic mission of Medicare remains the same: to provide a system for the delivery and payment of medical and hospital care for people age 65 and over (and for people with certain disabilities). This program is administered by the Health Care Financing Administration of the U.S. Department of Health and Human Services.

## ■ ORIGINAL MEDICARE PLAN

Medicare is a government insurance entitlement program that provides basic health insurance protection to an estimated 39 million Americans. In addition to providing medical benefits, the program acts to control the costs for these medical services through a system of regulations and procedures. As noted in Chapter 2, Medicare attempts to hold down the cost of medical care by limiting the scope of its coverage and its benefit amounts, thus making the consumer and the service provider more cost conscious and less likely to "overuse" or "overcharge" the program.

Contrary to popular belief, Medicare does *not* cover all medical expenses. Medicare does not pay for most routine physicals, eye and hearing exams, dental care, self-administered prescription drugs and many other medical products and services. In addition, many long-term health problems requiring custodial or private nursing care (like Alzheimer's disease) are not covered. Medicare coverage is also subject to deductibles, copayments and limitations.

The Original Medicare Plan has two distinct parts: Hospital Insurance (Part A) and Medical Insurance (Part B). Part A provides hospitalization insurance for inpatient hospital care, inpatient care prescribed by a doctor at a skilled nursing facility, home health care and care at a recognized hospice. Part B provides medical insurance for required doctors' services, outpatient services and medical supplies and many ser-vices not covered by Part A hospitalization coverage.

Eligibility for Medicare benefits is not determined by financial need. Practically everyone age 65 or older, as well as many people classified as disabled, is eligible for Medicare Part A and Medicare Part B. A person is eligible for Medicare benefits if he or she is/was:

- 65 or over and has qualified for Social Security or Railroad Retirement monthly cash benefits;

- entitled to benefits under the Social Security program for 24 months as a disabled worker, disabled widow(er) or as a child age 18 or over who was disabled before age 22;

- diagnosed as having permanent kidney failure and requiring dialysis or a kidney transplant; or

- born before 1929 and has few or no quarters of coverage under the Social Security system.

Coverage under Medicare Part A is automatic and premium free if individuals or their spouses are entitled to benefits under either the Social Security or Railroad Retirement systems or if they have worked for a prescribed period of time for a local, state or federal government. Part A coverage is financed through part of the Social Security (FICA) tax paid by workers and their employers. People who do not qualify for premium-free Part A coverage may purchase the coverage if they are at least age 65 and meet certain other requirements. People under age 65 who were previously entitled to disability benefits under Medicare and have the same disability but whose benefits were terminated because of the recipient's work and earnings may also purchase coverage.

Medicare Part B is voluntary and may be elected or rejected as the recipient wishes. Enrollment in Part B is automatic when the recipient is enrolled in Part A coverage. However, people may choose not to participate in this program by filing a "nonelection of Part B benefits" on a special government form mailed to all individuals qualifying for Part A. Part B coverage requires payment of a monthly premium that is deducted from Social Security benefits. These premiums fund only about one-fourth of the cost of the program; the federal government pays approximately 75 percent of the total program costs.

Medicare performs its health care function through a series of carefully laid out steps. There are rules, regulations and procedures that must be followed to ensure that the claim is paid, either to the Medicare recipient as reimbursement or to the care provider as direct payment. Now let's look at how Parts A and B of Medicare function, what they cover and what they don't.

## MEDICARE PART A: HOSPITAL INSURANCE

Medicare Hospital Insurance (Part A) pays for medically necessary inpatient care in a hospital, skilled nursing facility, psychiatric hospital or hospice. In addition, Part A pays for the cost of medically necessary home health care and 80 percent of the approved cost for durable medical equipment supplied under the home health-care benefit. Certain deductibles, copayments and limitations apply to Part A coverage.

In general, Part A hospitalization benefits cover the following:

- semiprivate room and board;

- regular nursing services;

- drugs furnished by the hospital;

- lab tests, X-rays and medical supplies such as dressings, splints and casts;

- blood transfusions, except for the first three pints, which are paid for by the Medicare recipient;

- use of durable medical equipment such as wheelchairs;

- use of the operating room, recovery room and special-care units, such as intensive care; and

- rehabilitation services, including physical therapy.

Part A covers basic inpatient hospital care, skilled nursing facility care benefits, home health care, hospice care and, to a limited extent, inpatient psychiatric care. Although coverage is fairly comprehensive, there are limitations, deductibles and copayments for each benefit period. This information is summarized in Illustration 3.1. Let's examine Part A benefits and limitations more closely.

### Inpatient Hospital Care

When an eligible person is hospitalized, benefits provided under Part A are subject to certain deductibles and copayments for each benefit period. Under Part A, a *benefit period* is defined as the length of time from which the patient enters the hospital until he or she has been discharged and out of the hospital for 60 days. Once the benefit period ends, a new benefit period can begin. If a person is readmitted to the hospital before the original benefit period ends, only the remaining unused benefits are available for that period. Let's look at how the benefit limitations apply to hospital care.

When an eligible person enters the hospital, Part A pays for all Medicare-covered services in a hospital (over the deductible) for the first 60 days. (The deductible per benefit period—$768 in 1999—is subject to change.) The benefit period begins on the first day a patient enters a hospital and ends when the patient has been discharged for 60 consecutive days. If a patient is discharged but returns to the hospital during the benefit period (that is, within 60 days of discharge), the deductible does not have to be paid again. On the other hand, if a patient is released from the hospital and returns 61 days later, Medicare deems that a new benefit period has begun and the deductible must be paid again.

## ILL. 3.1 ■ *Medicare (Part A): Hospital Insurance—Covered Services Per Benefit Period* [1]

| Services | Benefit | Medicare Pays** | Patient Pays** |
|---|---|---|---|
| **Hospitalization** Semiprivate room and board, general nursing and miscellaneous hospital services and supplies | First 60 days | All but $768 | $768 |
| | 61st to 90th day | All but $192 a day | $192 a day |
| | 91st to 150th day* | All but $384 a day | $384 a day |
| | Beyond 150 days | Nothing | All costs |
| **Posthospital Skilled Nursing Facility Care** Patient must have been in a hospital for at least three days, enter a Medicare-approved facility generally within 30 days after hospital discharge and meet other program requirements[2] | First 20 days | 100 percent of approved amount | Nothing |
| | Additional 80 days | All but $96 a day | Up to $96 a day |
| | Beyond 100 days | Nothing | All costs |
| **Home Health Care** Medically necessary skilled care, home health aide services, medical supplies, etc. | Part-time or intermittent nursing care and other services for as long as patient meets criteria for benefits | 100 percent of approved amount; 80 percent of approved amount for durable medical equipment | Nothing for services; 20 percent of approved amount for durable medical equipment |
| **Hospice Care** Full scope of pain relief and support services available to the terminally ill | As long as doctor certifies need | All but limited costs for outpatient drugs and inpatient respite care | Limited cost-sharing for out-patient drugs and inpatient respite care |
| **Blood** | Blood | All but first three pints per calendar year | For first three pints*** |

* 60 reserve days may be used only once.

** These figures are for 1999 and are subject to change each year.

*** To the extent the blood deductible is met under Medicare Part A during the calendar year it does not have to be met under Medicare Part B.

1. A benefit period begins on the first day a partient receives service as an inpatient in a hospital and ends after he or she has been out the hospital or skilled nursing facility for 60 days in a row or remains in a skilled nursing facility but did not receive skilled care there for 60 days in a row.

2. Neither Medicare nor Medigap insurance will pay for most nursing home care.

*Source: The National Association of Insurance Commissioners and the Health Care Financing Administration of the U.S. Department of Health and Human Services.*

If a hospital stay lasts longer than 60 days during one benefit period, Medicare continues to pay for covered services from the 61st to the 150th day. During this period, however, the patient also absorbs a portion of the cost by paying a daily amount called a *coinsurance payment* or *copayment*. The amount of the copayment changes with the length of the hospital stay. From the 61st to 90th day of hospitalization, one copayment is applied ($192 per day in 1999); from the 91st to 150th day of hospitalization, another higher copayment is assessed ($384 per day in 1999). After 150 days of hospitalization, the Medicare recipient pays for *all* hospitalization charges. Like the deductible, the copayment is subject to change each year.

Inpatient hospital care also affords a *lifetime reserve* of 60 days. These lifetime reserve days may be used whenever the eligible patient needs more than 90 days of inpatient hospital care in a benefit period. When a reserve day is used, Part A pays for all covered services except for a coinsurance payment noted earlier. Once exhausted, reserve days are not renewed.

### Skilled Nursing Care Facility (Nursing Home) Benefits

A *skilled nursing care facility* is an institution that treats people with complex nursing and rehabilitative needs, such as physical, occupational or speech therapy. In many cases, patients in skilled nursing care facilities have suffered a stroke or have had major surgery. They do not require the level of care that a hospital provides, but they do need around-the-clock supervision and skilled treatment. Others are admitted to such facilities because of a need for custodial or assisted care. For the purposes of Medicare, the distinction between skilled care and custodial care is important.

Care at a skilled nursing facility is covered by Medicare if both the facility and the patient's diagnosis and treatment plan meet Medicare's strict standards. Medicare nursing home benefits are available only if the following three conditions are met:

1. The patient must have been hospitalized for at least three days (measured as 72 consecutive hours in the hospital) prior to entering the nursing home and the patient must have been admitted to the nursing home within 30 days of the hospital discharge.

2. A doctor must certify that skilled nursing is required.

3. The services or care must be provided by a Medicare-certified skilled nursing facility (SNF); assisted living facilities, board-and-care homes, rest home and homes for the aged are not covered.

As a result of these requirements, the number of nursing home stays covered by Medicare is quite limited. To begin with, only about half of those entering a nursing home were previously in a hospital. Furthermore, coverage for most chronic and mental impairments is ruled out since the nursing home care must be for the same condition for which hospital care was needed and these conditions typically do not require a hospital stay before nursing home care is needed.

The requirement that the patient must receive skilled nursing care further restricts Medicare's coverage. Skilled nursing care is daily, restorative care, ordered by a physician and delivered by skilled personnel. For Medicare's purposes, "daily" is five days a week; "restorative" is rehabilitation treatment or therapy to assist an individual's continuing recovery; "ordered by a physician" means the primary doctor certifies the care is needed for the same condition for which hospital treatment was received; and "skilled personnel" means a qualified nurse—RN or LPN.

Usually, individuals receiving skilled care are recovering from an injury or illness that required a hospital stay. Such care is administered for short periods of time, rarely lasting longer than three weeks.

Custodial or assisted care—less intensive, yet the most often utilized—is not covered. Care is considered custodial when the care primarily meets personal needs rather than medical needs or when the care can be provided by individuals without professional training. It includes help in walking, getting in and out of bed, bathing, dressing and taking medicine. Medicare will not pay for this type of care; it pays for skilled nursing care only.

Those who meet Medicare's strict qualification standards will find that Medicare's benefits are quite limited. Medicare pays for 100 percent of all covered charges for the first 20 days. For the next 80 days, the patient is responsible for a daily copayment. (In 1999, the daily copayment for skilled nursing facility benefits is $96.) After 100 days, the patient is responsible for all charges. See Illustration 3.2 for the Medicare time line as it applies to nursing home residents.

---

### ILL. 3.2 ■ *Medicare Time Lines for Nursing Home Residents*

| **Medicare Pays** | **Medicare Pays** | **Medicare Pays** |
|---|---|---|
| all approved charges | all approved charges over the daily copayment | nothing |
| **Day 1** | **Day 21** | **Day 101** |
| Nursing home residents pay for nonapproved charges only. | Nursing home residents pay copayment and non-approved charges. | Nursing home residents pay all charges. |

### Home Health-Care Benefits

Health-care benefits for homebound patients are also available under Medicare Part A. However, here again, Medicare imposes strict standards before these benefits will be paid. The following four eligibility rules must be met:

1. A physician must prescribe and periodically review the need for home health care.

2. The patient must be homebound.

3. The care must be intermittent or part time.

4. The care must be provided by a skilled nurse who works for a Medicare-certified home health-care agency.

If these requirements are met, the full cost of part-time skilled nursing, physical therapy or speech therapy are covered. Part-time or intermittent home health aide services, occupational therapy, medical social services and medical supplies are also covered. Durable medical equipment, such as hospital beds, wheelchairs and oxygen equipment, if ordered by a physician, are also covered at 80 percent.

Normally, home health care under these guidelines is only needed for short periods of time. The typical period is about 21 days.

### Hospice Care Benefits

A *hospice* is an organization that furnishes a coordinated program of inpatient, outpatient and home care for terminally ill patients. Hospice care includes counseling, control of disease symptoms and pain relief.

Terminally ill patients can elect to receive hospice care, but only in lieu of other Medicare benefits. Under hospice care benefits, the full cost of physician and nursing services, medical appliances and supplies is paid for by Medicare. Medicare benefits for this care are available for as long as a doctor certifies the care is needed, up to 210 days for patients who are terminal (although, in some cases, patients may be recertified for benefits). The patient pays 5 percent of the cost of prescription drugs (not to exceed $5 for each prescription) and 5 percent of the cost of respite care (not to exceed five consecutive days or the current Part A deductible).

### Psychiatric Hospital Care Benefits

Inpatient care in a Medicare-participating psychiatric hospital is covered for up to 190 days. After the 190 days are used or inpatient hospital coverage is exhausted, Part A will not pay for additional inpatient care. However, if psychiatric care is received in a general hospital rather than a psychiatric hospital, Medicare treats it the same as other inpatient hospital care.

### Part A Exclusions

As noted earlier, Medicare does not cover all hospital or medical expenses. Specifically, Part A of Medicare excludes:

- personal convenience items such as television sets, radios and telephones;

- private duty nurses;

- private rooms (unless deemed medically necessary);

- custodial care in a skilled nursing facility; and

- full-time nursing care, drugs, homemaker services and meals delivered to the patient's home for home health-care benefits.

## MEDICARE PART B: SUPPLEMENTARY MEDICAL INSURANCE

Part B is the medical expense part of Medicare. Part B pays for covered medically necessary services no matter where they are received—at home, in a doctor's office, in a hospital or in a nursing home. As previously noted, although people are automatically enrolled in Part B when they enroll in Part A, they may elect to decline this coverage. If an individual elects Part B coverage, he or she must pay a monthly premium for that coverage ($45.50 in 1999).

People who initially do not elect Part B coverage may sign up for this coverage during an annual *general enrollment period* from January through March. If an individual enrolls during this period, the coverage become effective in July of the year in which he or she signs up. If an individual doesn't enroll at the earliest opportunity or drops out and enrolls again, he or she must pay a slightly higher premium to guard against adverse selection. The premiums are 10 percent higher for each full 12 months that the individual did not participate after he or she was eligible.

Part B covers the following:

- surgeons' and physicians' fees

- outpatient services

- medical lab fees

- ambulance costs

- some outpatient psychiatric care

In addition to a monthly premium, the recipient must pay an annual deductible before Part B benefits begin. (In 1999, the Part B deductible is $100.) After the annual deductible is met, Medicare will pay 80 percent of allowable charges for covered medical services and 100 percent of some costs, such as clinical diagnostic lab tests. Illustration 3.3 summarizes the coverage provided by Medicare Part B.

### Part B Exclusions

As noted earlier, not all medical services are covered under Part B. The following items and services are excluded:

- routine physical exams, eye or hearing exams and related tests;

- eyeglasses, hearing aids or dental care;

- services not medically necessary;

- most immunizations;

- diagnostic or therapeutic services of a chiropractor, except for conditions detected by an X-ray;

- full-time private nursing care in the home;

- homemaker services provided by a relative or household member; and

- most prescription drugs taken at home.

## ■ HOW CLAIMS ARE PAID

When a person becomes eligible for Medicare benefits and enrolls for those benefits, he or she receives a *Medicare card* showing a claim number and the effective dates for Part A and Part B coverage. Because the card is the only evidence that someone is covered by Medicare, it is vital that the participant keep the card in a safe place. In addition, the card contains a *claim number.* Without that claim number, a patient's claims will be denied.

Insurance companies or other organizations, such as Blue Cross/Blue Shield, contract with the government to process claims. Those who process Part A coverage claims are called *intermediaries*; those who process Part B coverage claims are called *carriers.* Hospital charges to be paid by Medicare are billed to these intermediaries or carriers who collect from Medicare. In most cases, physicians and other health-care professionals will submit charges directly to carriers by "taking assignment," which is discussed in more detail later. (Even if the doctor does not accept assignment, he or she must send the claim to the Medicare carrier on behalf of the patient.)

## ILL. 3.3 ■ *Medicare (Part B): Medical Insurance— Covered Services Per Calendar Year*

| Services | Benefit | Medicare Pays | Patient Pays |
|---|---|---|---|
| **Hospitalization** Physicians' services, inpatient and outpatient medical and surgical services and supplies, physical and speech therapy, diagnostic tests, durable medical equipment, etc. | Medicare pays for medical services in or out of the hospital | 80 percent of approved amount (after $100 deductible); 50 percent of approved charges for most outpatient mental health services | $100 deductible* plus 20 percent of approved amount and charges above approved amount**; 50 percent of approved charges for mental health services |
| **Clinical Laboratory Services** | Blood tests, biopsies, urinalysis etc. | Generally 100 percent of approved amount | Nothing for services |
| **Home Health Care** Medically necessary skilled care, home health aide services, medical supplies, etc. | Part-time or intermittent nursing care and other services for as long as patient meets criteria for benefits | 100 percent of approved amount; 80 percent of approved amount for durable medical equipment | Nothing for services; 20 percent of approved amount for durable medical equipment |
| **Outpatient Hospital Treatment** Reasonable and necessary services for the diagnosis or treatment of an illness or injury | Unlimited if medically necessary | 80 percent of approved amount (after $100 deductible) | Subject to deductible plus 20 percent of billed amount |
| **Blood** | Blood | 80 percent of approved amount (after $100 deductible and starting with fourth pint) | First three pints plus 20 percent of approved amount for additional pints (after $100 deductible)*** |

\* The Part B deductible is applied only once annually.

\*\* The amount by which a physician's charge can exceed the Medicare-approved amount is limited by law.

\*\*\* To the extent the blood deductible is met under one part of Medicare during the calendar year it does not have to be met under the other part.

*Source: The National Association of Insurance Commissioners and the Health Care Financing Administration of the U.S. Department of Health and Human Services.*

## Diagnosis-Related Groups (DRGs) and Prospective Payment System

Throughout much of its history, Medicare operated under the traditional "fee-for-service" system commonly found in Blue Cross/Blue Shield plans. Under "fee-for-service," hospitals and doctors set their own fees and Medicare paid the claims without questions. As costs increased rapidly through the 1970s, it became obvious that changes in this approach would have to be made. In the early 1980s, the concepts of *diagnosis-related groups (DRGs)* and *prospective payment system* were implemented by the federal government.

Basically, all patients are admitted to a hospital under a doctor's order because a doctor must diagnose the patient's condition and order a hospital stay to help cure that illness or injury. The doctor's diagnosis establishes the patient's DRG. Possible diagnoses are classified into 23 major diagnostic categories and then further subdivided into 477 additional categories. Virtually all hospital services fall into one of the 477 DRGs with a prospective payment schedule for each.

For example, if John is diagnosed as having a broken arm, John is admitted to the hospital under that DRG. A prospective price has been established by Medicare for that broken arm and that price is the amount the hospital will receive from Medicare for treating John, no matter how long or short his stay in the hospital may be or what services the hospital has to perform to treat him. If the DRG for John's injury says the hospital will receive reimbursement for five days but the hospital can discharge him in four days, the hospital still receives five days' reimbursement. On the other hand, if the hospital keeps John in for seven days they still get paid for only five days.

Obviously, diagnosis-related groups have given many care providers an incentive to discharge a patient as soon as possible after a procedure; the less time the provider spends with the patient, the more profitable the procedure becomes. The term "quicker and sicker" has often been used to describe the way Medicare patients are discharged from hospitals today. Since the patient often has less time to recover in the hospital, costs are controlled to some extent but the quick discharge may result in a longer recovery time at home or in a nursing home.

## Medicare-Approved Amount

The amount Medicare will pay for a physician is based on a national fee schedule that assigns a dollar value to each physician service based on work, practice costs and malpractice insurance costs. Basically, when a doctor's fee is submitted as a claim, the amount Medicare will pay for that service will be taken from the national fee schedule. After the deductible has been met, Medicare usually pays 80 percent of that amount. The patient pays the annual deductible and, in most cases, the balance due the physician.

If a person is eligible for Medicare at age 65 or older but is working for an employer with 20 or more employees, he or she is entitled to the same employer-sponsored health-care benefits as other employees. Therefore, if a person has such benefits,

Medicare becomes a *secondary payor* and pays those charges not covered under the employer's plan. These rules apply to a spouse at age 65 or older, regardless of the Medicare recipient's age. These rules also apply to any disabled Medicare enrollee who is covered by an employer-sponsored plan as a current employee or a family member, if the plan covers an employer with 100 or more employees. Finally, Medicare becomes a secondary payor if medical care can be paid under any liability policy, such as comprehensive general liability or automobile liability.

## Accepting Assignment

Physicians and suppliers may sign Medicare participation agreements stating they will accept the Medicare-approved amount as payment in full. Those health-care providers who *accept assignment* are paid directly by the Medicare carrier, except for the deductible and coinsurance amounts that the patient must pay. For example, assume that Mary Miller goes to a physician who accepts assignment and the Medicare-approved amount for the service she receives is $300. The physician can bill no more than $300 for the service. He or she submits charges directly to a carrier for the services provided and Medicare remits payment to the doctor. In this case, Mary is personally responsible for $140—$100 for the annual deductible plus 20 percent of the remaining $200, or $40. Medicare pays 80 percent of $200, or $160, of the physician's bill. After Mary has met the annual deductible, she will only be responsible for 20 percent of future Medicare-approved amounts for the remainder of the year.

All physicians and qualified laboratories who have signed participation agreements must accept assignment for Medicare-covered clinical diagnostic tests. Physicians must also accept assignment for covered services provided to patients with incomes low enough to qualify for Medicaid. Low-income people may qualify for limited financial assistance through Medicaid to pay for Medicare premiums, deductibles and coinsurance amounts, even if they otherwise do not qualify for Medicaid. (Medicaid is discussed in detail in Chapter 4.)

If a physician does not accept assignment, the patient must pay all permissible charges; however, the patient will be reimbursed by Medicare for its share of the approved amount. Physicians and other providers of services who do not accept assignment are nevertheless limited in the amount they can charge for covered services. If the actual charge is higher than the customary charge for a particular service, it may not be more than 115 percent of Medicare's allowable fee. Medicare patients do not have to pay charges that exceed the legal limit. In addition, when a physician knowingly charges more than these amounts, he or she is subject to sanctions.

## Coverage Limitations

It is clear that the coverage and benefits provided by Medicare are by no means comprehensive or complete. Because of deductibles, copayments and other limitations, there are many "gaps" in coverage. Many of the most obvious gaps are found in Medicare Part B. The first of these gaps is the annual deductible. The next gap is the difference between the actual fee a doctor charges and the allowable charge that Medicare covers. Any remaining excess charge within Medicare's legal limit must be paid entirely by the Medicare recipient. The third gap is the patient's 20 percent copayment charge of the allowable expense. The most popular way to fill these gaps is with a Medicare supplement or Medigap policy, sold by private insurance companies.

## ■ MEDICARE SUPPLEMENT INSURANCE

*Medicare supplement insurance* or *Medigap policies* are designed to pick up coverage where Medicare leaves off. The purpose of these policies is to supplement Medicare's benefits by paying most, if not all, coinsurance amounts and deductibles and paying for some health services not covered by Medicare, such as outpatient prescription drugs. Let's begin by looking at how Medigap policies were designed.

### Requirements for Medicare Supplement Policies

In late 1990, as part of the Omnibus Budget Reconciliation Act, Congress required the *National Association of Insurance Commissioners (NAIC)* to address the subject of Medicare supplement insurance policies. Specifically, this group's task was to develop a standardized model Medicare supplement policy, which would provide certain "core" benefits, plus as many as nine other policies. These model policies could then be adopted by the states as prototype policies for their insurers. The intent of this law was to reduce the number of Medicare supplement policies that were being offered for sale. It was also intended to help consumers understand and compare Medicare supplement policies (thereby helping them make informed buying decisions) by:

- standardizing coverages and benefits from one policy to the next

- simplifying the terms used in these policies

- facilitating policy comparisons

- eliminating policy provisions that could be misleading or confusing

The NAIC developed 10 Medicare standard supplement plans, ranging from the basic "core" policy, with a minimum of supplemental coverage, to policies with increasingly more comprehensive coverage. By June 30, 1992, nearly all states, U.S. territories and the District of Columbia limited the number of different Medigap policies that can be sold in any of these jurisdictions to no more than 10 standard benefit plans. (See Ill. 3.4.)

Each of the 10 plans developed by the NAIC has a letter designation ranging from "A" (the most basic policy) to "J" (the most comprehensive policy). Plan A is the "core" benefits plan; each of the remaining nine plans incorporates these core

## ILL. 3.4 ■ *Medicare Supplement Plans*

| A | B | C | D | E | F | G | H | I | J |
|---|---|---|---|---|---|---|---|---|---|
| Basic Benefits | Basic Benefits | Basic Benefits | Basic Benefits | Basic Benefits | Basic Benefits | Basic Benefits | Basic Benefits | Basic Benefits | Basic Benefits |
|  |  | Skilled Nursing Copayment | Skilled Nursing Copayment | Skilled Nursing Copayment | Skilled Nursing Copayment | Skilled Nursing Copayment | Skilled Nursing Copayment | Skilled Nursing Copayment | Skilled Nursing Copayment |
|  | Part A Deductible | Part A Deductible | Part A Deductible | Part A Deductible | Part A Deductible | Part A Deductible | Part A Deductible | Part A Deductible | Part A Deductible |
|  |  | Part B Deductible |  |  | Part B Deductible |  |  |  | Part B Deductible |
|  |  |  |  |  | Part B Excess (100%) | Part B Excess (80%) |  | Part B Excess (100%) | Part B Excess (100%) |
|  |  | Foreign Travel Emergency | Foreign Travel Emergency | Foreign Travel Emergency | Foreign Travel Emergency | Foreign Travel Emergency | Foreign Travel Emergency | Foreign Travel Emergency | Foreign Travel Emergency |
|  |  |  | At-Home Recovery |  |  | At-Home Recovery |  | At-Home Recovery | At-Home Recovery |
|  |  |  |  |  |  |  | Basic Drugs ($1,250 Limit) | Basic Drugs ($1,250 Limit) | Extended Drugs ($3,000 Limit) |
|  |  |  |  | Preventive Care |  |  |  |  | Preventive Care |

Source: National Association of Insurance Commissioners.

benefits and adds various other combinations of benefits. These combinations of benefits may not be altered by insurers nor may the letter designations be changed (though insurers may add names or titles to the letter designations).

In addition, insurers must use the same format, language and definitions in describing the benefits of each of the standard plans. The standardization of these benefit plans makes it easier for consumers to compare plans and premiums. Because each insurer's products are alike, they must compete with one another on the basis of service and price. Let's look briefly at each of the 10 standard plans and the benefits each provides.

### Plan A: Core Benefits

The basic plan, Medicare Supplement Plan A, is the "core" plan. It includes coverage for:

- the Part A coinsurance amounts for the 61st through the 90th day of hospitalization ($192 per day in 1999) and for each of Medicare's nonrenewable lifetime hospital inpatient reserve days used ($384 per day in 1999);

- 100 percent of the Medicare Part A eligible hospital expenses for 365 additional days after all Medicare hospital benefits are exhausted;

- the Part B coinsurance amount (generally 20 percent of Medicare-approved services) after the annual deductible is met; and

- the reasonable cost of the first three pints of blood each calendar year.

At a minimum, all Medicare supplement policies must contain these "core" benefits. In addition, any company that markets and sells Medicare supplement policies must make available this basic core Plan A as a separate policy.

### Plan B

Medicare Supplement Plan B must contain Plan A core benefits, plus coverage for:

- the Medicare Part A inpatient hospital deductible ($768 per benefit period in 1999).

### Plan C

Medicare Supplement Plan C must contain Plan A core benefits, plus coverage for:

- the Medicare Part A deductible;

- medically necessary emergency care in a foreign country;

- the daily coinsurance amount for skilled nursing facility care ($96 per day in 1999); and

- the Medicare Part B deductible ($100 per calendar year in 1999).

### Plan D

Medicare Supplement Plan D must contain Plan A core benefits, plus coverage for:

- the Medicare Part A deductible;

- medically necessary emergency care in a foreign country;

- the daily coinsurance amount for skilled nursing facility care; and

- "at-home recovery," which includes services to provide short-term assistance with activities of daily living for those recovering from an illness or accident.

### Plan E

Medicare Supplement Plan E must contain the core benefits of Plan A, plus coverage for:

- the Medicare Part A deductible;

- medically necessary emergency care in a foreign country;

- the daily coinsurance amount for skilled nursing facility care; and

- preventive screening or preventive medical care, such as physicals, tetanus and booster shots, flu vaccines and cholesterol screenings, up to $120 per year.

### Plan F

Medicare Supplement Plan F must contain Plan A core benefits, plus coverage for:

- the Medicare Part A deductible;

- medically necessary emergency care in a foreign country;

- the daily coinsurance amount for skilled nursing facility care;

- the Medicare Part B deducible; and

- 100 percent of Part B excess charges (that is, 100 percent coverage for the difference between the actual Medicare Part B charge as billed, subject to Medicare limitations, and the Medicare-approved Part B charge).

### Plan G

Medicare Supplement Plan G must include Plan A core benefits, plus provide coverage for:

- the Medicare Part A deductible;

- medically necessary emergency care in a foreign country;

- the daily coinsurance amount for skilled nursing facility care;

- "at-home recovery," as described for Plan D; and

- 80 percent of Part B excess charges (that is, 80 percent coverage for the difference between the actual Medicare Part B charge as billed and the Medicare-approved charge).

### Plan H

Medicare Supplement Plan H must contain Plan A core benefits, plus coverage for:

- the Medicare Part A deductible;

- medically necessary emergency care in a foreign country;

- the daily coinsurance amount for skilled nursing facility care; and

- the "basic" outpatient prescription drug benefit, which provides coverage for 50 percent of outpatient prescription drug charges, after a $250 annual deductible, up to $1,250 a year.

### Plan I

Medicare Supplement Plan I must include Plan A core benefits, plus coverage for:

- the Medicare Part A deductible;

- medically necessary emergency care in a foreign country;

- the daily coinsurance amount for skilled nursing facility care;

- "at-home recovery" services;

- 100 percent of Part B excess charges (up to the charge limitations set either by Medicare or state law); and

- the "basic" outpatient prescription drug plan, as described for Plan H.

### Plan J

Medicare Supplement Plan J, the most comprehensive of all the plans, must include Plan A core benefits, plus coverage for:

- the Medicare Part A deductible;

- medically necessary emergency care in a foreign country;

- the daily coinsurance amount for skilled nursing facility care;

- "at-home recovery" services;

- preventive screening and preventive medical care;

- 100 percent of Medicare Part B excess charges; and

- the "extended" outpatient prescription drug benefit, which provides coverage for 50 percent of outpatient drug charges, after an annual $250 deductible, up to $3,000 a year.

As you can see, no provision of any of these Medicare supplement plans duplicates benefits provided under Medicare—instead, each plan provides *supplemental coverage.* Of course, the more benefits a supplement plan offers, the more expensive it will be.

## ■ QUALIFYING FOR MEDIGAP COVERAGE

According to a federal law effective in 1991, people age 65 or older who enroll in Medicare Part B are afforded a six-month *open enrollment period* for purchasing Medigap insurance coverage. They may select any of the Medigap policies available in their state and they cannot be denied coverage because of health problems. In fact, insurers may not discriminate in the pricing of the policy or condition the issuance of the policy on good health. However, the insurer may exclude certain preexisting conditions, such as health problems treated within the six months before the policy went into effect. It is important, therefore, that agents carefully check their policies for any exclusions in order to explain such restrictions to their prospects and clients.

In general, people under age 65, disabled and enrolled in Medicare Part B are not eligible for open enrollment unless their state mandates otherwise.

### Protecting the Consumer

As stated earlier, the standardization of Medigap policies was intended to help consumers understand what these policies cover and, more importantly, what they do not cover. Consumers are now encouraged to do some "comparison shopping" before they purchase a Medicare supplement policy. Prospective insureds should compare benefits, the coverage limitations, the exclusions and the premiums of several insurers before they buy a policy. In many cases, policies that provide the same coverage will not necessarily have the same premiums.

As further protection for the consumer, purchasers have the option of reviewing their policies and canceling the coverage. Consumers can receive a refund of their premium if they notify the insurer within a specified number of days after the policy is delivered. In most states, this *free-look period* is 30 days, but some states have shorter periods.

Agents should know, and consumers should be cautioned, that although state insurance departments approve policies sold by insurance companies, this simply means that the company and the policy meet state law requirements. Neither the state nor federal governments sponsor Medigap policies. Anyone claiming to represent a government-sponsored Medigap insurance carrier should be reported to the state insurance department. This type of misrepresentation is a violation of state and federal law.

### Your Role as an Insurance Professional

Because the provisions of the Medicare program can be confusing, and the features and benefits of Medicare supplement policies so varied, an array of regulations and guidelines have been developed to support and assist agents who solicit Medicare supplement sales. These "do's and don'ts" were created by insurance agency officers, state insurance departments and federal agencies and affect your prospects, your policyholders, your carrier and you.

Basically, the following activities, if knowingly conducted to replace existing coverage with duplicate coverage, can lead to both federal and state criminal and civil penalties:

- selling Medicare policies with overlapping or duplicate coverage;

- excluding preexisting conditions under a policy;

- adopting illegal advertising, such as using any symbol of the U.S. government to imply that the government underwrites or sponsors the policy; and

- misrepresentation.

As is the case with any life or health insurance sale, the ability to meet needs based on the knowledge the agent has gained about the prospect is of paramount importance. When you clearly define these areas and know how your product works to fill the need, your sales efforts will be honest and successful.

## ■ MEDICARE+CHOICE

While Medicare is facing many challenges, the most pressing are the financial pressures resulting from changing demographics. Today, and in the future, the number of people becoming eligible for Medicare will increase rapidly and the number of workers paying taxes to support Medicare will decrease. Innovative solutions to this financial challenge must be developed and tested.

In 1997, Congress passed a law to reduce the financial strain on Medicare funds and provide Medicare beneficiaries with a variety of new health plan options. The Original Medicare Plan and Medicare supplement insurance, which is purchased from private insurance companies, are still available. However, new options are available beginning in 1999 through what is called the Medicare+Choice Program. These options include a variety of Medicare Managed Care choices, a private fee-for-service plan (PFFS) and a Medicare Medical Savings Account Plan (MSA).

Medicare's Managed Care system consists of a network of approved hospitals, doctors and other health-care professionals who agree to provide services to Medicare beneficiaries for a set monthly payment from Medicare. The health-care providers receive the same fee every month, regardless of the actual services provided. As a result of this arrangement, health-care providers try to manage care in such a way that they achieve a balance between budgetary and health-care concerns. The options available to Medicare beneficiaries include health maintenance organizations (HMOs), preferred provider organizations (PPOs) and provider-sponsored organizations (PSOs). Some HMOs and all PPOs offer a point-of-service option (POS). With a POS option, beneficiaries can use providers outside the network for an additional fee. HMOs and PSOs provide incentives for beneficiaries who use only the doctors and hospitals in the plan's network.

Although likely to be more expensive than managed care plans, a private fee-for-service plan (PFFS) offers a Medicare-approved private insurance plan. Medicare pays the plan for Medicare-covered services while the PFFS plan determines, up to a limit, how much the care recipient will pay for covered services. The Medicare beneficiary is responsible for paying the difference between the amount Medicare pays and the PFFS charges.

Medicare beneficiaries have the most control over their health-care expenditures with Medicare Medical Savings Accounts (MSAs). A Medicare+Choice MSA consists of two parts: a high-deductible insurance policy (the policy) and a savings account (the account). The policy pays for at least all Medicare-covered items and services after an enrollee meets the annual deductible of up to $6,000 (in 1999). Medicare pays the premium for the policy and deposits the difference between the premium and the fixed amount Medicare allots for each Medicare+Choice enrollee in the individual's account. Money in the account may earn interest or dividends. Money can be withdrawn from the account tax free to pay for services covered under the Medicare benefit package, as well as services listed as qualified medical expenses in the Internal Revenue Code. MSA funds also can be used to purchase long-term care insurance.

If a beneficiary does not use all of the money in his or her account during the year, the money, including interest, is carried over into the next year. A beneficiary who needs a lot of medical care may not have enough money in the account to meet the policy's deductible. In that case, the beneficiary will have to use his or her own money for medical bills until the policy's deductible is met. After that, the policy will pay some or all of the medical bills.

MSAs are available on a first-come, first-serve basis to 390,000 Medicare beneficiaries. It should also be noted that health-care providers can charge whatever they want above what is paid by the Medicare MSA policy. Furthermore, unlike other

## ILL. 3.5 ■ *Medicare Health Plan Options*

| OPTION | DESCRIPTION | CONSIDERATIONS |
|---|---|---|
| Original Medicare Plan | The traditional pay-per-visit or fee-for-service arrangement. | Individuals can go to any provider that accepts Medicare. Some services are not covered and individuals have to pay some out-of-pocket costs. |
| Original Medicare Plan with Supplemental Insurance Policy | The Original Medicare Plan plus one of the ten standardized Medicare supplemental insurance policies (Medigap) available through private companies. | Depending on the Medigap policy purchased, the individual will have coverage for some deductible and coinsurance costs and may have coverage for extra benefits not otherwise covered by Medicare. |
| Medicare Managed Care Plan | A Medicare-approved network of doctors, hospitals and other health care providers that provides care in return for a set monthly payment. May be an HMO, PSO or PPO or an HMO with a POS. | An HMO or PSO asks individuals to use only network providers. If individuals do, they may have little or no out-of-pocket cost for covered services.<br><br>A PPO or a POS lets individuals use providers outside the network for an extra out-of-pocket cost.<br><br>Some plans provide extra benefits. Some charge a premium. |
| Private Fee-for-Service (PFFS) Plan | A Medicare-approved private insurance plan. Medicare pays the plan a premium for Medicare-covered services. A PFFS plan provides all Medicare benefits. | The plan, not Medicare, decides how much to pay for the covered services. Providers may bill for more than the plan pays (up to a limit) and the beneficiary must pay the difference. Beneficiary may also have to pay a premium for a PFFS plan. |
| Medicare Medical Savings Account (MSA) Plan | A health insurance plan with a high annual deductible. Test program for up to 390,000 beneficiaries. Medicare pays the premium for the policy and deposits money into a separate account. Account funds are used to pay for medical expenses. | There are no limits on what providers can charge above what is paid by the policy. Enrollment is in November and for a year. |
| Religious Fraternal Benefit Society Plan | Offered only to society members by a religious fraternal benefit society. | |

Medicare+Choice options, individuals who choose an MSA must enroll in the Medicare MSA Plan for at least a year, from January to December. They can then withdraw by December 15 of the following year.

To be eligible for any of the Medicare+Choice options, a Medicare beneficiary must be enrolled in both Medicare Part A and Part B. Individuals with end-stage renal disease (kidney failure) cannot enroll in most Medicare+Choice plans. All programs are considered part of Medicare and will provide for all Medicare covered services. Medicare+Choice options do not replace the need for long-term care insurance.

## ■ SUMMARY

Medicare is the primary provider of medical and hospital care benefits for the elderly. Like other health-care systems, Medicare faces rapidly increasing expenses and is trying to contain costs through such innovative programs as Medicare+Choice. Keep in mind, however, that Medicare was designed to cover physician and hospital costs associated with acute illness and injuries. It was never intended to cover chronic conditions that require long-term care, whether at home or in a nursing facility.

To finance that level of care, there are three primary options: self-funding, Medicaid and private long-term care insurance. These are the subjects of our next two chapters.

## ■ CHAPTER 3 QUESTIONS FOR REVIEW

1. Which of the following statements regarding Medicare is correct?

   A. Medicare Part B—Supplement Medicare Insurance (SMI)—is voluntary.
   B. Under Medicare Part B, payment for physicians' services is unlimited.
   C. Enrollees are billed for premiums on Medicare Part A on a semiannual basis.
   D. Medicare Part A: Hospital Insurance carries no deductible.

2. In order to be eligible for Medicare's nursing home benefit, the claimant must first

   A. spend at least three days in a hospital
   B. enter a Medicare-certified skilled nursing facility
   C. have a physician certify that skilled care is required and being received
   D. do all of the above

3.  After a person qualifies for Medicare's skilled nursing home benefits, Medicare will pay 100 percent of all approved charges for

    A.  as long as the care is needed
    B.  20 days
    C.  100 days
    D.  150 days

4.  All Medicare supplement (Medigap) policies are designed to pay

    A.  all hospital and physicians' charges Medicare does not pay
    B.  some or all of Medicare's deductibles and coinsurance payments
    C.  benefits provided under Medicare Part A
    D.  benefits to those who cannot afford Medicare Part B coverage

5.  People age 65 or older who enroll in Medicare Part B may also select Medigap coverage during a(n)

    A.  open enrollment period
    B.  free-look period
    C.  grace period
    D.  free enrollment period

6.  Medicare is

    A.  a joint federal-state means tested program
    B.  a federal entitlement program
    C.  another term for Social Security
    D.  a full-service health-care program

7.  Medicare+Choice is designed to

    A.  standardize how people over age 65 receive care
    B.  replace the need for long-term care insurance
    C.  reduce the financial strain on Medicare
    D.  force more people into Medicare Part B

8.  All of the standardized Medicare supplement insurance offerings must cover

    A.  the reasonable cost of the first three pints of blood
    B.  at-home recovery
    C.  the daily coinsurance amount for skilled nursing facility care
    D.  a basic outpatient prescription drug benefit

# 4
# Medicaid and Medicaid Estate Planning

A s important as Medicare is to the elderly, it does not cover what people perceive to be their greatest health care risk: the risk of needing formal long-term custodial care in a nursing home. At costs that average $45,000 a year and more, few people can afford to finance this care on their own. Many believe the answer is Medicaid.

Medicaid, unlike Medicare, does provide for custodial and assisted care in a nursing home and it has become the largest payor of nursing home expenses. However, there are some distinct disadvantages to using Medicaid to cover these costs. In this chapter, we'll provide you with an overview of the Medicaid program and then look at Medicaid as a means of paying long-term care costs. Agents should understand that Medicaid is the primary competition they face in the long-term care insurance arena.

■ ■ ■ ■ ■

## ■ WHAT IS MEDICAID?

Government officials have long struggled to find a solution to the problem of affordable health care. In the early 1960s, President Kennedy proposed legislation to cover medical care for the poor and elderly. After many compromises, the problem of providing medical care was solved, in part, by the passage of the *Social Security Amendments of 1965.* Part of that legislation, called *Title XIX,* created a medical assistance program called Medicaid.

*Medicaid* is a government-funded, *means-tested* program designed to provide health care to poor people of all ages. The goal of Medicaid is to offer medical assistance to those whose income and resources are insufficient to meet the costs of necessary medical care. Individuals claiming benefits must prove they do not have the ability, or *means,* to pay for their own medical care. Applicants do this by completing a lengthy questionnaire, disclosing all assets and income. To qualify for Medicaid a person must be poor or become poor by spending down their assets.

When drafting the original Medicaid program, Congress's intent was to limit aid to the "deserving" poor, that is, those who are poor through no fault of their own. Therefore, Medicaid recipients generally fall into two categories:

1. pregnant women, children and families receiving "public assistance" or "welfare" under the *Aid to Families with Dependent Children (AFDC)* program; and

2. elderly, blind and disabled people receiving *Supplemental Security Income (SSI)*.

However, because many states have minimum income levels for AFDC recipients that fall below the U.S. poverty level, many poor people who technically fit into one of these two categories are still not eligible for Medicaid. The ineligible poor tend to be able-bodied people between the ages of 21 and 64, childless couples or two-parent families.

Individual states design and administer the Medicaid program under broad guidelines established by the federal government. The federal government contributes about 56 cents for every Medicaid dollar spent; state governments contribute the balance. Therefore, the extent of coverage and the quality of services vary widely from state to state. A core of services must be provided, but each state is able to design a benefit package that meets the needs of their residents through special requests or *waivers*. In general, Medicaid pays the bills for inpatient and outpatient hospital care, prescription drugs, physician services, lab and x-ray services and nursing home care, including custodial care. In addition, some states' plans provide for optional services such as home-based and community-based long-term care or care in an intermediate care facility.

Although Medicaid may be used to cover a number of medical needs, the focus of this chapter will be on Medicaid's nursing home benefits. Let's look at Medicaid's qualification requirements for these benefits.

## ■ QUALIFYING FOR MEDICAID NURSING HOME BENEFITS

Unlike Medicare, Medicaid does provide for custodial care or assisted care in a nursing home. To qualify, the potential recipient must:

• be at least age 65, blind or disabled (as defined by the recipient's state);

• be a U.S. citizen or permanent resident alien;

- need the type of care that is provided only in a nursing home; and

- meet certain asset and income tests.

Generally, people meeting these basic criteria will have their long-term nursing home care paid for by Medicaid. However, as explained earlier, individuals claiming a need for Medicaid must prove that they cannot pay for their own nursing home care. Each state (and even some counties within certain states) evaluates an individual's ability to pay by looking at the income and assets of the nursing home resident and his or her spouse. The specific limits for each of these sources vary by state and change annually. Although it is beyond the scope of this text to cite specific limits for each state, the next section provides some general guidelines.

### Income Limitations

In order to qualify for Medicaid in many states, the nursing home resident must first pass certain *income limitation tests*. For the purpose of these tests, a resident's *income* is defined as all the money that he or she receives from any source, such as Social Security benefits, pensions, annuities, investments and so on. (See Ill. 4.1.) Basically, if the resident has any income, Medicaid wants it to go for the cost of nursing home care.

The income limitation tests vary widely from state to state. In some states, any income over a certain limit—in many states this figure is $2,049 a month for 1999— totally disqualifies a patient from Medicaid assistance. In other states, if the nursing home resident's income is *more* than the cost of nursing home care, the resident must pay for the care. If his or her income is *less* than the cost of care, most or all of that income must go to the nursing home and Medicaid will make up the difference. For example, if the resident's monthly pension and Social Security benefits total $2,000

---

**ILL. 4.1 ■ *Sources of Income***

| | |
|---|---|
| Alimony | Long-term care insurance benefits |
| Annuities (when annuitized) | Private pension benefits |
| Child support | Railroad benefits |
| Contributions | Rental payments |
| Disability income benefits | Royalties |
| Dividends | Salary |
| Earnings | Social Security income |
| 401(k) benefits | State and local retirement benefits |
| Gambling winnings | Trust income |
| Gifts | Veterans' Administration benefits |
| Interest | Wages |

and the state's nursing home reimbursement amount is $3,000 a month, the resident pays $2,000 and Medicaid pays $1,000.

### Single Residents

Currently, 29 states and the District of Columbia allow a single person to qualify for Medicaid benefits regardless of his or her monthly income, as long as that income is less than the monthly nursing home bill. If the person entering a nursing home has available monthly income that exceeds the monthly cost of care, he or she must pay the nursing home directly. If the person's monthly income is less than the state's nursing home reimbursement rate (and provided the other requirements are met), Medicaid will make up the difference.

A small amount of the single resident's income can be held back to pay for personal needs or bills. The allowable amounts vary by state and range from $30 to $50 per month. Generally, this personal needs allowance is used for personal, nonmedical needs, such as books or magazines, toiletries and clothing.

Medicaid will also permit an individual to keep personal resources to pay:

- insurance premiums, including Medicare Part B and Medicare supplement insurance;

- medical expenses not paid by Medicaid, such as glasses, dentures, hearing aids and over-the-counter drugs; and

- housing expenses to maintain a home in anticipation of returning there within three to six months after entering a nursing home. (In most cases, this allowance is made only for single individuals and only if a physician certifies that the resident will be able to return to the home within six months.)

The remaining states have set limits on the amount of monthly income a single person can get and still qualify for Medicaid. These income limits are based on either the federal SSI benefit level or the cost of nursing home care in relation to a person's income.

### Community Spouse's Income Limitation

The Medicaid program does not apply the same income limitations to the *community spouse* or a *spouse-at-home* (the husband or wife who remains outside the nursing home) that it applies to the nursing home resident. Most states allow the community spouse to continue to work and to keep his or her monthly salary and/or other monthly income (such as Social Security benefits). In addition, the state usually permits the spouse to keep half of the couple's assets that generate income such as dividends or rent; however, the states have discretion in setting the amount from total joint income that the stay-at-home spouse may keep.

## Asset Limitations

In addition to the income limitations just described, Medicaid applicants in every state must pass certain *asset limitation tests*. *Assets* are basically anything of value that can be used to pay for nursing home care. This includes checking accounts, savings accounts, certificates of deposit (CDs), stocks, bonds, mutual funds, cars, recreational vehicles, jewelry, coin and stamp collections and real estate. Many states use the following definition: "cash or other liquid assets or any real or personal property that an individual (or spouse, if any) owns and could convert to cash."

Medicaid imposes limitations on the amount and type of assets that a Medicaid recipient may keep. Medicaid divides assets into two categories—countable and exempt—and uses the value of these assets to help determine Medicaid eligibility.

### Countable Assets

Before a nursing home resident can qualify for Medicaid benefits, he or she must exhaust certain *countable assets*. Generally, these items are assets that could be sold to pay for nursing home care. Countable assets include:

- cash, checking and savings accounts;

- stocks, bonds and CDs;

- IRAs, annuities or other retirements plans if the resident has access to and can liquidate the account;

- Treasury notes and Treasury bills;

- life insurance cash values; and

- vacation homes, second vehicles and every other item not specifically listed as exempt by Medicaid. (See Ill. 4.2.)

Asset exemptions vary by state, but generally, all countable assets are used to determine Medicaid eligibility and must be reduced to $2,000.

### Exempt Assets

Medicaid has determined that certain assets should not be counted when determining a person's eligibility for nursing home benefits. Consequently a person can keep these assets (no matter how much they are worth) and still be eligible for Medicaid benefits. These so-called *exempt assets* commonly include the following:

- *a house used as a primary residence* if the nursing home resident intends to return to the home; if a spouse lives in the home; if a blind, disabled or minor child lives in the home; if a child has lived in the home and cared for the

### ILL. 4.2   ■   *Countable Assets*

| | |
|---|---|
| Annuities | Mobile homes and lots |
| Antiques* | Mutual funds |
| Boats | Precious coins* |
| Burial plots and funds* | Precious metals |
| Cars and other vehicles* | Precious stones |
| Cash | Primary home* |
| Certificates of deposit | Real property* |
| Corporate bonds | Savings and checking accounts |
| Deferred compensation | Savings bonds |
| Farm equipment | Stocks |
| 401(k) accounts | Treasury bills |
| IRAs | Treasury notes |
| Jewelry* | Tools* |
| Life insurance cash values* | Trust funds |
| Livestock | Vacation homes and time shares |

* These assets may be exempt under certain conditions. See Ill. 4.3.

nursing home resident for at least two years prior to the resident entering the nursing home; or if a sibling has lived in the home and has maintained an ownership interest for at least one year;

- *household furnishings* (furniture, appliances and so on) if they are being used in the nursing home resident's home, and the home is excluded as just described;

- all *personal property;*

- *one car* if it is used to drive to work or as transportation to and from receiving medical care (many states limit the value of the car to $4,500 but if it has been adapted for a handicapped person, no value is stipulated);

- *one engagement ring and one wedding ring,* regardless of the value;

- *cash surrender value of life insurance,* if the face amount is less than $1,500 (in most states);

- *a cemetery plot* for the nursing home resident and his or her immediate family;

- *a burial trust fund* if it is an irrevocable trust (many states limit the value to under $1,500; some allow for a prepaid funeral in lieu of the burial trust fund); and

- *real property* if it is essential for support (such as land to grow food) and produces income, goods or services for one's daily activities. Many states limit the equity value of such property to $6,000. (See Ill. 4.3.)

### Protecting a Spouse's Assets

To address the problem of elderly impoverishment that so often results from the costs of long-term nursing home care, Congress enacted the *Medicare Catastrophic Coverage Act of 1988.* One of the objectives of this act was to keep the community spouse from destitution when the other spouse entered a nursing home. However, the subsequent repeal of much of that act left many people without the protection that was originally intended.

Part of the Medicare Catastrophic Coverage Act, called the *Spousal Impoverishment Act,* remains in effect. This act allows the community spouse to retain certain assets and income. In essence, most states require that the couple list all their countable assets regardless of who owns the assets, who earned them or how long they have been owned. Medicaid totals these combined assets as of the date the individual enters the nursing home and then assigns half of the value of the assets to each of the spouses. The community spouse is allowed to keep one-half of the total amount of assets as of the date the resident spouse enters the nursing home, within certain minimums and maximums that are adjusted annually for inflation. In 1999, Medicaid's minimum amount is $16,392 and the maximum amount is $81,960. (See Ill. 4.4.)

Let's look at how Medicaid's asset allowance affects a community spouse's assets. Assume that on September 1, 1999, the date that Bill enters a nursing home, Mary and Bill Jones have assets totaling $25,000. One-half of their total assets equals $12,500. This figure is less than the minimum asset allowance and so Mary will be permitted to keep the minimum asset amount, or $16,392, and Bill will be permitted to keep $2,000.

In other situations, the maximum asset allowance comes into play. For example, assume that Nancy and Joe Morgan have assets totaling $200,000 on September 1, 1999, the date Nancy enters a nursing home. In this case, one-half of the combined assets is $100,000, which is over the maximum allowed. Consequently, Joe will be permitted to keep only $81,960, the maximum allowed in 1999, and Nancy will be permitted to keep $2,000.

To further confuse the issue, states are also permitted to set the community spouse's allowable amount at any amount between Medicaid's minimums and maximums. Therefore, in the example of Mary and Bill Jones above, if their state determined that the minimum amount allowed is $20,000 instead of $16,392, Mary would be permitted to keep $20,000 and Bill would be permitted to keep $2,000.

---

### ILL. 4.3 ■ *Exempt Assets*

A primary residence or home if:

- the nursing home resident will return within six months;
- a spouse lives in the home;
- a blind, disabled or minor child lives in the home;
- a child lived in the home and cared for the nursing home resident for at least two years before the resident entered the nursing home; or
- a sibling has lived in the home and has maintained an ownership interest for at least one year.

All personal property, including antiques.

A car if:

- its value is less than $4,500*;
- it is used to drive to work;
- it is used as transportation to and from medical care; or
- it has been adapted for a handicapped person.

One engagement ring and one wedding ring.

Life insurance cash value if the original face amount of all policies totals less than $1,500.

A cemetery plot.

A burial trust fund if:

- the amount is less than $1,500* *and*
- it is in an irrevocable trust.

Real property if:

- the equity is less than $6,000* *and*
- it is essential for support *and*
- it produces goods or services for the resident's daily activities or it produces net income.

\* Some states do not have limits on these values.

---

### Spending Down Assets (Divestment)

As noted, regardless of what the marital assets are on the date the spouse *applies* for Medicaid, eligibility for Medicaid benefits is based on the couple's total marital assets as of the date the spouse *enters* the nursing home. As shown in Illustration 4.5, in order to qualify for Medicaid, the couple may be required to *spend* their assets *down* to the allowable limits.

---

### ILL. 4.4 ■ *Medicaid's Asset Allowance*

---

The community spouse may keep one-half of the total marital assets as of the date the resident spouse enters a nursing home, but not less than the minimum or more than the maximum amounts set annually by Medicaid. For example, in 1999, community spouses could keep assets valued between $16,392 and $81,960. (However, these amounts may be higher because individual states can adjust these minimum and maximum amounts.)

|      | Minimum  | Maximum  |
|------|----------|----------|
| 1994 | $14,522  | $72,660  |
| 1995 | $14,964  | $74,820  |
| 1996 | $15,384  | $76,740  |
| 1997 | $15,804  | $79,020  |
| 1998 | $16,158  | $80,760  |
| 1999 | $16,392  | $81,960  |

---

## ■ MEDICAID PAYMENT LIMITATIONS

Medicaid benefits are the fastest growing component of most states' budgets. This is due in large measure to the fact that Medicaid is paying costs for a significant portion of every state's nursing home residents. The states are faced with a dilemma: how to pay for quality care on a limited budget.

Payments to nursing homes are based on reimbursement schedules determined by the federal government, but individual states determine the final amount of reimbursement and payment due the nursing home. In most states, Medicaid pays the difference between the amount the nursing home charges and the amount of the nursing home resident's income that goes toward the cost of care. As an example, if the nursing home charges $2,000 per month and the nursing home resident's income is $1,000 (less the allowable expenses described earlier), the resident pays $1,000 and Medicaid pays $1,000 per month.

However, in order to control rising Medicaid costs, some states do not always reimburse a nursing facility for the full cost of providing care. In fact, Medicaid reimbursement is very low relative to fee-for-service levels. In other words, non-Medicaid (private pay) residents pay more for their care than the state pays for Medicaid residents. While the nursing home industry recognizes Medicaid reimbursement as an important component in their income mix, the majority of facilities prefer to have individuals who can pay their own way.

In addition, Medicaid payments to the nursing home are not always timely. One state remits payment as much as nine months behind schedule. Generally, nursing homes have small profit margins and late payments can weaken their financial stability.

## ILL. 4.5 ■ *Medicaid's Asset "Spend Down" Examples*

Although the maximum and minimum allowable assets will vary by state and change annually, assume that the following amounts apply:

| | |
|---|---|
| Maximum allowable assets for community spouse: | $81,960 |
| Minimum allowable assets for community spouse: | $16,392 |
| Maximum allowable assets for nursing home spouse: | $ 2,000 |

### Example 1

Community spouse with assets above the maximum allowance.
$200,000 in combined assets

| Community Spouse | | Nursing Home Spouse |
|---|---|---|
| $100,000 | Assets | $100,000 |
| – 81,960 | Less maximum allowance | – 2,000 |
| | Amount over maximum allowance | |
| $ 18,040 | that must be spent down | $ 98,000 |
| $ 81,960 | TOTAL ASSETS AFTER SPEND DOWN | $ 2,000 |

$200,000 in assets becomes $83,960; total spend down of $116,040.

### Example 2

Community spouse with assets between minimum and maximum allowance.
$100,000 in combined assets

| Community Spouse | | Nursing Home Spouse |
|---|---|---|
| $ 50,000 | Assets | $ 50,000 |
| – 81,960 | Less maximum allowance | – 2,000 |
| | Amount over maximum allowance | |
| $ - 0 - | that must be spent down | $ 48,000 |
| $ 50,000 | TOTAL ASSETS AFTER SPEND DOWN | $ 2,000 |

$100,000 in assets becomes $52,000; total spend down of $48,000.

**ILL. 4.5 ■** *Medicaid's Asset "Spend Down" Examples (Cont.)*

### Example 3

Community spouse with assets under the minimum allowance.
$20,000 in combined assets

| Community Spouse | | Nursing Home Spouse |
|---|---|---|
| $ 10,000 | Assets | $10,000 |
| − 16,392 | Less minimum allowance | − 2,000 |
| ($ 6,392) | | $ 8,000 |
| | Amount over maximum allowance | |
| $   - 0 - | that must be spent down | $ 8,000 |
| ($ 6,392) | | |
| | Amount transferred from nursing | |
| + $6,392 | home spouse to community spouse | − 6,392 |
| | | |
| $ 16,392 | TOTAL ASSETS AFTER SPEND DOWN | $ 2,000 |

$20,000 in assets becomes $18,392; total spend down of $1,608.

### Example 4

Nursing home resident without a community spouse.
$20,000 in combined assets

| | |
|---|---|
| Assets | $ 20,000 |
| Less maximum allowance | − 2,000 |
| | |
| Amount over maximum allowance that must be spent down | $ 18,000 |
| | |
| TOTAL ASSETS AFTER SPEND DOWN | $ 2,000 |

$20,000 in assets becomes $2,000; total spend down of $18,000.

Therefore, many nursing homes have difficulty providing adequate care for Medicaid patients. In order to maintain profitability, many nursing homes reduce staff or eliminate programs, which, in turn, has a direct effect on the quality of care Medicaid residents receive.

Finally, Medicaid does not reimburse nursing homes for "luxuries" such as telephones or televisions in rooms. If Medicaid patients cannot afford to pay for their own telephone or television, they must use those located in common areas. This obviously results in less privacy for the resident. In addition, the resident's personal needs (newspapers, magazines, clothing, hearing devices, eyeglasses and haircuts) are limited to a "personal needs allowance" of about $30 per month.

### Medicaid Access

In addition to limiting the amount of Medicaid reimbursement, states also attempt to control their costs by restricting the supply of nursing home beds. States can either limit the number of beds they will certify for Medicaid and/or the number of nursing home construction permits they approve. This creates a situation in which more people are vying for fewer beds.

Some nursing homes do not accept individuals who must use Medicaid to pay for their care. As a result, finding a nursing home for a Medicaid patient can be extremely difficult. The lucky recipients go to a nearby facility; the less lucky ones may be required to receive care hundreds of miles away from their homes and family.

Many times a Medicaid recipient requires more care than the average nursing home is able to provide. Those with behavioral problems or Alzheimer's disease are the most difficult to place. Without access to a good nursing home, the individual must stay in a hospital or in the community until an appropriate nursing home bed becomes available. It may take a few days or as long as six months for a bed in an appropriate facility to become available. And that bed may be located far from the individuals' family and friends. In most cases, private pay patients can find a bed in less time and closer to the area they desire.

In some states, nursing homes can refuse to accept a patient with Medicaid financing but they are not allowed to evict a Medicaid recipient if their facility has Medicaid-certified beds. Therefore, many nursing homes across the country are decertifying their Medicaid beds as a Medicaid resident leaves. These facilities have apparently concluded that Medicaid's red tape and lower payments make it more profitable to have an empty private pay bed than to fill it with a Medicaid resident.

## ■ PROBLEMS WITH MEDICAID ESTATE PLANNING

In the past, some individuals would "plan" to become eligible for Medicaid. The goal of this planning was to take countable assets (those that must be reduced in order to qualify for Medicaid) and to make them exempt. This typically involved such steps as transferring assets to other individuals or to a Medicaid trust. However, there are a number of reasons why such planning to qualify for Medicaid is not a good idea. Perhaps the most important reason is that there are now criminal penalties in place for those transferring assets in order to qualify for Medicaid.

### Criminal Penalties

With the passage of the Health Insurance Portability and Accountability Act of 1996 (HIPAA), and with the further clarifications made in the Tax Relief Act of 1997, criminal penalties can be levied against anyone who receives a fee for knowingly and willfully advising someone to dispose of assets in order to become eligible for Medicaid. If convicted of a misdemeanor, the advisor is subject to a fine of up to $10,000, up to one year in prison or both. If convicted of a felony, the advisor could receive up to five years in prison, up to a $25,000 fine or both. Those who previously promoted using loopholes to qualify their clients for Medicaid must recognize that much of their advice is now against the law. This could have serious ramifications for those providing Medicaid estate planning advice in the legal, accounting or financial services professions.

### Periods of Ineligibility

Perhaps the most common means of Medicaid planning was the transfer of otherwise countable assets to family or friends. Once the assets were given away, they were not countable for the purposes of determining Medicaid eligibility. However, the government has moved to close this loophole by providing that an individual's Medicaid eligibility will be delayed if he or she transfers assets for less than their market value during a specified look-back period. The look-back period is 36 months prior to either the date of application for benefits or to the date of entering the nursing home, whichever is later. In the case of the transfer of assets to a trust, the look-back period is 60 months. Some states are using a 60-month look-back period for all asset transfers.

How long is the individual's eligibility delayed? The ineligibility period is determined by dividing the amount of the asset transfer by the average monthly private patient cost of nursing home care in the state. For example, if Jane Smith transfers $35,000 in assets during the look-back period and the average monthly cost of nursing home care in Jane's state is $3,500 then Jane would be ineligible for 10 months ($35,000 ÷ $3,500 = 10 months). The result is that the Medicaid applicant pays for his or her own care for the same amount of time that the transferred assets would have covered.

### The Loss of Financial Independence

So the transfer of assets does not guarantee immediate Medicaid eligibility. However, the transfer does guarantee that the individual is now without legal control over those assets. Even if the assets were transferred to a trusted son or daughter, the individual is now perhaps put in the position of going to the son or daughter to ask for money. Emotionally, this loss of financial independence at a time when the individual's physical independence is already threatened can be very difficult to handle. Furthermore, if the son's or daughter's financial needs change it may prove difficult for even the best-intentioned child to use the assets as Mom or Dad would want them to be used.

While transferring the assets to a trust rather than a child may solve some of these problems, it creates others. Financial needs or circumstances may arise that were not anticipated by the trust document. Now the individual has a trustee making important decisions regarding his or her assets. The individual has given up control and independence to the trustee who may be a virtual stranger.

## The Loss of Choice Regarding Facilities

Even after someone financially qualifies as a Medicaid nursing home resident, the worries don't end. All of a sudden, the individual loses his or her ability to choose a nursing home.

Not all nursing homes accept Medicaid residents. There are many facilities built for private pay residents only. The rationale for this policy is simple: if Medicaid doesn't reimburse for the full cost of care (as we discussed above, it doesn't in most states), then private pay residents subsidize Medicaid residents. A private pay facility that does not admit Medicaid patients can provide care at a lower cost because its residents are not subsidizing the care provided to Medicaid patients.

Furthermore, not all nursing homes have room for a Medicaid resident. Most facilities allocate a certain number of beds for Medicaid, Medicare, and private pay residents. A nursing home administrator may find it more profitable to leave a private pay bed empty for a short period of time than to fill it with a Medicaid resident. This is especially true with regard to the better facilities. It will become an even greater problem as nursing home occupancy rates rise. Nursing homes will be more selective about their residents; they will select those residents with the potential to provide the nursing home with the highest net income.

If a Medicaid bed is not available at the time someone needs one, there will be a search for an available Medicaid bed. One could open up down the block from someone's favorite facility or it may be on the other side of town or even in the next county. People may have to wait at home or in the hospital until a Medicaid bed becomes available.

It is illegal to evict a Medicaid beneficiary out of a nursing home that accepts Medicaid residents. What happens when this person needs to enter a hospital to recover from a heart attack, stroke or broken hip? Medicaid will only pay the nursing home to hold the bed for a week or two. After that time, the bed may be given to another patient and the recovering Medicaid patient starts the process of looking for a facility all over again.

You as an advisor must understand (and you must help your clients to understand) that if Medicaid is paying the client's bills, then the client is at the mercy of Medicaid in many important ways.

## Medicaid Estate Recoveries

When Medicaid planning efforts were successful in the past, an individual could have his or her long-term care costs paid by Medicaid and, at death, still leave a sizable estate to his or her beneficiaries. The government and other taxpayers were footing the bill for an individual's long-term care costs when that individual had substantial resources. In an effort to address this inequity, federal law requires each state to have an estate recovery program.

Estate recovery programs are designed to recover the state's costs from the Medicaid recipient's estate or his or her spouse's estate. The state can recover an amount equal to the total medical assistance paid. States are allowed to recover money from countable assets, exempt assets, transferred assets and assets in trust. Payment of funeral expenses is the only allowable claim prior to a medical assistance claim. Once a Medicaid beneficiary dies, the state will likely freeze all bank accounts (a countable asset), put a lien on a home (an exempt asset) and void a change in ownership (transferred asset). States have the right to collect insurance or annuity proceeds from beneficiaries. Although states may recover costs directly from a surviving spouse, they will generally wait and recover from the surviving spouse's estate.

Money that was transferred to an individual even before the "look-back period" took effect can be recovered—there is no statute of limitations or grandfather clauses. If Mom gave her son $25,000 five years before she went to a facility, it would not be a countable asset when Mom applied for Medicaid. Once Mom dies, though, the state can bill the son for the $25,000. In one case, a mother gave her son a farm five years before entering a facility and then qualified for Medicaid. Her son sold the farm and bought a house in town. After his Mom died, the son got a big bill from the estate recovery program and sold his home to pay it.

States may also recover money from trusts. States like trusts because there is a complete accounting of the Medicaid beneficiary's money in the trust. They know who got how much and where to go to recover the amount of money they paid for the benefit of the individual.

This type of estate recovery program was pioneered by the state of Oregon. They found that for each tax dollar invested in estate recovery, they get fourteen dollars back. Estate recovery then is an excellent way for the state to increase revenues without increasing taxes. For example, California recovered almost $22 million in 1993. As state estate recovery programs show success in recovering assets from Medicaid beneficiaries estates, they will become more aggressive in "following the money." This can be seen in Wisconsin's estate recovery program.

Wisconsin has delegated the responsibility of estate recovery to the counties. Counties receive a percentage of the amount they collect. So now local governments have a financial incentive to monitor individual cases—from the time someone first applies for Medicaid assistance until the day they die. In order to qualify for Medicaid in Wisconsin, an Estate Recovery Program Disclosure Sheet must be completed. The state, county and "client" all get a copy. This information can be used to recover money after the Medicaid beneficiary dies.

As an advisor, it may be worthwhile to find out exactly what your state and county are doing regarding estate recovery. Your local Medicaid office may have a brochure on their estate recovery program. When this information is relayed to your clients, they will have a better understanding of Medicaid's limits and the value of long-term care insurance.

## Ethical Questions Associated with Medicaid Estate Planning

In addition to the possibility of criminal penalties, the use of Medicaid estate planning to fund nursing home costs creates certain moral, ethical and malpractice risks for attorneys and other financial advisors. The Medicaid eligibility requirements, transfer-of-asset rules and income limitations are fairly complex. Even experienced attorneys may find themselves confused by state and federal policies that change frequently. In fact, one expert has estimated that nearly 9 out of 10 attorneys give incorrect advice about Medicaid estate planning options.[1]

There may be a conflict of interest for advisors who find it difficult to determine whether their client is the elderly parent or the heir to the family "fortune." Many adult children attempt to shift the burden of nursing home costs to the government while maintaining their share of the parents' estate. The attorney who is acting on behalf of the adult child may, in fact, condemn the parent to an inferior Medicaid-approved nursing home.

Finally, there are ethical and moral questions for the individuals involved. Is it appropriate for middle-class individuals to use health-care benefits that were originally intended for poor women and children? Some people argue that when someone is permitted to protect his or her assets while receiving Medicaid benefits, at least four groups suffer:

1. the nursing home resident who will likely receive lower quality care;

2. the truly needy who have only a predetermined amount of money allocated for their needs;

---

[1] Stephen Moses, Center for Long-Term Care Financing, Seattle, WA.

3. the nursing home because it loses money on the Medicaid reimbursement payment; and

4. taxpayers whose tax dollars are helping the middle class rather than the needy.

All these ethical and moral problems compound the legal and practical problems we have already discussed regarding Medicaid planning.

## ▮ SUMMARY

Medicaid is a joint federal and state program to pay health-care expenses for the poor. In order to qualify for Medicaid benefits, an individual must meet certain asset and income limitation tests. In the past, Medicaid estate planning has been used to shield assets from devastating nursing home bills; however, providing advice on how to transfer assets to qualify for Medicaid is now illegal. Even if certain planning steps are found to be legal, there are financial, emotional and ethical disadvantages to the type of planning involved in qualifying for Medicaid.

As the U.S. population ages, it seems likely that the government will find it increasingly difficult to fund long-term nursing home care. Given the financial and emotional costs of qualifying for Medicaid coverage, consumers are looking for other ways to pay for long-term care. In Chapter 5, we'll look at the logical solution to this problem—long-term care insurance.

## ▮ CHAPTER 4 QUESTIONS FOR REVIEW

1. Medicaid is a government-funded program designed to provide medical assistance for

   A. retired government employees
   B. low-income people who meet certain asset and income limitation tests
   C. elderly people who are not covered by Medicare
   D. disabled people who do not have Medigap coverage

2. All of the following are considered to be exempt assets when determining an applicant's eligibility for Medicaid EXCEPT

   A. a wedding ring
   B. a burial trust fund
   C. an individual retirement account
   D. reasonable household furnishings

3. The at-home spouse of a nursing home resident is often referred to as a

   A. care recipient
   B. custodial spouse
   C. care manager
   D. community spouse

4. Eligibility for Medicaid benefits is based on a couple's marital assets

   A. before entering the nursing home
   B. before applying for Medicaid
   C. upon entering the nursing home
   D. after qualifying for Medicaid

5. Medicaid is

   A. a joint federal-state means-tested program
   B. a federal entitlement program
   C. another term for Social Security
   D. a full-service health-care program

6. A Medicaid period of ineligibility occurs when

   A. an applicant has family available to provide care for a limited time
   B. an applicant can afford to pay for his or her own care
   C. income temporarily exceeds the state limit
   D. assets are transferred during the look-back period

7. A community spouse is able to keep additional

   A. assets and income
   B. income only
   C. assets only
   D. neither assets nor income

8. Receiving a fee for providing advice on disposing of assets to qualify for Medicaid is

   A. legal if the advice is provided by a lawyer
   B. legal if the advice is provided during the lookback period
   C. illegal
   D. illegal only when the advice is provided by an unlicensed financial advisor

# LTC Policy Features

T o many, relying on family or friends or becoming impoverished to qualify for Medicaid are unattractive solutions to their long-term care needs. Yet these people must understand that the daily cost of a nursing home, once less than an average hotel room, has skyrocketed. Today, funding a year's stay in a nursing home is out of the reach of many people who need that kind of care. For them, the solution may be long-term care (LTC) insurance.

Though long-term care insurance policies aren't a recent innovation, *quality* long-term care insurance is relatively new. As the need for long-term care insurance has grown, insurers have reevaluated their products and responded with coverages that are better designed and more comprehensive than their early counterparts. In addition, today's policies are far less restrictive with regard to the conditions or events that trigger payment of benefits. More and more insurance companies are beginning to offer quality long-term care coverage.

In this chapter, we'll look at typical features and benefits of LTC policies and provide guidelines to help you evaluate such provisions. We'll discuss how and when a long-term care policy's benefits are triggered and the kinds of care providers these policies cover. Options to individually-sold, stand-alone LTC insurance policies are also discussed. As an agent, you'll have to review various LTC policies to determine which best fit your clients' needs and objectives.

■ ■ ■ ■ ■

## ■ THE EVOLUTION OF LONG-TERM CARE POLICIES

Long-term care insurance began to appear after Medicare was enacted in 1965, although the products offered then bear little resemblance to today's products. Early LTC insurance mirrored Medicare's requirements for benefits: that is, coverage was provided only to those who received skilled care in a Medicare-certified skilled nursing facility after spending three days in a hospital. The benefit periods were limited to a year or two and the elimination periods coordinated with Medicare's 20-day and 100-day benefit payments. Typically, these early policies had the following coverage restrictions:

- A three-day prior hospital stay was required before nursing home benefits were payable.

- There were limitations on the length of time after a hospital stay the recipient could wait before entering a nursing home in order to receive benefits.

- Alzheimer's disease or similar forms of senility or irreversible dementia were often excluded.

- Certain types or levels of care were required before custodial care benefits were payable.

- Contracts were not always guaranteed renewable.

- Inflation protection was rarely available.

While those early long-term care policies would not meet the needs of today's market, Medicare is also an unattractive long-term care provider. In 1988, Congress passed the Medicare Catastrophic Health Care Act, which eliminated Medicare's three day prior hospitalization requirement and expanded the Medicare benefit maximum to 150 days. However, consumers realized that Medicare was not designed to pay for nursing home care and that they had to pay higher Medicare premiums for this and other limited expansions. The 1988 act that passed with great fanfare was repealed in 1989. These developments regarding Medicare, along with the rapidly rising nursing home costs, made consumers and insurers aware of the huge financial risk that the average nursing home stay posed.

Competitive pressures and consumer demands encouraged insurers to offer more features and benefits in order to attract more policyholders. Insurers have found that consumers are willing to pay slightly higher premiums in return for a better product that covers additional risks. Today, long-term care insurance policies typically cover skilled, intermediate and custodial care in state-licensed nursing homes. They also offer coverage for home health services provided by state-licensed and/or Medicare-certified home health-care agencies. In addition, many policies cover adult day services and other care in the community. The aging population and an increased incidence of chronic illness have produced an enormous market for LTC insurance policies. As the need for coverage continues to grow and change, the policies themselves will evolve as well.

### ILL. 5.1 ■ *Consumer Protection*

In order to qualify for favorable tax treatment under HIPAA, an LTC policy must have certain consumer protection features. While you as the agent will not be drafting policies yourself, it may be helpful for you to understand what benefits were considered important enough to be included in this legislation. These protections include:

- All contracts must be guaranteed renewable.
- Preexisting conditions can be excluded up to a maximum of six months after issue. (If a new contract replaces another contract, the new contract must recognize the previous contract's satisfaction of the insured's six-month preexisting condition.)
- Contracts cannot require prior hospitalization before paying nursing home benefits or require prior institutionalization before paying home care benefits.
- Contracts cannot exclude any specific illnesses (such as Alzheimer's disease).
- Contracts must provide protection against unintentional lapse because of a physical or cognitive impairment.
- Companies cannot utilize "post-claims" underwriting.
- Contracts providing home care benefits cannot restrict allowable care to only skilled care, and must provide coverage for a meaningful length of time.
- Contracts must offer inflation protection.
- Companies must offer a nonforfeiture option.

Most reputable companies in the LTC insurance industry were already meeting these consumer protection standards. Many states had adopted these requirements before the passage of HIPAA.

## Tax-Qualified and Nontax-Qualified Plans

A new class of long-term care insurance policies called *tax-qualified long-term care insurance* was established with the passage of the Health Insurance Portability and Accountability Act of 1996 (HIPAA). Policies that meet standards set forth in this act state on their cover and in marketing materials that the policy is intended to be a qualified plan. The word "intend" or "intended" is used because the federal government does not have a mechanism for certifying that policies are "qualified." However, a policy that clearly does not meet the standards cannot state that it is "intended to be a qualified plan."

A tax-qualified long-term care policy (TQ) is any insurance contract that provides only coverage of qualified long-term care services and meets the following additional requirements:

- The contract must be guaranteed renewable.

- The contract must not provide for a cash surrender value or other money that can be paid, assigned, borrowed or pledged.

- Refunds under the contract (other than refunds paid upon the death of the insured or complete surrender or cancellation of the contract) and dividends may only be used to reduce future premiums or to increase future benefits.

- The contract must meet certain consumer protection standards. (See Ill.5.1.)

- The contract must coordinate benefits with Medicare (unless Medicare is a secondary payor) or the contract is an indemnity or per diem contract.

*Qualified long-term care services* include necessary diagnostic, preventive, therapeutic, curing, treating, mitigating and rehabilitative services as well as maintenance and personal care services that are required by a *chronically ill individual* and are provided in accordance with a plan of care prescribed by a licensed health-care practitioner.

A chronically ill individual is any individual certified within the previous 12 months by a licensed health practitioner as (1) being unable to perform at least two activities of daily living for a period expected to last at least 90 days owing to a loss of functional capacity, (2) requiring substantial supervision to protect the person from threats to health and safety because of severe cognitive impairment or (3) having a similar level of disability as designated by regulation.

Under the ADL trigger, the policy must take into account at least five of the following ADLs in determining whether an individual is chronically ill: eating, toileting, transferring, bathing, dressing and continence.

Plans that do not meet these requirements are nontax-qualified long-term care insurance (NTQ). These plans are easily identified by one or more of the following characteristics:

- physical impairment does not need to be expected to last at least 90 days;

- physical impairment requirement can be met with just one ADL impairment;

- physical impairment requirement can be met with an impairment with two or more of any ADLs;

- fewer than five ADLs can be assessed in determining whether an individual is chronically ill;

- physical impairment requirement can be met with an impairment of instrumental activities of daily living (IADLs) only;

- the physical impairment requirement can be met without reference to the need for "substantial" assistance;

- the insured can qualify for benefits:
  - because of a "medical necessity";
  - without a "severe" cognitive impairment; and
  - without a plan of care submitted to the insurance company;

- benefits reimburse for actual charges but do not coordinate with Medicare[1];

- plan pays benefits for services received from unskilled providers or family members[1];

- plan pays benefits for services not related to caring for the insured;

- plan pays for capital improvements to a home; or

- plan includes a cash payment type of return of premium at lapse.

There are those who believe it is easier to qualify for benefits with a nonqualified plan. They say there could be as many as 40 percent more claims qualifying for benefits under nonqualified plans while others say there is a negligible difference between the number of claims qualifying for benefits under nonqualified and qualified plans. If it is easier to qualify for benefits under a nonqualified plan, the premiums for a nonqualified plan will be higher than those for a qualified plan from the same company. (The company or actuary designing a plan with the expectation to pay more benefits needs to charge extra for it if proper pricing techniques are used.) The amount of the premium increase is directly proportional to the additional valid claims that are expected.

There is much debate concerning which type of policy is better: a tax-qualified (TQ) or nontax-qualified (NTQ) policy. Distinctions between TQ and NTQ plans will be pointed out and explained throughout this chapter.

## ■ STANDARD FEATURES OF LONG-TERM CARE POLICIES

The *National Association of Insurance Commissioners (NAIC)* is an association of the top insurance administrators from each state. As you will recall from our discussion of Medicare supplement insurance in Chapter 3, the NAIC meets regularly to discuss various insurance issues. The NAIC proposes recommendations and *model acts* that are intended to create better insurance laws and promote uniformity among the states. While state legislators will often look at the NAIC's

---

[1.] A tax-qualified long-term care insurance plan (TQ) can also pay benefits for unskilled providers or family members and does not have to coordinate benefits with Medicare if the benefits are paid without regard to actual cost. These types of plans are normally referred to as *indemnity* plans. Plans that are concerned with actual cost are referred to as *reimbursement* plans. These plans are discussed in Chapter 6.

recommendations when drafting or adopting state regulations or laws, the NAIC has no power to enforce its recommendations.

As with Medicare supplement policies, the NAIC has developed minimum standards for long-term care policies that attempt to balance the consumer's interest with the insurance company's ability to successfully market quality coverage. The model act and regulations exemplify the type of language state insurance departments should use in regulating long-term care policies. On a regular basis, the NAIC updates its model act and regulation to reflect changes occurring in the industry.

Most insurers have developed their LTC products to meet or exceed the NAIC's guidelines. As an agent, you will want to carefully review policy language, terms and conditions to be certain that the policy or policies you are offering provide comprehensive protection and benefits for your prospects and clients. Let's begin by looking at some of the features shared by all LTC policies.

### Free-Look Period

Most states require a *free-look period* of 30 days. This allows consumers to review and return the LTC policy if they are dissatisfied for any reason. If the policy is returned within the specified time period, the consumer receives a full refund of premium.

### Guaranteed Renewability

When long-term care insurance was first introduced, it was a *conditionally renewable* contract. This gave insurers wide latitude to raise rates and/or cancel coverage. Today, quality LTC policies are *guaranteed renewable.* This means that the insurer cannot cancel the policy and that the insurer cannot require the insured to provide evidence of insurability in order to renew the policy. The insured may cancel a policy by requesting cancellation in writing or by simply not paying the premium when it is due.

A guaranteed renewable contract also provides that premiums cannot be raised unless there is a rate increase for all policyholders in a particular group. *Noncancellable policies,* which guarantee that premiums will not rise, are rare in the LTC insurance industry.

The NAIC model provides that no LTC policy can be canceled, nonrenewed or otherwise terminated solely on the grounds of the insured's age or health. Most states either follow these NAIC guidelines or have created their own state statutes to guarantee renewability.

## Level Premiums

Premiums for long-term care insurance are typically based on the product design (which the prospect controls), the prospect's health status (which he or she controls to a lesser degree) and the prospect's age (which he or she controls by deciding when to purchase an LTC policy). Obviously, the younger the buyer, the less he or she pays for insurance. Although rates vary by company, generally speaking, a 50-year-old will pay about half as much as a 60-year-old insured; a 60-year-old insured will pay half the cost of a 70-year-old; and a 70-year-old will pay about one-third less than an 80-year-old insured for the same insurance policy. In most cases, regardless of the insured's age at the time of purchase, the premiums remain level for the life of the policy.

Simply stated, a *level premium* takes into account all of the anticipated increases in premium over the lifetime of a policyowner or over the entire term of the policy. It does this in effect by charging additional amounts in the early years of the policy and setting aside these additional amounts in a fund known as a *reserve*. Then, in the policy's later years, this reserve, consisting of excess premium dollars plus investment income from the excess premiums, is used to pay the claim. Consequently, the policy's premium can remain level throughout the policy term.

Most insurers use *class rates* to determine premiums for LTC policies. Insurers are able to identify "classes of insureds" in their long-term care insurance business. A class of insureds can be based on a geographic region such as a state, age at issue such as *all over age 70,* underwriting category such as *all preferred risks* or benefit design options such as *all with an unlimited maximum.* Based on its claims experience, rates for an entire class may be adjusted up or down. However, no single policy can be experience rated or canceled because of the individual insured's age, health status or claims experience. Inadequate rates and the need to increase premiums can generally be attributed to poor underwriting prior to policy issuance or bold actuarial assumptions, rather than rising long-term care costs.

## Waiver of Premium

Policies typically include a *waiver of premium* provision that permits the policyholder to stop paying premiums while he or she is in a nursing home for a specified period of time and the insurer has begun to pay benefits. However, only a few policies waive premiums if care is received at home.

## Preexisting Conditions Limitation

Many insurers include a *preexisting conditions limitation* to help protect themselves from early claims arising from conditions known to the insured. When a company uses medical underwriting before policy issuance (discussed in detail in Chapter 7), serious preexisting conditions such as stroke or heart disease, usually disqualify the applicant. Less serious preexisting conditions, such as a broken arm or a history of minor allergies, are usually covered after a waiting period of up to six months following the effective date of the policy. Most policies today require no waiting period before a preexisting condition is covered.

## ■ LONG-TERM CARE BENEFIT TRIGGERS

All forms of insurance have triggers for determining when benefits are paid. A *benefit trigger* is an event or condition that must occur before benefits are paid. For example, a fender dented in an accident would be a benefit trigger for an automobile insurance policy. Damage from a fire or flood would be a benefit trigger for a home insurance policy. Someone's death would be a benefit trigger for a life insurance policy.

Determining benefit triggers for long-term care policies is not so simple. When long-term care policies were introduced, insurers frequently required at least three days of prior hospitalization or skilled nursing home stays before the LTC policy benefits were "triggered." Although policies no longer require prior hospitalization, TQ policies require a licensed health-care practitioner's certification that nursing home or home care is required because of a physical or severe cognitive impairment.

### The Functional Model

Today's policies use a *functional model* to measure the insured's ability to function independently in the community. This encompasses both physical and cognitive measurements. Without using a cognitive measure, claims for Alzheimer's disease patients (who may be able to complete most activities of daily living [ADLs] but who need assistance and supervision throughout the day) could be denied. It is important, therefore, that the insurer measure both the applicant's physical and cognitive abilities before paying benefits.

#### *Physical Assessment*

The basis of physical impairment research is a 1963 study by Sidney Katz in which he developed a measurement of physical functioning called *activities of daily living (ADLs)*. These ADLs have been used to (1) predict the length of hospital stays, the use of services and the need for health and supportive care among the elderly, (2) determine disability compensation and (3) chart changes in health status.

Activities of daily living provide an excellent means to assess an individual's need for nursing home care, home health care or other health-related services. A policy should indicate what number and/or type of ADLs will be used to trigger benefits; when the insured cannot independently perform these ADLs, benefits will be paid to cover expenses for assistance with those activities.

**ILL. 5.2 ■ *The Impairment Continuum—Activities of Daily Living***

This illustration shows the progression of impairments included in the activities of daily living.

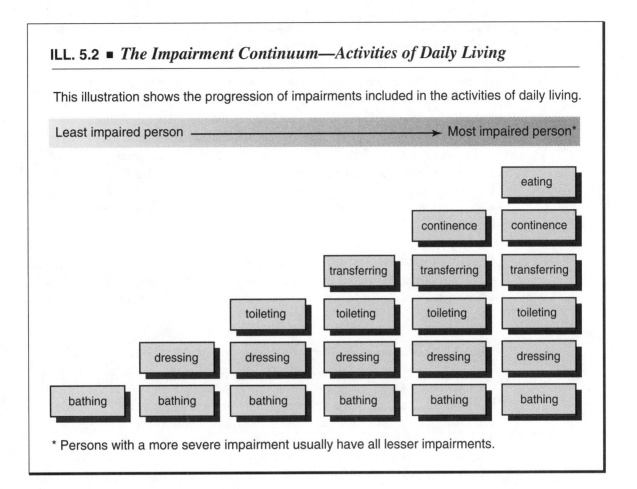

Least impaired person ⟶ Most impaired person*

* Persons with a more severe impairment usually have all lesser impairments.

As you may recall from Chapter 1, individuals tend to become physically impaired in a specific order because of chronic conditions. As indicated in Illustration 5.2, impairment tends to progress from only problems with one or two activities to problems with all the activities of daily living. Understanding the impairment continuum will help the agent to understand the physical assessment. When comparing policies, the agent should note *where* on the impairment continuum an insurer is likely to pay benefits, not just *how many* ADLs need to be impaired.

For example, some companies do not assess bathing or one of the earlier lost ADLs. If these early impairments are not assessed, the level of impairment that will trigger benefits may be toileting. The result is that benefits are not paid until the "on demand" level of care is needed.

The company should evaluate the insured's normal method of performing the ADL. For example, if the insured normally lives alone and uses a bathtub for bathing, the ability to use the tub and wash alone should be assessed. However, some insurers will not pay benefits unless the insured first installs special equipment (such as grab bars) or changes habits (requiring showers instead of baths). Changing habits or installing equipment should be the insured's option—not the company's right. Agents should look for these policy restrictions.

A new issue has arisen regarding the assessment of ADLs and an individual's impairment; namely, whether an individual requires "hands-on" assistance or "standby" assistance to complete an ADL. For example, let's look at transferring. "Standby" assistance requires a caregiver to be present as the insured gets out of bed and moves to a chair. "Hands-on" assistance requires the caregiver to hold or help lift the insured out of bed and lower him or her into a chair. These distinctions become important when comparing and pricing LTC products because a policy that covers only those individuals requiring hands-on assistance would provide fewer benefits.

**Benefit Triggers Under HIPAA.**   Insurance companies offering TQ policies must use ADLs as one of their benefit triggers. HIPAA requires insurers to trigger benefits when an individual is impaired in at least two of the following: bathing, dressing, toileting, transferring, continence and eating.

HIPAA has also standardized the level of assistance that must be present before qualifying for benefits under the ADL trigger. The claimant must be receiving "substantial assistance." HIPAA does not define "substantial assistance," but the IRS has issued a Notice stating that it refers to "hands-on" assistance as well as "standby" assistance. This level of assistance must be expected to last at least 90 days. (This does not require all TQ policies to have a 90-day elimination period but rather requires the licensed health-care practitioner performing an assessment to use his or her best judgment to determine whether an impairment will last 90 days.) These two requirements are integral parts of the law's intent to allow only chronically ill individuals to qualify for tax-free benefits.

### Cognitive Assessment

Comprehensive tests have been developed to measure common cognitive impairments such as intellectual instability or memory loss. These types of cognitive assessments are important because companies that perform only physical assessments of the cognitive condition may miss some people who are physically able to pass the tests but forget how or why to perform the tasks or cannot perform them safely on their own. Typically, these tests include a "delayed word recall" test that measures the applicant's short-term memory loss. The applicant might be asked to study a list of words for a few minutes and then recall the list from memory. These tests may also ask questions that are easily answered by individuals with adequate short-term and long-term memory capabilities but are difficult for individuals losing their ability to think, perceive, reason or remember. To be assured that a cognitive measurement will be used at claim time, the agent can look for specific terms in the contract: *think, perceive, reason, remember, calculate, orientation* and *memory.*

The policy should also indicate whether benefits will be paid if the insured is too mentally incapacitated to remember to perform the task. Many people are physically able to perform all ADLs but require constant supervision, prompting or cuing in order to complete them safely. The agent should be certain that the contract he or she sells has specific language stating the company will pay for cognitive impairments independently from the physical measure. For example, if the insured is physically able to dress but must be told how to dress because of memory loss, the contract should allow the insured to qualify for benefits under the cognitive measurement.

HIPAA requires TQ plans to trigger benefits when an individual requires substantial supervision to protect the individual from threats to health and safety due to severe cognitive impairment. According to the IRS Notice regarding HIPAA, severe cognitive impairment means a loss or deterioration in intellectual capacity that is (1) comparable to Alzheimer's disease (and similar forms of irreversible dementia) and (2) measured by clinical evidence and standardized tests that reliably measure impairment in the individual's short-term and long-term memory; orientation to people, places and time; and deductive and abstract reasoning. This "severe cognitive impairment" must result in the insured needing "substantial supervision," which means someone is present throughout the day to protect the insured from threats to his or her health and safety. An NTQ plan is free to define a cognitive impairment using other terms.

### The Assessors

Who measures ADLs and cognitive abilities varies among insurers. Although it may not be clear from the contract language, some companies will use an insured's physician to determine the claimant's ability; other companies use their own specially trained employees to make the assessment; still others use a third party such as an outside consultant or assessment team.

An individual's personal physician often has not been trained to measure ADLs and may lack a sense of urgency about completing the assessment. An insurance company employee seldom is objective because he or she is working for the insurer. Using properly trained, third-party assessors living in the claimant's community will provide the most timely, objective and consistent measure of a claimant's ability to remain independent.

HIPAA requires that the assessment be performed by a licensed health-care practitioner but permits the insurer to select the individual. An NTQ plan can use any assessor it chooses.

## ■ DEFINITION OF PROVIDERS OF CARE

Another aspect of long-term care policies is the extent of coverage as determined by how the provider of care is defined. Agents should examine their policies carefully

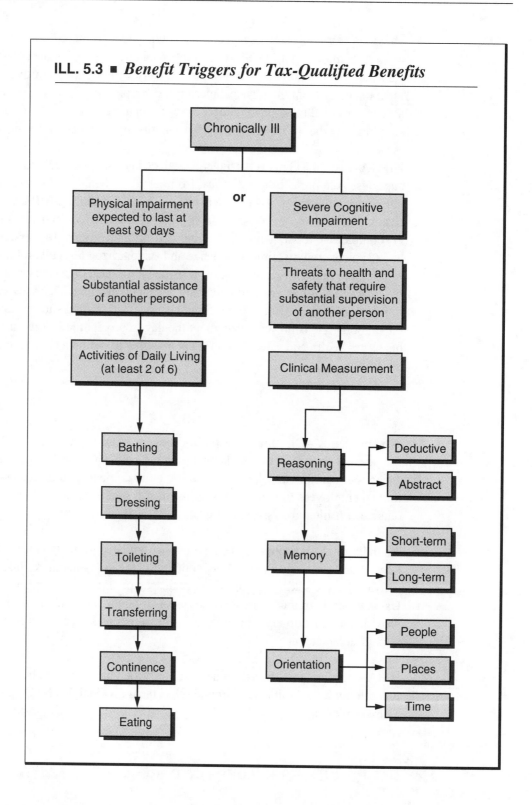

**ILL. 5.3 ■ *Benefit Triggers for Tax-Qualified Benefits***

Chronically Ill

Physical impairment expected to last at least 90 days

or

Severe Cognitive Impairment

Substantial assistance of another person

Threats to health and safety that require substantial supervision of another person

Activities of Daily Living (at least 2 of 6)

Clinical Measurement

Bathing

Dressing

Toileting

Transferring

Continence

Eating

Reasoning

Deductive

Abstract

Memory

Short-term

Long-term

Orientation

People

Places

Time

because these are critical components when comparing policies. At one time, LTC policies followed Medicare's definition but now coverage is provided for a broader range of providers. The providers commonly covered by LTC policies are nursing homes, alternate care facilities, home health-care agencies and adult day centers.

## Nursing Homes

Regardless of how much they have improved over the years, nursing homes still have a negative image. In an effort to improve the public's perception of these homes (as well as improve the actual care provided), many LTC policies now require that a nursing home be state licensed and Medicare certified, maintain proper medical records, have a certain number of beds and have a physician and/or registered nurse on duty or on call at all times. When the agent is comparing policies, he or she should look for a plan that requires licensing as well as other reasonable requirements.

## Alternate Care Facilities

Most companies offering long-term care insurance have seen care providers evolve over the past 10 years and have expanded their coverage to account for the changes. Possibly the biggest change in the long-term care provider network is the advent of *alternate care facilities*. These facilities provide less intense care than a nursing home. They are also referred to as assisted-living facilities, community-based residential facilities (CBRF), adult foster care homes, personal care homes or residential care facilities for the elderly.

Alternate care facilities provide personal and environmental services but also offer the independence many individuals need. Typically, the residents need personal care or assistance with activities of daily living along with limited amounts of health care. Prepared meals, housekeeping, laundry services and preventive health services (such as blood pressure checks) are provided to assist the residents. The facility will have a nurse on call and keep health records (including the name of a physician) on file for each resident.

Some insurers include these facilities as part of their home care plans while others include them as part of their nursing home plans. In either event, insurance benefits are payable when a claimant is unable (rather than unwilling) to remain independent. Measuring the difference between ability and willingness is difficult; as a result, some companies have delayed providing benefits in alternate care facilities. Furthermore, many companies will reduce the amount payable or available to the claimant because the cost for care in these facilities is less than a nursing home.

## Home Health-Care Agencies

Home health-care (HHC) agencies provide a variety of services including nursing care; nutrition services; physical, speech and occupational therapy; home health aid; and medical care. However, most insurers restrict coverage of the types of services provided by HHC agencies.

Insurers typically divide covered services into personal and medical care categories. *Personal care* includes assistance with daily living activities such as bathing, dressing and personal hygiene. Normally, a family member will complement the work of a home health aide or personal care worker in completing these tasks. *Medical care,* such as administering medications, skin care and catheter treatments, must be administered by a qualified nurse.

Be aware that some insurers offer stand-alone home health-care plans that can easily be misunderstood or misconstrued as long-term care plans. While home health-care is typically the first type of long-term care that insureds use, it is not always the last. Under a stand-alone HHC plan, HHC benefits will end once the insured enters a nursing home. Imagine telling your client, "You are too sick to receive benefits with this home health-care plan. You should have bought a nursing home plan as well."

The best LTC policies will provide benefits only for high-quality HHC. However, measuring quality can be complicated. Some insurers require that HHC agencies be Medicare certified and/or state licensed. This type of requirement can create some problems. Many of the best HHC agencies do not want Medicare patients because Medicare covers only a portion of the actual cost of providing care. Therefore, a policy requiring Medicare certification can severely limit the insured's freedom of choice because only about half of HHC agencies are Medicare certified.

Similarly, keep in mind that some states do not license HHC agencies. In these states, an insurer requiring licensing by the state will not pay HHC benefits. To avoid these problems, some state insurance departments require insurance companies to adopt uniform language before their home care policies will be approved. The agent should look for a policy that has prudent restrictions on HHC provider requirements.

### Adult Day Centers

When caregivers are employed or must be away from the impaired person, they frequently turn to adult day centers (ADCs). Insurers usually require that such centers be licensed by the state, have no overnight accommodations, have regular hours of operation and maintain certain patient-to-staff ratios. In addition, some insurers require that a registered nurse, dietician, therapist or physician be on the ADC staff. Generally, when comparing policies, the fewer ADC restrictions, the better.

### ■ POLICY LANGUAGE AND OUTLINES OF COVERAGE

As legal contracts, insurance policies tend to be lengthy and contain a number of detailed clauses and provisions. Like all legal contracts, LTC policies are open to interpretation. Therefore, every provision must be set forth in clear and definite terms to protect the policyowner's and the insurer's rights. It is essential that the language be as clear and unambiguous as possible. Through the years, court decisions, legislative mandates and individual state governments have played important roles in shaping the language of insurance contracts.

All states mandate that the insurers provide the consumer with an *outline of insurance coverage* to make comparison shopping easier. Outlines must meet standards of full and fair disclosure and describe the policy's benefits and coverage, premium cost, exclusions, restrictions, renewability requirements and eligibility conditions. However, outlines of LTC coverage or company brochures simply do not provide all the information an insurance professional will need to make a valid comparison between policies. Therefore, it is best to obtain a sample or actual contract when comparing LTC policies. Sample policies are available from most companies or from the state insurance department.

## ■ TAX TREATMENT OF LONG-TERM CARE INSURANCE

The Health Insurance Portability and Accountability Act (HIPAA) was signed into law in August 1996. This law set standards that long-term care insurance policies issued after December 31, 1996, must meet in order to qualify for favorable tax treatment. This created a new class of long-term care insurance known as Tax-Qualified Long-Term Care Insurance or TQ.

Under the new law, qualified long-term care insurance policies are now treated in the same manner as accident and health insurance contracts. That is, amounts received under a TQ are excluded from income as amounts received for personal injuries and sickness. On per diem contracts, the amount of the exclusion is capped at $175 per day for 1997; this amount will be indexed for inflation in future years.

Claimants who own a TQ policy are now assured their benefits will receive favorable tax treatment. Every dollar they receive from the insurance company can go toward paying for care. HIPAA and the IRS have not addressed the issue of how benefits from an NTQ plan are treated.

All long-term care insurance claimants will receive an IRS Form 1099LTC from the insurance company paying their benefits. This form shows the amount received in benefits—whether from a TQ, NTQ or "grandfathered" plan. The additional forms and instructions used to complete the forms only describe how to fill out the information for a TQ or grandfathered plan. The instructions specify qualified (and this term is in bold type) benefits are free from taxation.

NTQ plans are not specifically mentioned in the instructions, which leaves NTQ insureds unsure how to account for their benefits. Some believe the NTQ benefits are the same as any accident or sickness insurance; others believe the benefits are taxable income because they are not specifically listed as tax-free income.

Another argument is that if NTQ benefits are taxable income, expenses incurred in receiving care are medical expenses and can offset the tax. But the IRS is considering only allowing a deduction for the medical component of care and not the room and board part of the cost. This would create a significant tax liability when receiving NTQ benefits for care in a facility—especially an assisted living or other alternative to a nursing home which does not provide much medical care.

---

### ILL. 5.4 ■ *Typical LTC Coverage Offered by Insurers*

| | |
|---|---|
| *Services covered:* | Skilled, intermediate and custodial nursing home care |
| *Home health care:* | Health-related and personal care |
| *Adult day services:* | Optional |
| *Daily benefit:* | $40–$250 per day for nursing home care or home health care |
| *Benefit eligibility:* | Physical or severe cognitive impairment |
| *Maximum benefit period:* | Unlimited |
| *Alzheimer's disease:* | Covered |
| *Elimination periods:* | 0–20 and 90–100 days |
| *Renewability:* | Guaranteed |
| *Preexisting conditions:* | 6 months |
| *Age limits for purchasing:* | 50–84 (some companies issue at age 40) |
| *Inflation protection:* | Optional |
| *Waiver of premium:* | Standard |
| *Free-look period:* | 30 days |
| *Marketing:* | Company or independent agents |

---

Many older Americans do not pay much money in taxes. Their income is limited and their deductions are high, so what difference does it make whether NTQ benefits are taxed? This argument does not take into consideration the fact that someone receiving a year's worth of long-term care insurance benefits is likely to receive a large sum of money—$30,000 to $50,000 or more—that is reported on IRS Form 1099LTC. If NTQ benefits are taxed, this will require the claimant to pay some additional tax.

At the writing of this text, neither Congress nor the IRS appear motivated to rule on the issue although the insurance industry continues to lobby for a clarification. They may leave it up to the judicial system and the tax courts to finally make a determination on how NTQ benefits are treated. There will be people outraged at the decision no matter what it is, when it is made or who makes it.

No company or agent wants to provide the wrong advice and no one has all the information necessary to make a definite determination on how benefits from a NTQ plan are treated for tax reasons. For this reason, it is important to let buyers of NTQ plans know both the positives (it may be easier to qualify for benefits) and negatives (the taxation of benefits is undetermined) of these plans. Buyers of TQ plans have the taxation issues clearly spelled out for them.

---

**ILL. 5.5 ■ *Grandfathered Qualified Policies***

---

**W**e have been discussing the standards that policies issued after December 31, 1996, must meet in order to be considered TQ policies. What about policies issued before or on that date? HIPAA provides for grandfathering of such policies. Generally speaking, a policy issued before January 1, 1997, that was approved as long-term care insurance in the state where the policy was issued will receive the same favorable tax status as a TQ policy.

---

## Deductibility of Premiums

On the premium side, there are tax incentives for those who buy TQ policies. Individuals or couples who itemize their tax deductions are entitled to deduct unreimbursed medical expenses that exceed 7.5 percent of their adjusted gross income. As a result of the 1996 legislation, TQ policy premiums can now be treated as a medical expense for purposes of the medical expense deduction—up to certain limits. (See Ill. 5.6.)

Let's look at an example of how this works. Bill and Mary Cook each own a TQ policy; Bill's TQ policy premium is $2,200 and Mary's is $2,700. In 1999, Bill is 71 and Mary is 67. During 1999, they both purchased new eyeglasses and had full physicals, and Bill got new dentures; all this cost them $1,400. Their combined Medicare Part B premium was $1,050. None of these expenses were reimbursed. Their unreimbursed medical expenses for 1997 would be as follows:

| | |
|---|---|
| Eyeglasses, physicals, dentures | $1,400 |
| Medicare Part B premium | $1,050 |
| Amount of Bill's LTC premium that is deductible | $2,200 |
| Amount of Mary's LTC premium that is deductible (from Ill. 5.6) | $2,120 |
| Total | $6,770 |

Assume their adjusted gross income was $44,000. They may deduct unreimbursed medical expenses that exceed $3,300 ($44,000 × 7.5% = $3,300). In this case, the Cooks can deduct $3,470 ($6,770 – $3,300 = $3,470).

While there may not be many people who will benefit from this tax break today (it is estimated that only 5 percent of taxpayers will deduct premiums), the deductibility of TQ premiums will become more important in the future. As TQ policyholders age, it is likely that their income will level off or decrease while their unreimbursed medical expenses will increase (due to rising medical expenses, reductions in employee/retiree benefits, or changes in Medicare). The result: unreimbursed medical expenses will exceed the 7.5 percent level and the tax deduction for TQ premiums will become

---

### ILL. 5.6 ■ *Amount of TQ Policy Premium Treatable as Medical Expense*

The following amounts of TQ policy premium are the maximum that can be included with other unreimbursed medical expenses in 1999.* If a couple files a joint return, these amounts are per person.

| Age | Amount |
|-----|--------|
| 40 or younger | $210 |
| 41–50 | $400 |
| 51–60 | $800 |
| 61–70 | $2,120 |
| 71 and older | $2,660 |

*This amount will be indexed for inflation.

---

available. Whether one can deduct NTQ premiums is unclear. Some say yes; others say no.

### Other Tax Issues Involving TQ Policies

We should also note another provision relating to the deductibility of TQ premiums. Self-employed individuals may take a deduction for a certain percentage of their health insurance expenses. HIPAA made this deduction applicable to TQ premiums. (See Ill. 5.7.) Again, the deductibility of NTQ premiums is uncertain.

### ■ GROUP LONG-TERM CARE INSURANCE

In addition to individual long-term care policies, agents may also offer group long-term care insurance to their business clients. More and more businesses include group LTC insurance in their employee benefits program because it can be used to attract and retain valuable employees. But group LTC is different from most group insurance you are accustomed to selling. Most group LTC plans give employers the option of either funding the plan or acting as a *sponsor* who channels the employees' premiums to the insurer. Typically, employees pay the entire cost of the plan. Insurers are often willing to tailor LTC plans to meet the needs of the employees because these plans are attractive; group coverage is less costly for the insurer to administer than individual plans. In addition, group LTC coverage is often an entree into selling the employer other types of business and individual coverages.

According to the Health Insurance Association of America (HIAA), more than 440,000 LTC policies have been sold through employer-sponsored groups since 1987. HIAA projects that enrollment in these plans will reach 68 percent by the year 2000. Amazingly, the large employer marketplace for LTC products is under-penetrated and the 10-employee to 200-employee market has been largely ignored by agents. The opportunity for sales in these markets is virtually untapped. However, the agent must overcome two major hurdles when marketing LTC insurance to employers:

- Many employers are unaware of the financial and emotional drain on an employee who is caring for a family member.

- Employers are not expanding benefits for employees or retirees.

These obstacles can be overcome. Employers must be shown the impact that long-term care considerations have on the employee *and* the employer. Almost one-quarter of all workers provide some type of care for their older relatives. These people tend to give up job opportunities, turn down overtime and spend more time away from work because they must care for others. Employers are beginning to understand how LTC considerations have an impact on their workforce and ultimately affect the employer. Employer-sponsored group coverage can minimize the impact that caring for family members has on an employee's well-being and job productivity.

In most cases, the underwriting for group long-term care is the same as with the individual plans. The offer is usually made to current employees (who sometimes get a guaranteed issue offer), parents of the employees and retirees of the sponsor. The benefit triggers and benefit design are usually the same as with individual long-term care policies although some sponsors limit the choices that are available.

## Reimbursement Benefit

The *reimbursement benefit* plans available to employers cover specified, licensed health-care services up to a daily maximum. Plans will normally cover one or more of the following:

- nursing home care, including skilled and custodial care

- a short respite period for a nonprofessional caregiver

- home health-care through a licensed agency

- licensed adult day services

Care from nonlicensed caregivers, family or friends is usually not covered.

---

### ILL. 5.7 ■ *Self-Employed Health Insurance Deduction*

For tax years beginning after December 31, 1996, the deductible percentage of health insurance expenses for self-employed individuals, their spouses and their dependents is as follows:

| Tax Year Beginning In | Percentage Deductible |
|:---:|:---:|
| 1999–2001 | 60% |
| 2002 | 70% |
| 2003 and after | 100% |

---

### Cost

As with individual LTC insurance plans, the integration of benefits and triggers affects the plan value and the cost. However, the premium for most group plans is level and based on the insured's age at the time of purchase and the coverage selected. Comparisons among plan options are difficult, but a nursing home–only option with a maximum daily benefit of $100 might cost a 50-year-old employee about $30 a month. A 40-year-old employee would pay substantially less.

It is important that your group LTC insurance carrier has the willingness, flexibility and expertise to accommodate the employer group you target. For example, if you target small retail businesses whose average employee is 40 years old, you need to be certain that your LTC carrier is willing to write coverage for people in their early 30s. If not, you will lose half your prospects. After you are certain that your insurer can meet your market's need, your future success will depend on your willingness to invest your time and effort in educating your business prospects about the need for group LTC insurance and your product's ability to meet that need.

### Tax Treatment of Group Long-Term Care Policies

After HIPAA, a number of tax advantages are available for an employer-sponsored TQ plan. First, employer-paid premiums for employees are tax deductible for the employer. The employer contributions are excludable from the employee's income. However, such premiums are not excludable from an employee's income if they are provided through a cafeteria or other flexible spending arrangement. Benefits received from TQ plans are not income taxable. These features should help you demonstrate the value of TQ plans to employers and their employees.

## ■ LIFE INSURANCE RIDERS

Until quite recently, traditional whole life insurance policies provided cash benefit payments only in the event of an insured's death or surrender of the policy. The only way the insured could access the policy's cash value while he or she was living was through a policy loan or policy surrender. In the event the insured was faced with a life-threatening medical condition, the life insurance policy, by design, could provide no financial relief.

Today, some insurers offer an *accelerated benefits rider* for their life insurance policies. This rider allows the early payment of some portion of the policy's face value if the insured suffers from a terminal illness or injury. The death benefit, less the accelerated payment, is still payable at the insured's death. For example, a $250,000 policy that provides a 75 percent accelerated benefit would pay up to $187,500 to the terminally ill insured, with the remaining $62,500 payable as a death benefit to the beneficiary when the insured dies.

Recognizing the needs of the elderly, more insurers are beginning to offer accelerated benefits, either as policy riders or as provisions in the life insurance policies themselves. Accelerated payments can be made in a lump sum or in monthly installments over a specified period, such as one year.

### Tax Treatment of Accelerated Death Benefits

Life insurance proceeds payable upon death generally are excluded from the beneficiary's gross income. There was some question whether accelerated death benefits, which are paid while the insured is still alive, should be similarly excluded. Under the legislation passed in 1996, it is clear that accelerated death benefits under a life insurance contract may be excluded from gross income if the insured is terminally or chronically ill provided certain requirements are met. The requirements relate to such matters as how one defines a chronically or terminally ill individual. As an agent, you will want to check with your company or companies to see that those who do offer such riders meet the requirements set forth in HIPAA.

### Using Accelerated Death Benefits to Fund LTC

Even though accelerated death benefits are now clearly not taxable in some situations, the use of accelerated death benefits to pay long-term care costs is still not ideal. First, not all insurers offer an accelerated death benefit rider. Even for those whose insurer does offer the rider, the use of this life insurance benefit for long-term care costs presents at least two problems:

1.  *The living benefits on a life insurance policy may be quite limited.* The accelerated benefits are limited to the amount of life insurance in force. Let's say a family had $100,000 of life insurance with an accelerated benefit rider

attached with a maximum payout of $50,000. Today, that payout would cover just over one year's stay in most nursing homes.

2. *Life insurance is purchased for reasons other than paying for LTC.* Many individuals do not have sufficient life insurance as it is. Using a portion of that life insurance to cover long-term care costs will leave very little to achieve the policy's main purpose.

    Consider the same family in the previous example. Let's say they used $50,000 of the accelerated death benefit for nursing home care and receive only $50,000 at the insured's death. This is not a great deal of money to replace a family's breadwinner. A stand-alone LTC insurance plan would have left the life insurance program intact for the loved ones left behind.

### Reasons to Use Life Insurance Riders

A life insurance rider is an effective option for people too young to qualify for long-term care insurance. The chances they will need to access the benefits are small, but clients are pleased that coverage was provided if they are disabled by an illness or accident. Riders may also be a good choice when a policy is paid up and the insured is approaching retirement. These people often cancel their life insurance and use the cash for retirement. However, an accelerated benefit rider could convince the insured to retain his or her coverage. Some professionals recommend increasing the life insurance amount to reflect the addition of the accelerated benefits.

The riders work with a stand-alone policy to provide additional funds to be used to offset rising nursing home costs. They may also be packaged with a nursing home–only plan to provide home care benefits. The elimination period could be extended on the stand-alone plan when combined with a life rider. However, paying for the life insurance with the accelerated benefit option is not the most cost-effective way to provide the benefits. In addition, life insurance accelerated benefits riders do not work when the life insurance proceeds have already been allocated, such as an estate planning situation or when a buy-sell agreement is in place or when attempting to maximize pension benefits for a family. Your clients will benefit most by purchasing the coverage that is designed specifically to meet their needs—a long-term care insurance policy.

## ■ SUMMARY

One of the most difficult decisions a family can face is to place a spouse, parent or other elderly relative in a nursing home. In addition to the emotional trauma, this decision may cause financial hardships when the family must pay for formal long-term care in a nursing home. As an agent, you can help to ease this burden with an LTC insurance policy. You can assist your clients by reviewing various LTC policies and helping them choose one that best fits their needs and objectives.

As you've learned, LTC policies have many similar benefits and features. However, it is the differences among policies that both you and your clients must carefully consider. In Chapter 6, we'll look at benefit design options.

■ **CHAPTER 5 QUESTIONS FOR REVIEW**

1. Provisions in long-term care policies that are used to determine when an insured qualifies for benefits are called

   A. reserves
   B. preexisting conditions
   C. accelerated benefits
   D. benefit triggers

2. Which of the following is NOT a factor that the insurance company uses to determine the premium for an LTC policy?

   A. The prospect's annual income
   B. The prospect's health status
   C. The prospect's age
   D. The LTC product design

3. Most long-term care insurance policies are

   A. guaranteed renewable
   B. noncancelable
   C. conditionally renewable
   D. indemnity plans

4. A tax-qualified plan (TQ) must pay benefits when a claimant

   A. has a severe cognitive impairment
   B. is chronically ill
   C. needs substantial assistance with at least two ADLS, expected to last at least 90 days
   D. complies with all of the above

5. ADLS were developed by

   A. insurance companies to pay NTQ benefits
   B. Congress with the passage of HIPAA
   C. researchers to measure physical functioning
   D. none of the above

6. With a TQ plan, qualified long-term care services must

   A. be for diagnostic, preventive, therapeutic, curing, mitigating and rehabilitation
   B. include alternate living facilities, home health-care and adult day centers
   C. be delivered for at least 90 days before any benefits can be paid
   D. all of the above

7. When using the functional model to trigger LTC benefits, the insurance company should measure the insured's

   A. need for medically necessary care
   B. cognitive and physical ability to complete the activities of daily living
   C. cognitive impairments only
   D. ability to pay for LTC

8. Before qualifying for benefits under a TQ policy, a claimant must be expected to need substantial assistance with ADLs for a period of

   A. 30 days
   B. 60 days
   C. 90 days
   D. 120 days

# 6

## LTC Benefit Design Options

L ong-term care insurance products have evolved from highly restrictive nursing home–only coverage that mirrored Medicare's benefit trigger to a variety of plans that can include home health-care delivered by either family members or professionals. One of the attractive features of today's LTC products is the flexibility the buyer has to select from a variety of policy options, thereby designing the plan that will best fit his or her needs and budget.

As discussed in the last chapter, the Health Insurance Portability and Accountability Act of 1996 (HIPAA) established standards that long-term care insurance must meet in order to qualify for favorable tax treatment. In addition, states must approve long-term care insurance contracts to make sure they comply with state laws and regulations. Despite these federal and state requirements, there is still room for innovative product design, as we will see in this chapter.

In this chapter, we will discuss the options the insured has when selecting various other policy provisions. When comparing LTC policies and making recommendations to prospective buyers, agents must understand these options.

■ ■ ■ ■ ■

### ■ BENEFIT DESIGN OPTIONS

In Chapter 5, we discussed policy features that are standard from one policy to the next. Policyholders do not have much input or choice regarding these features. For example, the long-term care applicant does not choose the length of the free-look period he or she would like to have.

The policy features we will now discuss are those that the consumer or policyholder will be able to affect depending on the important choices he or she makes regarding the long-term care policy. These choices will determine the type and amount of coverage the policy provides and will also have a significant impact on the premiums he or she will pay.

The agent must find a policy that meets a client's coverage needs—and his or her budget. When an agent is proposing the purchase of a long-term care policy, he or she must help the client address three basic coverage issues:

1. When should benefits be paid?

2. How much should be paid?

3. How long should payments be made?

The answers to these questions will form the design of a long-term care policy.

## ■ STANDARD OPTIONS

When designing a policy, the agent helps the applicant select from among five standard options that determine the providers of care that are covered, an elimination period, a benefit amount, increasing or level benefits, and a benefit period. All companies offer basically the same options, although different terms may be used. After the benefit trigger is pulled, these options become important.

### Providers of Care

As explained in Chapter 2, long-term care can be provided by home care agencies, senior centers, traditional nursing homes and a variety of other care providers. An LTC policy should clearly define *what* services are covered, *who* may provide these services and *where* these services may be provided in order for benefits to be paid.

Home care options have evolved dramatically in the past 10 years. Home care started out as a recovery benefit from the nursing home benefit then was integrated with the nursing home benefit. Companies are now offering home care options that are integrated with a nursing facility plan. The same elimination period, benefit maximum and inflation options apply to both benefits. The daily benefit is normally a percentage of the nursing home benefit—50 percent, 75 percent or 100 percent are common. This allows a claimant to manage one risk (needing long-term care) versus two risks (nursing facility care and home care).

Although the NAIC Model does not define home health care, such care typically includes services provided by a registered nurse, a licensed practical nurse or a licensed therapist. Some policies also cover personal assistance or home health aides who perform "homemaker" duties, such as laundry or cooking, in addition to assistance with bathing or personal hygiene. When comparing policies that include home health care, look for exclusions or restrictions that limit custodial home care only to care given in conjunction with skilled care.

Many policies also offer adult day services, respite care and case management services. *Adult day services* are usually provided at senior or community centers; these services may be recreational in focus or may include occupational and physical therapy. Organized programs may provide meals and transportation and offer temporary relief for caregivers. When caregivers need longer periods of relief, *respite care* permits a short institutional stay for the insured or provides for the services of a temporary caregiver while the regular caregiver rests or attends to other business.

Finally, many policies now include *case management* services to identify and coordinate care among various agencies. When the case manager works for the insurance company, this "service" may actually become a *gatekeeper*—that is, a way to ensure that covered services are provided only to insureds who genuinely need them or to prevent inappropriate use of certain services. Case managers who work for the insurance company may also attempt to shift claims away from the insurance company and toward Medicare.

### Needs Assessment

In assessing what types of care your client needs, answers to the following questions will be helpful:

- Do you have family nearby to care for you if you should need care at home?

- Does your family work outside the home?

- Do they still have children living at home with them?

- Have you talked with your family about caring for you?

- How many hours a day would you like someone to come in to help you so your caregiver can take a break?

- Do you think you could pay $50 per day (cost of a couple of hours of home care) for someone to care for you at home without putting a huge dent in your budget?

- Would you prefer to pay now so that benefits will be available if you happen to need care in your home?

### Elimination Period

Long-term care policies typically include *elimination periods* (also known as *deductible* or *waiting periods*). The elimination period is the number of days that must pass after the insured enters a nursing home or starts to receive home health care before LTC benefits are payable. Like dollar deductibles in other forms of insurance, having the insured pay the initial costs helps to reduce the total policy premium. The applicant may select the elimination period under his or her policy, and the agent should advise the applicant carefully on this issue. The elimination or waiting period is designed to offer insureds a choice in protection. The insured can choose a short elimination period, which provides protection from the beginning of the nursing home stay (a zero-day elimination period provides what is called *first dollar protection*). Or the insured can choose a longer elimination period, which provides protection later in the stay as expenses mount.

Common elimination options are 0, 20, 30, 90, 100 and 180 days. The longer the elimination period, the lower the premium. However, electing to reduce premiums by purchasing a longer waiting period is not always the best choice on a cost/benefit basis.

To illustrate this point, assume that Adam and Ben purchase LTC policies from the same company with a $100-a-day benefit and a four-year benefit period. Adam selects a 90-day waiting period at an annual premium of $1,110. Ben selects a 30-day waiting period and pays $1,320—a premium difference of $210. Now, assume that both are injured in an accident and must spend 100 days in a nursing facility. If the facility charges $100 a day, Adam and Ben will each have accumulated $10,000 in charges. However, with the 90-day waiting period, Adam is responsible for $9,000 out of pocket while Ben (with a 30-day period and a higher premium) pays $3,000. In this case, the extra $210 in premium was worth it.

HIPAA put a new wrinkle in how an elimination period is satisfied. A TQ plan cannot pay benefits unless the claimant is expected to need care for at least 90 days. This doesn't mean all elimination periods need to be at least 90 days though. Using examples is the best way to explain this concept.

Let's use the example of an insured who has a TQ plan with a 20-day elimination period and has asked the insurer to assess a claim. If the licensed health care practitioner who performs the assessment (as required of a TQ plan in HIPAA) thinks the claimant will need care for at least 90 days, benefits begin accruing on day 21. That's the easy one to understand. Now for the twists.

What happens if the claimant has a speedy recovery and no longer needs care after 45 days? Because care was expected to last 90 days, the claimant keeps all the benefits. The key is how long care was *expected* to last when the licensed health care practitioner assessed the claim.

What happens if the licensed health care practitioner thinks the claimant will get better within 60 days, and he or she does? Benefits will not be paid. What happens if complications arise during the 60-day recovery and care is actually received for 120 days? In other words, the licensed health care practitioner's recovery estimate was wrong. The insurance company will have the claimant reassessed and benefits will be paid retroactive back to the 21st day if the claimant is still chronically ill.

The intent of this "gatekeeper" is to be sure tax-free long-term care insurance benefits are paid only when people need *long-term* care. Congress decided any care delivered for less than 90 days was *short-term* care. Congress wanted to avoid duplicating benefits under Medicare, which provides benefits for the first 100 days of a skilled nursing care for those recovering from a hospitalization. Congress did not think a tax-qualified plan should provide benefits that are provided by the government. Again, Congress wanted people to benefit from their insurance not improve their financial situation.

NTQ plans do not have this type of requirement with their elimination period. If someone buys an NTQ plan with a 0-day elimination period and receives three days of care, three days of benefits are payable. This is one area where it can be argued that it is easier to qualify for benefits with an NTQ plan than with a TQ plan. Those who still favor a TQ plan will side with Congress—Medicare pays for short-term care; private insurance need not duplicate it.

It is important to note whether a plan's definition of the elimination period requires consecutive days for home health care, adult day services or both, because such a policy is unlikely to pay benefits until late in the care cycle. Further, if either home health care or adult day services are received only a few days a week, the care may not meet the consecutive days requirement. Look for an elimination period that enables the insured to accumulate days over a period of time. The longer the amount of time that insureds are given to accumulate days toward the elimination period, the better the plan.

The agent should be certain that home health care and adult day services count as a full day of care. The agent should also determine whether all providers count against a single elimination period. Some products have separate elimination periods for HHC and nursing home care to qualify for benefits.

### Needs Assessment

In determining the appropriate elimination period, agents should ask their clients questions such as:

- Do you have low or high deductibles on your homeowner's or automobile insurance?

- Can you afford to pay for the first few months of your care or will you need help after the first few weeks?

- How would paying the first $10,000 of your care (assuming a 100-day elimination period where cost is $100 per day) affect your spouse's lifestyle? Your estate?

- How much have you set aside to pay for your long-term care costs?

- Would you like to reduce your current premium with the understanding that you will have to pay more out of your pocket if you happen to need care?

- How do you feel about having only your long-term care covered?

## Benefit Amount

The benefit amount is the number of dollars an insurer pays a claimant. There are two methods for paying the claimant: the per diem plan and the reimbursement plan.

Per diem or indemnity contracts pay a predetermined dollar amount regardless of the actual cost of care. For example, if the daily benefit amount is $125 per day and the facility charges $110 per day, the insurance company will pay the full $125 per day. The claimant determines what to do with the extra funds. Typically, policies offer daily benefit amounts ranging from $40 to $250 or more a day. Obviously, the higher the daily benefit and the longer the benefit period, the higher the policy premium. Applicants usually select the daily benefit amount and length of coverage according to their own needs and the cost of the coverage.

A per diem contract does not have to coordinate benefits with Medicare to be considered a TQ plan. However, recall from our earlier discussion of the taxation of TQ benefits that the tax-free benefits amount under a per diem contract is $175 per day for contracts issued after August 1, 1996. (The full benefit amount is tax free for contracts issued prior to that date.) The $175 per day is increased each year based on an inflation rate.

A reimbursement plan pays actual charges up to a certain limit. As an example, if the daily benefit amount is $125 per day and the facility charges $110 per day, the insurance company will pay just $110 per day. The savings will be reserved for future claims. A reimbursement plan is normally less expensive than a per diem plan because fewer dollars will be paid out over the short term. Regardless of which plan is offered, the higher the benefit amount, the higher the cost of the insurance.

Reimbursement plans must coordinate with Medicare to be considered TQ. That is, the TQ plan must not cover expenses that are reimbursable by Medicare except when Medicare is a secondary payor or when the TQ contract makes payments per diem or on another periodic basis without regard to actual expense.

### Needs Assessment

What is the right amount of daily benefit to offer? There are two schools of thought. The first says the daily benefit amount should offer the current full cost of care. The other says insureds should minimize the cost of their insurance by developing a "copayment" plan.

Under the current full cost-of-care thinking, if a good facility in the community is charging $125 per day then perhaps your prospect will want $125 per day from the

---

### ILL. 6.1 ■ *Assessing a Prospect's Daily Benefit Amount Needs*

Common Living Expenses

| | |
|---|---|
| • Mortgage/rent | $_____/month |
| • Utilities | $_____/month |
| • Food | $_____/month |
| • Insurance | $_____/month |
| • Taxes | $_____/month |
| • Transportation | $_____/month |
| • Medical expenses | $_____/month |
| • Other expenses | $_____/month |

| | |
|---|---|
| Total living expenses | $_____/month |
| *Plus* Nursing Home Costs | $_____/month |
| *Equals* Expenses When Care Is Needed | $_____/month |

*Less* Common Sources of Income

| | |
|---|---|
| • Pension | $_____/month |
| • Social Security | $_____/month |
| • Savings/Investments | $_____/month |
| • Other | $_____/month |

| | |
|---|---|
| Total Income | $_____/month |
| *Equals* Minimum Monthly LTC Benefit | $_____/month |

---

insurance company. Of course, this coverage will cost more in terms of premium than a plan where the insured will, in effect, copay some portion of the $125 cost.

Those who want to minimize the cost of their insurance develop a "copayment" plan. The copayment concept would look at your prospect's current living expenses, adding in the cost of care. This is then compared to the prospect's income. The difference equals the minimum monthly benefit amount that your prospect should have if they wanted all their excess income to go toward the cost of care. (See Ill. 6.1.) Of course, not everyone wants to do this.

### Needs Assessment

You should be prepared to ask your prospect questions to determine the appropriate level of benefits for their personal situation.

- Do you have a low or high deductible on your auto insurance?

- Do you want the same type of design for your long-term care insurance?

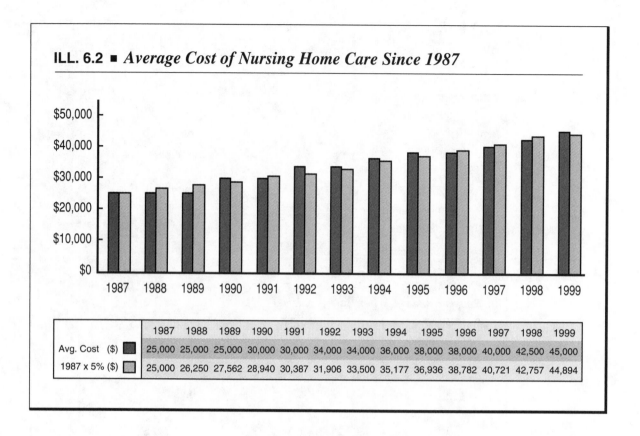

**ILL. 6.2 ■ *Average Cost of Nursing Home Care Since 1987***

|  | 1987 | 1988 | 1989 | 1990 | 1991 | 1992 | 1993 | 1994 | 1995 | 1996 | 1997 | 1998 | 1999 |
|---|---|---|---|---|---|---|---|---|---|---|---|---|---|
| Avg. Cost ($) | 25,000 | 25,000 | 25,000 | 30,000 | 30,000 | 34,000 | 34,000 | 36,000 | 38,000 | 38,000 | 40,000 | 42,500 | 45,000 |
| 1987 x 5% ($) | 25,000 | 26,250 | 27,562 | 28,940 | 30,387 | 31,906 | 33,500 | 35,177 | 36,936 | 38,782 | 40,721 | 42,757 | 44,894 |

- How do you feel about using some of your own income to pay for your care?

- Do you prefer a plan that will pay a flat dollar amount regardless of the actual cost of care or one that simply reimburses you for actual charges?

- Do you know how needing care might effect your budget? (If they don't use the worksheet in Ill. 6.1.)

- Would you like your insurance benefits to cover the full cost of care or just a portion?

- Do you want a plan that will definitely pay tax-free benefits, or are you willing to take a risk that your benefits will be taxed?

The answers to these questions will help you and your client select an appropriate benefit amount.

### Increasing Benefits

Nursing home costs are likely to increase over time. The average cost of nursing home care in 1987 was approximately $25,000 per year. This cost has gradually increased by approximately 5 percent each year. (See Ill. 6.2.) In the Health Care

Financing Administration's projections for nursing home cost increases in the future, it uses between a 4.7 percent and a 6.6 percent increase over the next 10 years.

If nursing home costs continue to average a 5 percent increase, the cost of care will double every 15 years. In other words, the cost of care will average four times today's average cost in 30 years—the time a 55-year-old buying the product today is likely to need care. The following table shows an approximation of the rising cost of nursing home care using a 5 percent increase.

|  | Annual Cost | Daily Cost |
|---|---|---|
| Currently | $45,000 | $125 |
| 10 years | $75,000 | $205 |
| 20 years | $120,000 | $325 |
| 30 years | $195,000 | $535 |

The NAIC Model Act and HIPAA require all insurers to offer a 5 percent compounded annually inflation option. Applicants have the choice to accept, decline or accept an alternative to this option. Through policy riders, insurance companies use two basic methods to increase benefits: automatic increase riders or offers to purchase additional coverage.

### Automatic Increase Rider

The *automatic increase rider* raises the benefit amount to be paid automatically in conjunction with cost-of-living increases. The amount of increase is normally based on a predetermined inflation rate. All companies offer a 5 percent increase. In addition to offering the 5 percent increase, some companies offer less. Some companies use the Consumer Price Index (CPI) or the Medical CPI to determine the annual increases.

The most common form of automatic increase rider (and the one recommended by the NAIC) is a *compound benefit increase option (CBIO),* which increases the daily benefit annually on the policy's anniversary by 5 percent of the previous year's benefit. Some companies also offer a 5 percent *simple benefit increase option (SBIO),* which works similarly but is based on an annual increase of 5 percent of the original daily benefit. Compounding the rate each year provides larger annual increases and costs a little more than the simple increase. As shown in Ill. 6.3, compounding increases will double the benefit amount approximately every 15 years while simple increases take about 20 years to double.

Automatic increase riders normally do not automatically increase the premiums; actually, the cost of the rider is built into the policy's original premium. In essence, insureds are *prepaying* for future benefits. However, because adequate reserves must be built in the early years of the policy, insureds pay *more* for their overall protection in the early years of their long-term care policy. The longer an insured owns the policy, the *less* he or she pays for their overall coverage over that time. In other words,

**ILL. 6.3 ■** *Simple Benefit vs. Compound Benefit Increase Options*

| Policy Year | Daily Benefit with SBIO (5% Simple Increases) | Daily Benefit with CBIO (5% Compound Increases) |
|---|---|---|
| 1 | $100 | $100.00 |
| 2 | $105 | $105.00 |
| 3 | $110 | $110.25 |
| 4 | $115 | $115.76 |
| 5 | $120 | $121.55 |
| 10 | $145 | $155.13 |
| 15 | $170 | $198.00 |
| 20 | $195 | $252.70 |
| 30 | $245 | $411.61 |

the compound inflation option is the most effective way to purchase coverage and keep up with the rising cost of care.

### Purchasing Additional Insurance

As an alternative to an automatic increase rider, some companies offer insureds a *pay-as-you-go option.* (See Ill. 6.4.) An insured may purchase additional coverage in the future, usually at the insured's attained age rates and without evidence of insurability.

This option permits the insured to purchase additional insurance when his or her health deteriorates and he or she can no longer pass underwriting requirements. This option requires additional premiums when the benefit increases and so it may cost more over the life of the policy. However, this option does allow the insured to increase coverage to more closely match the actual increase in nursing home costs.

### Needs Assessment

To determine whether your client would benefit from one of these options, you should ask:

- How long do you plan to keep this coverage?

- How much do you think nursing homes will charge then?

- How do you anticipate paying for that care?

- Would you be interested in an option that enables you to keep up with rising costs when you need care?

- How do you feel about paying additional amounts now for additional future benefits?

- Do you feel you'll be able to afford to purchase additional coverage in the future?

## Benefit Maximum

Policies contain one of two types of benefit maximums: one measures benefits according to a certain number of years and the other measures benefits according to a certain dollar amount. Per diem plans normally pay for a number of years while reimbursement plans pay until a certain dollar amount is paid out.

### Benefit Maximum Based on Period of Time

When choosing a benefit maximum based on a number of years, common options are two, three, four and six years. Many companies offer unlimited benefit periods. The length of time for which benefits are paid is expressed in years, but companies actually count the number of days. Thus, a two-year plan will pay for 730 benefit days. The longer the benefit period, the higher the premium.

Some people like the peace of mind that lifetime benefits provide. There is a certain peace of mind knowing that benefits will not run out—that they'll never get a last check. However, reducing the benefit period to three or even two years can cut the premium significantly.

When an applicant chooses less than lifetime benefits, he or she might consider a company that offers a *restoration of benefits* clause. Under such a provision, if the insured receives care in a nursing facility and recovers, the policy benefit is restored to its original level after the insured is certified "treatment free" for a period of at least six months. A restoration of benefits clause helps to prevent short nursing home stays from using up the insured's coverage.

The agent should also review how care is "credited" against the daily benefit maximum. Some policies may count three days of care during a week as a full week of care. This is not acceptable; three days of care should count as three days of care. On the other hand, some insurers count certain providers (such as HMOs) at less than a full day of care against the benefit period. This is a bonus for the insured, but should not be given much weight when comparing policies because it is rare and may also involve some additional restrictions.

## ILL. 6.4 ■ *Pay-As-You-Go vs. Prepayment Plans*

| | Age | | | | | | | |
| --- | --- | --- | --- | --- | --- | --- | --- | --- |
| | 55 | 60 | 65 | 70 | 75 | 80 | 85 | 90 |
| **Pay-As-You-Go Plan** | | | | | | | | |
| Daily Benefit (purchasing additional coverage) | $100 | $130 | $165 | $210 | $265 | $340 | $410 | $410 |
| Cumulative Premium | $512 | $3,502 | $7,861 | $14,884 | $27,515 | $52,398 | $100,047 | $155,152 |
| **Prepayment Plan** | | | | | | | | |
| Daily Benefit (with 5% compounded annual increases) | $100 | $128 | $163 | $208 | $266 | $339 | $433 | $552 |
| Cumulative Premium | $1,080 | $6,480 | $11,880 | $17,280 | $22,680 | $28,080 | $33,480 | $38,880 |

This compares the cost effectiveness of a long-term care insurance contract that purchases additional coverage (pay-as-you-go) with automatic increases (prepaid). The amounts of annual increases are consistent but not exact because the pay-as-you-go option is limited to purchases in $5 increments.

In the first year, both plans offer $100 per day. The prepayment plan costs about twice as much as the pay-as-you-go plan.

As the insured ages, the daily benefit increases about the same under both options. The pay-as-you-go plan is purchasing additional coverage at an ever-increasing age. We assume the insured remains insurable. Also, unless the company offers an option to increase benefits during a claim, the pay-as-you-go option will not increase in benefits during a claim.

The cumulative premium of the two plans has a cross over in cost effectiveness between ages 70 and 75 in this example. In other words, if the insured lives beyond age 75, prepaying for the additional increases will be the most cost-effective way to purchase additional coverage.

Finally, the cost of care will not stop increasing when someone turns age 85. But most insurers do not offer the coverage after ages 79 or 84, so the opportunity to purchase additional coverage is limited. With the prepaid option, the increases continue until death or lapse regardless of age.

### Benefit Maximum Based on Dollar Amount

The other type of benefit maximum uses a set dollar figure to draw upon for claims. This design is usually found with contracts that pay actual charges up to the daily benefit amount. This design allows contracts to pay benefits for a longer period than originally expected if actual charges are less than the daily maximum because the unused amounts remain in the benefit pool for future use.

The amount of money available is usually the product of the daily benefit times a length of time selected. If someone has a plan paying $125 per day with a three-year maximum, the amount available for claim would be $136,875 (125 × 1,095 days).

Let's say this is a typical reimbursement plan and the person who bought it goes into claim status where the actual cost of care is $100 per day for three years. The benefits would continue beyond the three years selected because only $109,500 ($100 per day for 1,095 days) was paid in benefits. The difference between the actual amount paid and the maximum available in this example would be $27,375, which would be available for a future claim or continuation of the current claim.

What would happen if the insured has the 5 percent compounded annually inflation option? Would the benefits be used up more quickly? So as not to decrease the benefit maximum available and penalize the claimant for making a prudent purchase years ago, all options to increase the daily benefits also increase the maximum benefit available. With many companies, the new maximum available is equal to the number of unused days times the daily benefit available.

Here is how the numbers would work in the previous example if the claim happened in the tenth policy anniversary and the cost of care is equal to the daily benefit.

|  | Daily Benefit Payable* | Number of Days Remaining | Benefit Maximum Available | Annual Benefits Paid |
|---|---|---|---|---|
| Year 10 | $204 | 1,095 | $223,380 | $74,460 |
| Year 11 | $214 | 730 | $156,220 | $78,110 |
| Year 12 | $225 | 365 | $82,125 | $82,125 |

*Amounts rounded to the nearest dollar.

The total benefits paid were $234,695, although the amount available when the claim started was less. This provides the claimant with the full benefits promised at the time of purchase. Again, this is designed to not penalize claimants for purchasing the inflation option.

### Needs Assessment

How do you determine which benefit maximum is best for your client? Ask questions such as:

- Do you have longevity in your family?

- Have any members of your family spent an extended period in a nursing facility?

- An average stay in a nursing home is almost three years. Do you want to cover the average stay or are you more concerned with the financial risk an extended stay would pose?

- Have you thought about what nursing homes will be charging in the future? Do you feel a benefit maximum of $150,000 would cover an average stay at the time you will be using it?

- When do you want your last check?

The answers to these questions will help you and your client select an appropriate benefit maximum.

## ■ NONFORFEITURE OPTIONS

When insurance policies are sold, the assumption, of course is that the policyowners will continue to pay the premiums for the duration of the premium-paying period. Insurance policies that cover a period of any considerable number of years with the rate constructed on a level premium basis automatically creates a reserve.

What happens if policyowners cancel their LTC contracts and stop paying premiums? Do they forfeit all they have paid? As part of their long-term care insurance policy, all companies now offer *nonforfeiture options*. Insurers usually offer two options to policyowners:

1. return of premium option

2. shortened benefit period option

Let's discuss these two options.

The *return of premium option* returns to the insured a percentage of the entire premium paid when the coverage is canceled. If the policy has been in force a long time and large amounts of premium have been paid, more money is returned to the insured. Typically, a policy would return nothing in the first five years, 15 percent of the premium about the fifth year and an additional 3 percent of the premium for each year thereafter. After about 35 years, the insured would get all of his or her premium back by surrendering the policy. At this time, it is unclear whether a TQ policy will be permitted to contain this option. However, HIPAA does permit the next option to be included in the TQ policy.

When the insured chooses to let his or her coverage lapse, the *shortened benefit period option* provides a guarantee that the coverage will still be available if needed. This coverage will provide a reduced maximum benefit (dollar amount) or a shorter benefit period. The extent of this benefit is based on the amount paid for it and the period of time the policy is in force. Typically, companies will calculate premiums paid from issue until lapse; that amount of money is then available for future claims. The providers covered, daily benefit amount and elimination period remain the same.

## ■ OTHER BENEFIT OPTIONS

In addition to the above, many companies offer other benefit options to attract qualified applicants. The more services that are covered, the more expensive the policy. Some prospects will want to be fully covered for every contingency but will be unwilling (or unable) to pay the added cost. Therefore, both you and your prospects should weigh the advantages of the following "bells and whistles" available in some policies:

- *Ambulance benefits.* Medicare or private insurance often picks up the cost of transporting patients with chronic conditions. Generally speaking, there is little advantage in purchasing ambulance benefits under an LTC policy.

- *Coordination of benefits with Medicare.* Plans that reimburse for actual costs up to the daily benefit maximum must coordinate with Medicare in order to be tax qualified. The per diem contracts have the option either to coordinate benefits with Medicare or to pay in addition to Medicare. Plans that coordinate with Medicare will be a little less expensive than those that pay in addition to Medicare.

- *Bed reservation benefit.* The daily benefit continues with the intent to pay for an unoccupied nursing home bed in the event an insured must enter the hospital. The facility reserves the bed until hospital discharge.

- *Survivorship benefit for married couples.* Some companies provide a paid-up policy for the surviving spouse of a deceased insured after the couple has paid premiums for a minimum of 10 years. It is not clear whether this option can be added to a TQ policy.

- *Coverage for Alzheimer's disease.* Although some insurers cite coverage for Alzheimer's disease as a special coverage option, policies sold today must include coverage for this disease. However, since Alzheimer's disease can only be positively diagnosed during an autopsy, the agent should be certain that the policy includes coverage for Alzheimer's disease and "similar forms of senility." The best policies will include a cognitive impairment trigger as discussed earlier.

### ILL. 6.5 ■ *Long-Term Care Policy Comparison Checklist*

**THE COMPANY:**

Ratings      A.M. Best _____          Moody's _____

             Standard & Poor's _____     Duff & Phelps _____

Special Underwriting Requirements _____

   Attending Physician Statement    Y ____  N ____  Ages ____
   Face-to-Face                     Y ____  N ____  Ages ____
   Phone Interview                  Y ____  N ____  Ages ____

TQ                                  Y ____  N ____

Coordinate with Medicare            Y ____  N ____

Premium                             $ _____ / year

**BENEFIT TRIGGER:**

ADLs:

   Walking                          Y ____  N ____
   Bathing                          Y ____  N ____
   Dressing                         Y ____  N ____
   Toileting                        Y ____  N ____
   Transferring                     Y ____  N ____
   Continence                       Y ____  N ____
   Eating                           Y ____  N ____

Level of Impairment _____

   Hands-on _____  Standby _____

Cognitive Impairment                Y ____  N ____

Assessor:

   Third Party                      Y ____  N ____
   Company Rep                      Y ____  N ____
   Physician                        Y ____  N ____
   Licensed Health Care Practitioner  Y ____  N ____

**DEFINITION OF PROVIDER:**

   Nursing Home _____
   Home Health Care Agency _____
   Adult Day Center _____
   Respite Care _____
   Other "Gatekeepers" Used _____

## ILL. 6.5 ■ *LTC Policy Comparison Checklist (Cont.)*

### BENEFIT DESIGN OPTIONS:

| | |
|---|---|
| Base Benefit Amount | If yes, how much? |
|     Nursing Home Care | $ _____ / day |
|     Alternate Facilities | $ _____ / day |
|     Home Health Care | $ _____ / day |
|     Adult Day Center | $ _____ / day |
|     Respite Care | $ _____ / day |
|     Other _____ | $ _____ / day |
|     Other _____ | $ _____ / day |
|     Indemnity Benefits | Y _____ N _____ |
|     Actual Cost of Care | Y _____ N _____ |
|     Usual and Customary Charges | Y _____ N _____ |
| Elimination Period | _____ days |
|     Nursing Home | Y _____ N _____ |
|     Home Health Care | Y _____ N _____ |
|     Integrated | Y _____ N _____ |
|     Accumulation Period | _____ days |
| Increasing Benefits | Y _____ N _____ |
|     Automatic Increase | Y _____ N _____ |
|     Percent Increase | _____ % |
|         Compound Increases | Y _____ N _____ |
|         Simple Increases | Y _____ N _____ |
|     Purchase Option | Y _____ N _____ |
|     Percent Available to Buy | _____ % |
|     Time Period and Frequency to Purchase | _____ |
|     Purchase at Attained Age | Y _____ N _____ |
|     Evidence of Insurability Required | Y _____ N _____ |
| Nursing Home Benefit Maximum | |
|     Benefit Period | _____ days, or |
|     Dollar Maximum | $ _____ |
|     Restoration of Benefits | Y _____ N _____ |
| Home Health Care Benefit Maximum | |
|     Benefit Period | _____ days |
|     Dollar Maximum | $ _____ |
|     Restoration of Benefits | Y _____ N _____ |
| Integrated Benefit Maximum | |
|     Benefit Period | _____ days |
|     Dollar Maximum | $ _____ |
|     Restoration of Benefits | Y _____ N _____ |

- *Reinstatement due to cognitive impairment.* Some companies now reinstate lapsed policies if the lapse is due to the insured being cognitively impaired and unable to remit payment. This is usually a one-time benefit limited to six months after the initial lapse.

- *Waiver of premium for married couples.* Some companies provide a waiver of premium for a healthy spouse when one goes into claim and waiver of premium status. Because a healthy spouse receives a benefit, it is unclear whether this benefit is available under a TQ plan.

- *Shared benefit maximum.* A few companies allow spouses to share a benefit maximum. If both husband and wife buy a three-year plan and one spouse uses his or her entire maximum, the claim can continue to be paid by reducing the healthy spouse's benefit maximum.

- *Spousal premium discount.* Most companies offer a discount for insureds who are married. The amount of discount varies from 10 percent to 50 percent and may apply to one or both policies. Some companies require that both own long-term care insurance from the same company while others just need to know the applicant has a spouse.

- *Limited pay.* Although pricing of long-term care insurance is in its infancy, companies are offering long-term care insurance with options to pay premiums for a short time. This varies from a single premium to paying for 10 years.

This is only a partial list of the many options that LTC companies offer to attract applicants. Although the right combination of "bells and whistles" can be a determinant in the decision to go with one policy or another, it is best to remember that without a solid base policy from a reputable company, these unique policy features are of little value.

Initially, given the number of companies offering LTC policies, the task of comparing LTC policy features and benefits may seem overwhelming for most agents. However, after you evaluate some sample policies, you will have a better understanding of the language, coverage, gatekeepers, covered providers and how and when benefits are paid. The more policies you evaluate, the easier policy comparison becomes. You may find Ill. 6.5 useful as you begin your study of LTC policies and benefit options.

## ■ SUMMARY

When comparing LTC policies, the agent must look at how and when a policy's benefits are paid, the kinds of providers these policies cover and the various options from which the insured may select. Only when you fully understand these policy provisions can you make sound recommendations to your prospects.

As part of your LTC study, you'll want to understand the underwriting process so that you can explain it to your clients. In Chapter 7, we'll look at how insurance companies underwrite long-term care and how the method selected affects the type and quality of coverage the insured receives.

## ■ CHAPTER 6 QUESTIONS FOR REVIEW

1. The most common form of inflation rider for LTC policies is a(n)

   A. simple benefit increase option
   B. automatic increase rider
   C. compound benefit increase option
   D. purchase option

2. Under a restoration of benefits clause, if an insured receives care in a nursing facility and recovers, the policy benefit is restored to its original benefit level as soon as the insured

   A. is discharged from the facility
   B. is certified "treatment free" for a period of at least six months
   C. is certified "chronically ill"
   D. pays the higher attained age premium

3. Benefits that repay the insured for the actual cost of care or for "reasonable and customary" charges up to a certain limit are called

   A. indemnity plans
   B. benefit periods
   C. daily benefits amount
   D. reimbursement plans

4. If an insurance company offers a three-year benefit maximum, benefits will be paid for how many days?

   A. 365
   B. 730
   C. 900
   D. 1,095

5. The daily benefit amount on a per diem contract

   A. is paid regardless of actual charges
   B. is reimburses for actual charges
   C. is must coordinate with Medicare
   D. none of the above

6. The most cost-effective way to keep pace with rising nursing home costs is to

   A. purchase additional coverage over time
   B. purchase an automatic benefit increase option
   C. not worry about it
   D. save extra money in retirement

7. The elimination period on a TQ plan

   A. must be at least 90 days
   B. must be less than 90 days
   C. can be any length of time
   D. cannot begin until Medicare's benefits are exhausted

8. A nonforfeiture option on long-term care insurance must

   A. return premiums at lapse
   B. return premiums at death
   C. provide a shortened benefit period
   D. be offered in most states

9. A benefit maximum

   A. is frozen during a claim regardless of other benefits payable
   B. is the number of days or amount of money payable to a claimant
   C. cannot be restored with a TQ plan
   D. is reduced when an inflation option is chosen

# 7

# LTC Insurers

**A**s an insurance professional, you'll want to offer your prospects and clients the best comprehensive long-term care insurance product from a reputable company at a fair price. This may not be as simple as it seems because no policy is likely to offer every feature your clients want at a price they can afford. To further complicate the issue, there are now more than 120 private insurance companies offering a variety of long-term care policies. Though some uniformity among these policies is beginning to emerge, the fact remains that with so many insurers and so many policies to choose from, consumers may have a difficult time making the right selection. This is where a knowledgeable agent can offer much-needed assistance.

In this chapter, we'll discuss how insurance companies underwrite long-term care policies and how that affects the type of coverage an insured receives. We'll also look at ways to help you and your clients select a quality company that offers quality LTC policies.

■ ■ ■ ■ ■

## ■ EVALUATING LONG-TERM CARE INSURERS

In Chapter 6, we discussed the variety of options available under different policies offered by different companies and how to choose the best policy for the customer. In this chapter, we will discuss how to choose the best insurer. We will look at four important criteria you and your clients should consider when choosing an LTC insurer: financial strength, reputation, service and cost.

## Financial Strength

The true financial health of a life insurance company cannot be determined merely by looking at its annual report or its size. However, the company's growth (or lack of growth) over a number of years can reveal some important information. Some factors to consider in assessing financial strength are the types of business written, the company's business trends over the years, its underwriting and investment strategies, the adequacy of its reserves and its ratio of policyholders' surplus to liabilities. Most importantly, the general quality of the company's management should be considered because it determines the company's direction.

If you wish to review a company's detailed financial information, it can usually be obtained from the state insurance department. In addition, a company's annual financial statements, ratings and analysis are published by various rating companies, such as A.M. Best. This company grades the financial stability of insurance companies from A++ to F. The worse the rating, the greater the risk that the company will not be around when the insured needs to file a claim.

Some consumers have expressed concern about Best's close ties to the life insurance industry and want insurers to obtain another rating. This has prompted many insurers to seek ratings from companies such as Standard & Poor's (S&P), Moody's Investors Service (Moody's) or Duff & Phelps (D&P). These organizations have excellent reputations for providing objective ratings of a company's financial situation after a thorough examination of the accounting and investment records and after meeting with senior management. Although these companies are known for their *bond rating* services (based on systems of gradation for measuring the relative investment quality of bonds), they also rate insurers using symbols that range from the highest quality (least risk) to the lowest investment quality (greatest risk). Insurance companies must bear the cost of these "second opinions" so not all insurers get ratings from all rating agencies.

As shown in Illustration 7.1, A.M. Best uses ratings that range from A++ to F (in liquidation). Standard & Poor's rating system ranges from AAA to R (placed in liquidation). Moody's offers similar gradings, but with ratings that range from Aaa to C. Finally, Duff & Phelps' ratings range from AAA to DD.

Although there are many variables to consider when you are selecting an LTC policy, you will probably want to select a policy from a company that meets these two criteria:

1. Historically, the insurer should have very high ratings from at least two of the four major rating firms.

2. The insurer should not have a poor rating from any of the four major rating firms.

You should be aware of the rating differences among these rating companies and what each rating means. Whenever possible, consult multiple sources to get other

### ILL. 7.1 ■ *Insurance Company Rating Systems*

|  | A.M. Best | Standard & Poor's | Moody's | Duff & Phelps |
|---|---|---|---|---|
| Superior to Good | A++, A+<br>A, A–<br>B++, B+ | AAA<br>AA+, AA, AA–<br>A+, A, A– | Aaa<br>Aa1, Aa2, Aa3<br>A1, A2, A3 | AAA<br>AA+, AA, AA–<br>A+, A, A– |
| Fair to Financially Weak | B, B–<br>C++, C+<br>C, C–<br>D | BBB+, BBB, BBB–<br>BB+, BB, BB–<br>B+, B, B– | Baa1, Baa2, Baa3<br>Ba1, Ba2, Ba3<br>B1, B2, B3 | BBB+, BBB, BBB–<br>BB+, BB, BB–<br>B+, B, B– |
| Nonviable, Under State Supervision, in Liquidation or Failed | E<br>F | CCC<br>R | Caa<br>Ca<br>C | CCC<br>DD |

Note: These ratings are not equivalent to one another.

views of an insurer's financial condition. If the insurer offers the needed coverage but the agent doubts the insurer's ability to remain solvent, another insurer should be selected. Not all insurers are properly financed or expertly managed by qualified personnel. The agent should avoid insurers that are underfinanced, underreserved and undermanaged.

## Reputation

Many life and health insurance producers represent only one insurance company. If you are one of those producers, your prospects and clients may have selected the company you represent on the basis of the insurer's advertising or general reputation. Well-known and recognized companies are generally good choices for LTC products. Thus, your clients may have chosen to do business with you because companies with good reputations usually attract high-quality representatives. Or the consumer's choice of your company may represent their trust in you.

If you represent several insurers, state insurance departments usually compile records of consumer complaints or claim denials that will give you an overall impression of a specific company. You may also obtain information about an insurer from magazine articles, trade journals or other agents. With more than 120 companies from which to choose, there is no reason to offer your clients a policy from a company with a poor reputation.

## Service

The third criteria you and your clients should consider when selecting an insurer is its reputation for prompt and fair claims settlement. One of the vital factors in clientele-building is the manner in which claims are handled. Your eventual success may be related directly to the quality of the claim service your client receives. After all, when illness or disability occurs, the contract comes to life and the LTC policy demonstrates its benefits in action.

As part of its service, an insurer should also allow its policyholders to convert their original LTC policies if the company offers new or improved coverage. Some insurers inform policyholders of improvements in their original policies and permit them to switch policies. Others will require replacement at the insured's older attained age in order to obtain the enhanced coverage. A few companies will actually add an amendment to the original policy that reflects the product enhancement(s). Unfortunately, this option is no longer available on grandfathered plans (plans that were issued before January 1, 1997, and receive favorable tax status under HIPAA).

## Cost

Finally, you must consider the cost of LTC coverage. Cost will vary by company and is a function of coverage and actuarial assumptions. Although most consumers are pleased when their premiums are low, they are never happy to learn that a loss or illness is not covered. Be wary of companies that offer seemingly broad coverage at lower than average premiums. Low premiums can indicate a company's strict attitude toward claims payments, its high lapse assumptions, its inadequate reserves or other strategies to develop a block of business quickly. It is imperative that costs adequately reflect the coverage provided.

Lapse rates are a significant factor in pricing long-term care insurance. A lapse occurs when someone stops paying premiums either because of death or they no longer want the coverage (a voluntary lapse). The more people that lapse, the fewer people that will have the coverage when claims are likely to occur. Using a lapse rate that turns out to be higher than actual experience will result in an underpriced product; while underestimating a company's lapse rate will result in an overpriced product.

| Ultimate Lapse Rate | % That Still Own Their Coverage After 20 Years | % That Still Own Their Coverage After 30 Years |
|---|---|---|
| 2.5% | 60% | 47% |
| 5 | 36 | 21 |
| 8 | 20 | 8 |
| 10 | 13.5 | 4 |

If a company projects a 10 percent ultimate lapse rate and experiences a 5 percent rate, it will have almost three times as many people owning the coverage after 20 years and five times as many with the coverage after 30 years. This puts pressure on the company's ability to maintain level premiums.

A company's lapse assumption can be dramatized with two standard riders that are directly effected by lapses. An increasing benefit option at 5 percent compounded annually has significantly higher rates for companies with low lapse rates, while a nonforfeiture benefit has much lower rates. In other words, premiums are higher when more people keep their coverage longer and benefits are paid when a lapse occurs. Consider the following, for example, where Company A assumes a low lapse rate while Company B assumes an average lapse rate.

| Plan | Company A vs. Company B |
|------|-------------------------|
| Base | + 5% |
| Base with increasing benefits | +39% |
| Base with nonforfeiture | –8% |
| Base with both | +20% |

Offering a product with a high lapse rate is more susceptible to premium increases than one with a low lapse rate. Unfortunately, companies do not disclose their lapse rate assumptions to agents—but they can be found in actuarial memorandums filed with state insurance departments. Most companies' experience with long-term care insurance is relatively limited because of the small number of sales and short time in the business. This creates a situation where neither the company nor the agent know if the lapse assumptions are accurate. If the rates are overestimated, a premium increase is likely.

The severity of the premium increase(s) is proportional to the level of overestimating the ultimate lapse rate. While rate increases can result in higher lapse rates (a strategy called *shock lapse rates*), the people who keep the coverage are likely to be uninsurable with other companies, which creates a risk pool of unhealthy people more likely to file claims. This puts added pressure on the company's pricing assumptions.

An underestimate in ultimate lapse rates is likely to have fewer claimants than expected over the long run, which results in a need for price decreases. This is because companies must pay out a certain percentage of premiums received in benefits to the insureds. This is called a *loss ratio* and is mandated by the state.

Although lapse rate is one of the many assumptions actuaries make when pricing long-term care insurance, a company that guesses the wrong ultimate lapse rate can still have stable premiums if other assumptions produce better actual results than expected.

Research will help you identify quality insurers. Look at the companies and their contracts. Ask companies about their pricing assumptions and their actual to expected ("A to F") experience. Today, the choices in coverage and benefits are more extensive than ever before. With a little time and an open mind, the task of finding a long-term care plan that you can confidently recommend to your clients can be rewarding for both you and your clients.

## ■ UNDERWRITING OBJECTIVES

As you know, most definitions of *insurance* typically contain two fundamental ideas: (1) insurance involves a transfer of risk for a consideration and (2) insurance seeks to achieve a spread of similar risks subject to the same peril to increase predictability of losses. In other words, a number of similar individuals contribute money in the form of premiums to a fund, or "pool," that is used to pay for the losses of those individuals. Insurance companies tend to select and evaluate members of these groups carefully to assure that money flowing into the pool does not flow out too quickly. This process of selection and evaluation is called *underwriting* and it is the process that ensures that funds will be available when a claim is submitted.

Originally, *underwriters* were individuals who accepted risk transfers and backed them with their own fortunes; the underwriter was the insurer. More commonly now, private insurance companies act as insurers and delegate underwriting tasks to specialized underwriting departments.

The major goal of underwriting is to pool risks into a profitable, growing book of business. A *book of business* is the set of all policies currently in force with an insurer of a particular kind of insurance (such as automobile policies or LTC policies), a certain class of business or all policies written by an insurer.

As part of their duties, underwriters identify and evaluate hazards. Generally, LTC underwriters are looking for applicants who are in reasonably good health and who can take care of themselves. The ideal applicant is also usually socially active and commonly does volunteer work or engages in active hobbies. As younger people buy LTC insurance, underwriters are finding that more insureds are still in the workforce.

Underwriters also consider current health conditions and, based on this condition, determine the likelihood that the applicant will need care in the near future. Most companies have coverage restrictions for applicants who have limitations in the activities of daily living (bathing, dressing, eating, transferring, continence or toileting), instrumental activities of daily living (preparing meals, shopping, managing money, housework and so on) or memory loss.

## ■ THE LONG-TERM CARE UNDERWRITING PROCESS

The *underwriting process* is the procedure that underwriters use to evaluate applicants and approve the issuance of LTC coverage for those applicants. The process begins with a review of a rather detailed *LTC application*. As shown in Illustration 7.3, in addition to identifying information about the proposed insured, such as the complete name, address, age and so forth, the application elicits information about the applicant's recent medical history and benefits selection. If the agent feels that the applicant meets the company's general guidelines for LTC coverage, he or she completes and submits the application directly to the home office along with the applicant's initial premium.

To determine whether the applicant meets the company's underwriting standards, underwriters typically follow a set of underwriting criteria. Usually this criteria has been formulated by the company's senior management, product developers, actuaries and underwriters. In general, companies do not issue coverage on a nonstandard basis though they may make adjustments for existing health problems or for older individuals.

Generally, the agent is cautioned to refuse an application from a prospect if certain drugs are taken or if specific medical conditions exist. Many companies refuse to issue coverage for applicants whose past or current medical conditions increase the likelihood of skilled, intermediate or custodial care. These conditions commonly include, but are not limited to:

- cancer

- heart problems or stroke

- diabetes with sight or severe problems or amputation

- drug or alcohol abuse

- ADL or IADL deficits

- Parkinson's disease

- Alzheimer's disease

- prior nursing home admission

- arthritis

- HIV infection or AIDS

Applicants are also usually questioned about the types of medication they are taking and the duration of that treatment. Underwriters are particularly interested in learning about anticonvulsants (which may indicate epilepsy or recent seizure), antianginals (which indicate heart disease) and dementia drugs (which are used to improve the intellectual and interpersonal skills of those suffering from primary progressive dementia and Alzheimer's disease). These questions regarding medications are important because there are situations where applicants are taking medications without knowing the purpose of the drug.

---

### ILL. 7.2 ■ *Questions for Choosing an LTC Insurer*

What is the company's overall reputation?

What is the company's underwriting philosophy?

How well is the company's investment portfolio managed?

What is the company's financial rating?

Can the policy be converted?

---

The philosophy, procedures and requirements of the insurance company will determine which of two types of underwriting will take place: post-claim underwriting or underwriting before issue. Let's look at each of these methods in more detail.

## Post-Claim Underwriting

Most insurance companies have elaborate underwriting procedures that include considerations of past and present physical health. However, some companies simply ask limited medical questions and typically do not request the applicant's medical records. These companies issue policies within a week or two based on the information found on the application. No further investigation is done until a claim is submitted.

After the insured submits a claim, the company's more extensive *post-claim underwriting* begins. The underwriter will request an *Attending Physician's Statement (APS),* which provides details of recorded medical information along with a copy of the insured's original application for insurance. Upon receipt, the application is screened for any "misrepresentation" of information found (or not found) on it. The claims representative can then deny the claim and/or rescind the policy based on the "new" information received. The company claims ignorance of facts it could have obtained earlier.

Here's how post-claim underwriting can affect coverage. Assume that according to company guidelines, LTC coverage cannot be issued to an applicant who has diabetes mellitus. However, the company's application—which is limited in scope— makes no reference to diabetes nor does the agent mention to the applicant that diabetes will prevent the coverage from being issued. After the insured enters the nursing home, he or she submits a claim under the policy. The underwriter then requests an APS; it reveals the insured's history of diabetes. At that point, the claims representative denies the claim or the underwriter rescinds the policy on the grounds that if the company had this information when the application was received, it never

## ILL. 7.3 ■ *Sample Application*

**XYZ Life Insurance Company of America**

| Mailing Address: Chicago, IL 60601 | XYZ Life Insurance Company of America | *Long-Term Care Insurance Application and Statement of Health* |

Proposed Insured's Name (first, middle, last) | Birthdate | Sex | Social Security Number

Home Address _____ City _____

State _____ Zip Code _____ Home Phone (_____) _____ Work Phone (_____) _____

1. Actively at work? ❑ Yes, _____ hours per week ❑ No, reason (e.g., retired) _____
2. Occupation (or former occupation if retired) _____
3. Annual income $_____
4. Payment option: ❑ Monthly ❑ Quarterly ❑ Semi-annual ❑ Annual

### Plan Information

I have selected the following plan benefits:

1. Daily Benefit: $40 – $200 (select in $10 increments only) $_____
2. Benefit Waiting Period ❑ 20 days ❑ 60 days ❑ 100 days ❑ 365 days
3. Total Benefit Multiplier ❑ x1000 ❑ x2000 ❑ Unlimited
4. Benefit Increase Option ❑ Option A 200% ❑ Option B 300% ❑ No
5. Home Health Care/Adult Day Care ❑ 50% ❑ 75% ❑ No

### Medical Information

Circle any specific information that may apply

Personal Doctor _____ Address _____
Date Last Seen _____ Reason/Findings _____

|  | Yes | No |
|---|---|---|
| 1. Height _____ft. _____in. Weight _____lbs. | | |
| 2. Have you gained or lost more than 10 pounds in the last year? Reason? _____ | ❑ | ❑ |
| 3. Are you currently under any medication, treatment, observation, or therapy? | ❑ | ❑ |
| 4. In the last five years, have you: | | |
|   a. Needed assistance of any kind to perform everyday living activities (e.g., walking, dressing, eating, toileting, bathing)? | ❑ | ❑ |
|   b. Used a wheelchair, walker, cane, or any other device designed to assist with mobility? | ❑ | ❑ |
|   c. Had a heart attack, heart surgery, high blood pressure, heart murmur, irregular heartbeat, or other cardiovascular disease or disorder? | ❑ | ❑ |
|   d. Had shortness of breath, asthma, bronchitis, emphysema, pneumonia, or other disease of the lungs? | ❑ | ❑ |
|   e. Had cancer, tumor, cyst, leukemia, lymphoma, or Hodgkin's disease? | ❑ | ❑ |
|   f. Had Alzheimer's disease, dementia, memory loss, depression, or mental illness; fainting spells or dizziness, Parkinson's, tremors, epilepsy, seizure, stroke, or paralysis? | ❑ | ❑ |
|   g. Had colitis, liver, or digestive tract disease or disorder? | ❑ | ❑ |
|   h. Had arthritis or joint disorder; osteoporosis; back or spinal disorder; loss of limb; disorder of the muscles or bones? | ❑ | ❑ |
|   i. Had diabetes or other endocrine disease; any infection or disorder of the eyes or skin? | ❑ | ❑ |
|   j. Had kidney or urinary tract disorder, sexually transmitted disease, or breast disorder? | ❑ | ❑ |
|   k. Been confined to or been advised to enter a nursing home, or received treatment from a home health care agency or adult day care facility? | ❑ | ❑ |
|   l. Had treatment for alcohol or drugs, or been told by a doctor, counselor, therapist, or other medical specialist of the need to reduce or discontinue the use of alcohol or drugs? | ❑ | ❑ |
| 5. Other than noted above, have you in the last five years seen a doctor, counselor, or therapist; had any other illness, surgery, diagnostic test, or treatment? | ❑ | ❑ |

*Continued*

## ILL. 7.3 ■ *Sample Application (Cont.)*

6. During the last 10 years, have you tested positive or received treatment for AIDS, AIDS-related complex (ARC), or immune disorder?

7. Do you have a family history of heart or kidney disease, diabetes, or cancer?

|  | **Yes** | **No** |
|---|---|---|
| 6. | ❑ | ❑ |
| 7. | ❑ | ❑ |

Give details of *yes* answers to medical questions 2 through 7. List the question number and give full details in the space provided below. If more space is needed, attach a separate signed and dated sheet.

| Question Number | Nature of Illness or Injury, Treatment, Testing, Medication, or Medical Attention, etc. | Date | | Duration | Diagnosis, Results, Findings, or Remaining Effects | Names and Addresses of Physicians or Hospitals |
|---|---|---|---|---|---|---|
| | | Mo. | Yr. | | | |
| | | | | | | |
| | | | | | | |
| | | | | | | |
| | | | | | | |
| | | | | | | |

### Statement of Understanding and Authorization

I authorize any medical practitioner, any medically related facility, insurance company, the MIB, Inc., or any other organization, institution, or person to give XYZ Life Insurance Company of America or its reinsurers any information about me including physical or mental history and information about drug or alcohol use. I authorize XYZ Life Insurance Company of America to release any such data to MIB, Inc., or as required by law. I have received a copy of the "Notice of Information Practices" which includes a description of MIB, Inc. This authorization is valid for two years from date of application.

I understand that, except as the Conditional Receipt provides, no insurance will become effective (1) unless medical history is evaluated and found satisfactory by the Company, (2) the first premium is paid, and (3) a payment method is accepted by the Company and my financial institution.

❑ This application is COD or     ❑ I have paid $_____. If money was paid, I have been given the Conditional Receipt. I have read, understand, and agree to the terms of the Conditional Receipt.

I represent that all information, statements and answers recorded on the front and back or attached to this application are full, correct and true to the best of my knowledge. **I understand that omissions or misstatements could cause an otherwise valid claim to be denied or cause the insurance, if issued, to be canceled as if never effective**. I agree that a photostat of this form is as valid as the original.

Any person who, with intent to defraud or knowing that he is facilitating a fraud against an insurer, submits an application or files a claim containing a false or deceptive statement is guilty of insurance fraud.

Signature of Applicant _____

Date Signed _____     Signed at _____
                               (City)                                      (State)

### Agent's Statement

Signature                          Date                        Agent's
of Agent _____  Signed _____  Code _____

Agent's Name _____  Agent's Soc. Sec. No. _____

Street _____  City _____  State _____  Zip _____

1. List policies sold to the applicant that are still in force _____
2. List policies sold to the applicant in the past
   five (5) years that are no longer in force _____

### (ONA/RBG/GRP OFF Use Only)

Field Representative's Signature _____  Date Signed _____

Marketing Office Name _____

| Rep Code | Office Code |
|---|---|
| | |

(Home Office Use Only)

Account Number _____  Policy Date _____

would have issued coverage. Instead of policy benefits, the insured receives a return of premiums.

Companies that engage in post-claim underwriting feel that this process reduces their expenses. Rather than requesting an APS for each applicant, the insurer needs to request and pay for only those needed at the time a claim is submitted. But denying claims based on a consumer's ignorance of the insurer's underwriting guidelines can tarnish the reputation of that insurer, the insurance industry and yourself.

## Underwriting Before Issue

The types of long-term care companies you want to represent are issued by insurance companies that screen applications for completeness, medical history, corresponding treatment and date of medical consultations *before* issuing LTC coverage. Policies issued by underwriters who look for pre-issue conditions and give the applicant an opportunity to correct or clarify the information are more likely to provide the benefits promised than policies issued by post-claim underwriters. Even if an error is noted after the application is accepted, in most cases the company will pay the benefits due—unless there was an obvious intent by the applicant to hide a serious medical or cognitive condition. Illustration 7.3 contains an abbreviated LTC application, which shows the type of information that should be sought (although the typical LTC application is slightly longer.)

It is important to do business with a company that will thoroughly investigate an applicant's medical records. This is simply a prudent business practice that is necessary to understand the nature of the risk. Companies that intend to remain in business for a long time will regularly request an APS that details past medical information on a new applicant. Unless an underwriter can consider the applicant's past and present physical and mental health, it is unlikely that an appropriate decision about the applicant can be made.

After reviewing a physician's records, many underwriters request a *personal history interview (PHI),* a telephone service designed to obtain supportive medical or general underwriting information from the applicant and/or physician. Personal history interviews have been proven effective in risk assessment because they can help clarify statements on the application, resolve conflicting information in the physician's records and give an indication of the applicant's cognitive capabilities. The interviews are relatively inexpensive for a company to perform and can save a company from some costly future claims if an impairment is discovered that would prohibit policy issuance. The agent should not view a request for the applicant to have a PHI as a personal criticism of his or her underwriting practice. Rather, the interview is intended to prevent costly underwriting errors that could happen with any applicant.

For certain older ages, *face-to-face assessments* may also be requested to determine an individual's physical and cognitive abilities. These assessments are performed by individuals trained in geriatrics who can detect deterioration or loss in a person's intellectual or physical capacity. They may review the individual's medical history and perform various tests to measure fine motor skills and self-care activities. Clinical evidence and standardized tests are given to reliably measure an applicant's cognitive impairment in the following areas:

- short-term or long-term memory;

- orientation as to person (who he or she is), place (where he or she is) and time (such as day, date and year); and

- deductive or abstract reasoning (loss can occur from Alzheimer's disease or similar forms of senility or irreversible dementia).

Before coverage is issued, such assessments will likely be required of applicants whose health history is incomplete, who show signs of memory loss or who are over a certain age.

### Errors in the Application

When an underwriter reviews and compares the application to the APS, he or she may note one or more discrepancies. There are at least four reasons the information in the medical records would not agree with the information on the application:

1. The applicant may not have known about the condition. This is common when a doctor feels there is an onset of senility and does not want to alarm the patient but simply makes notes in the patient's medical records.

2. The applicant does not tell the agent about a condition because he or she does not feel a medical condition is significant or because he or she may honestly have forgotten that a previous medical treatment took place.

3. The applicant knows that a medical condition exists but does not tell the agent because he or she hopes the insurance company will not discover the condition.

4. The applicant may tell the agent about a medical condition or about the use of a prescription medication but the agent does not include the information on the application. The agent may feel it is unimportant or knows it will prevent the coverage from being issued. Agents should record all conditions disclosed by the applicant.

## Explaining the Underwriting Process to Prospects

You'll want to know the underwriting practices of the company you represent and communicate that information to the applicant. It is best to explain that the company you represent uses the information on the application to assess the applicant's eligibility for coverage and therefore, the application must be accurate and complete. But underwriters will frequently need additional information from the applicant. This is especially true if the prospect has a history of illness.

You will also want to explain that all the information obtained as part of the underwriting process will be treated as confidential. The insurance company will not release this information to anyone without the applicant's authorization. In addition, the applicant has the right to access any information that is obtained from his or her physician.

Companies that assess an applicant before issuing a policy will reduce the frequency of underwriting errors. However, careful underwriting prior to issue takes longer than post-claim underwriting. That time will be further extended when:

- a physician delays sending the APS to the insurance company;

- an APS does not provide adequate information and actual records need to be ordered and reviewed; or

- an APS refers to a specialist or other physician the applicant has seen recently for a specific condition; those medical records must then be ordered, received and reviewed.

It may take some time for the physician's office to copy the necessary medical information and send it to the insurance company. Even after the underwriter receives and reviews the APS, he or she may need additional information. If there are discrepancies between or among records, that information must be clarified.

Remain patient during the underwriting process. Underwriting commonly takes 30 days and, in fact, may take longer if the case is unusual. However, if underwriting a single, healthy applicant consistently takes five weeks or longer, you may want to speak with the underwriter to determine what you can do to help speed up the process. In some cases, the application may be incomplete. In other cases, the underwriter will ask you to check with the physician or specialist to be certain that the applicant's records were copied and sent.

## ■ SUMMARY

The LTC products you have to offer today have improved significantly over those offered even five years ago. Insurers are gaining valuable experience and are willing to offer the better plans. A strong company standing behind the policy you sell gives you confidence and enhances your reputation of offering only quality products that will provide the benefits originally promised.

In the next chapter, we'll explore some common myths about the need for long-term care insurance. In addition, we'll also look at the various segments that make up the long-term care market and suggest ways you can enter that market.

■  **CHAPTER 7 QUESTIONS FOR REVIEW**

1.  According to the text, the primary objective of underwriting is to

    A.  provide the best coverage at the least amount of premium
    B.  pool like risks into a profitable book of business
    C.  select only those individuals who will not have losses
    D.  preserve the reputation of the insurance company

2.  When a company chooses to use post-claim underwriting, it generally results in

    A.  increased initial underwriting expense
    B.  decreased underwriting errors
    C.  decreased initial underwriting time and expense
    D.  fewer misrepresentations in the application

3.  Underwriting time will generally NOT be extended when

    A.  the applicant forgets to tell the agent about a specialist he or she has seen within the past month
    B.  a physician's office fails to send copies of the applicant's medical records to the insurer
    C.  the application contains all the information requested
    D.  additional medical records must be ordered

4.  An insurance company's financial stability and claims paying ability is

    A.  impossible for an agent to evaluate
    B.  seldom important when considering LTC coverage
    C.  an indication of its overall ability to remain in business
    D.  determined by the number of agents who represent and sell its policies

5.  When selecting an LTC insurer, you should consider all of the following EXCEPT its

    A.  overall reputation
    B.  financial rating
    C.  location of the home office
    D.  policy pricing

6.  The financial strength of an insurance company is important to

    A.  the agent
    B.  the client
    C.  the agent and client
    D.  none of the above

7. The cost of long-term care insurance is a function of

   A. many actuarial assumptions, including ultimate lapse rates
   B. the level of service provided by the agent
   C. the ratings received from A.M. Best
   D. the quality of the marketing materials

8. A company with a high nonforfeiture premium and a low inflation rider premium

   A. is expecting low lapse rates
   B. has accurately priced their product
   C. will be able to guarantee premiums
   D. is susceptible to future rate increases

9. Underwriting long-term care insurance

   A. is designed to pool like risks together
   B. is normally done at the time of the claim
   C. does not consider volunteer work or hobbies
   D. all of the above

10. Normal underwriting of long-term care insurance takes

   A. 72 hours
   B. one week
   C. 30 days
   D. 7–8 weeks

# The Market for LTC Insurance

T oday's aging population, coupled with the public's growing awareness of the need for long-term care, creates opportunities for the agent who can offer a long-term care product that will meet a client's needs and objectives. However, as every good agent knows, before you can successfully market a product, you must understand the attitudes, perceptions and values of your prospects. You must also remember that every situation is different; what may be an effective approach for one prospect is not always appropriate for another. In this chapter, we'll look at the vast market for long-term care insurance and ways you can help your clients protect themselves against what may be the largest unfunded financial risk they face in their retirement years—the need for long-term care.

■ ■ ■ ■ ■

## ■ THE "NEW" INSURANCE MARKET

In the past, the traditional client was a family, headed by a male in his 20s or early 30s, who provided most if not all of the family's income. But times changed and so did the demographics of the traditional insurance market. There are more two-income families now than ever before; there are also many more single-person households. And while serving the needs of older people or the anticipated future needs of middle-aged people used to be just a secondary market for the insurance industry, it may soon equal the traditional primary market. The agent who understands the opportunities presented by the mature market will be successful in the fastest growing market of the future—long-term care insurance.

Insurance professionals selling long-term care insurance will do well to avoid assumptions about the older market that they seek to serve. Although older people share some similar characteristics, gerontological research shows that people become more dissimilar as they age. For example, some will be healthy; some will face chronic illness. Some will retire while others will remain in the workforce. They may be married, widowed, divorced or single. The financial profiles range from impoverished elderly who subsist on welfare to a large number of "semi-millionaires" between the ages of 50 and 70, though most fall somewhere between these two extremes.

As explained later in this chapter, the market for long-term care insurance consists of a number of market segments. However, your primary long-term care insurance prospects will be individuals over age 50 who are usually at the peak of their income-earning years and, as such, are best able to afford long-term care insurance premiums. This is the market we call the "empty nesters." As a whole this group owns three-quarters of all U.S. financial assets. It also accounts for one-fourth of the total population of the United States. In addition, individuals over the age of 50:

- control one-half of all U.S. discretionary spending;

- purchase almost one-half of all luxury cars sold;

- spend more on health and personal care products than any other age group;

- purchase more than one-third of all over-the-counter medicinal products;

- read newspapers and are better informed than any other age group;

- want detailed information that allows them to take charge of their buying decisions;

- are well-informed purchasers; and

- show a high concern for quality and value over the cost of a product.

You can use demographics such as these as a useful tool for defining your long-term care target market. For example, you might target college-educated professionals who are 50 to 65 years old. Or you might select your prospect base by income, type of business, geographical area and so forth. Let's take a closer look at the potential market.

## ■ THE LONG-TERM CARE MARKET

Currently, there are about 34 million Americans aged 65 and over; they constitute about 13 percent of the entire population and their numbers are growing at a rate of 12 percent per year. Of these 34 million people over age 65, 43 percent will spend some time in nursing homes. However, only about 5 percent of this group currently has LTC insurance. Obviously, a large percentage of the 65-and-over group has yet to be reached. And the 65-and-over group will grow. Currently, there are 72 million Americans age 50 and older—about 27 percent of the U.S. population. In addition,

**ILL. 8.1  ■  *The 50+ Population***

Currently, the 72 million people who make up the age 50+ population also . . .

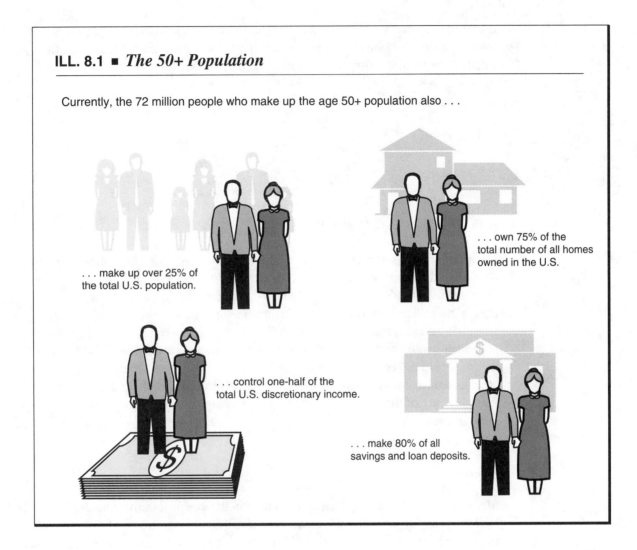

. . . make up over 25% of the total U.S. population.

. . . own 75% of the total number of all homes owned in the U.S.

. . . control one-half of the total U.S. discretionary income.

. . . make 80% of all savings and loan deposits.

there are more than 82 million baby boomers (those born between 1946 and 1964) who, when they begin to reach age 65, will become the largest retired population in U.S. history. The solution to the problem of long-term care for many in this vast market is affordable long-term care insurance coverage.

Most people can purchase quality insurance protection at affordable rates; then when the need arises, benefits can be provided without depleting family income or assets. As an agent, you can provide this needed protection. Your sales efforts should begin by identifying qualified prospects.

## ■  QUALIFYING THE LONG-TERM CARE PROSPECT

Now that you have a basic understanding of the long-term care market, let's narrow the focus and take a look at what qualifies an individual as a long-term care prospect. As you know, not everyone is a bona fide prospect for life insurance; the same is true for long-term care insurance. In order to market and sell LTC effectively, you must identify who among the many in the market are qualified buyers. Essentially, true long-term care prospects must meet certain criteria in three areas:

1. age

2. ability

3. assets

## Age

Long-term care insurers set minimum and maximum age limits for policy issuance. Typically, these limits range from age 40 to age 84, though some companies offer coverage to individuals as old as 99 and as young as 21. (In Pennsylvania, all companies must offer coverage to individuals who are at least 16 years old.) Agents would do well to prospect among individuals who fall between the typical age limits. Individuals younger than 50 typically have other insurance needs with which they are (or should be) concerned and the likelihood that they would need nursing home care in the near future is slim. Those older than 80 are not likely to qualify for coverage because of their health or the fact that premiums for this age group are frequently unaffordable.

## Ability

*Ability* can be defined as the capacity to remain independent in the community. Underwriting for long-term care insurance is different from that of life or medical insurance because the applicant's ability to function is analyzed. Underwriters look for diseases, injuries or illnesses that could lead to loss of independence. For example, arthritis may not affect underwriting for life insurance, but it would be an important factor in long-term care underwriting. In general, individuals with signs of a chronic condition that would likely lead to a loss of function will not qualify for coverage. Further, as individuals age, their likelihood of qualifying for LTC coverage decreases because chronic conditions begin to set in as we age.

## Assets

Those who meet the age and ability requirements must also have assets. This is important for two reasons. First, an individual with assets has the ability to pay the premium. Second, an individual with assets has something or things that he or she wants to protect. In this respect, "assets" should not be limited to financial assets.

For instance, certain individuals may not have a great deal in the way of financial assets. For these individuals, qualifying for Medicaid would not require much if any financial sacrifice. If not financial assets, what are the assets these individuals are protecting—intangible assets such as pride and dignity. They may well take pride in having provided for themselves and their family without any help. They may not want to rely on family members or the government for help. They may wish to be able to make their own decisions regarding their long-term care. This pride and independence is an asset that LTC insurance helps preserve.

Now that we have looked at the factors that help determine who makes a good LTC prospect, let's look at how these factors apply within the specific sales segments that make up the LTC market.

### The Baby Boom Generation

The members of the huge post-World War II generation—the baby boomers—usually begin to think seriously about retirement savings, asset protection and financial planning around age 45. Even though most enjoy higher lifetime earnings than their parents, baby boomers may have delayed saving for retirement. It follows then that they also have a growing concern that certain "entitlement" programs such as Medicare and Social Security will be limited or unavailable for them when they retire. They may already be supporting their own aged parents (as well as supporting their children in some cases), placing a strain on their financial and personal wherewithal. Having felt the burden and responsibility of caring for elderly parents, and having seen first hand the effects of a chronic condition on an aging parent, baby boomers are often deeply concerned about the cost of their own catastrophic illness and long-term care.

Baby boomers are well aware that medical advances have eliminated many contagious diseases and have contributed to increased life expectancy. This group can expect to live into their 80s or 90s. But there is a downside to a longer life. While the diseases that used to cause early death are being successfully treated, they are being replaced by diseases that render people incapable of performing the simple activities of daily living. And as we've seen, in many cases the family cannot take care of the elderly because of physical, emotional or financial limitations.

The major problems facing this group—increased longevity, changes in Social Security benefits and company pensions and rising health-care costs—will increase the amount of personal income needed during retirement. Unfortunately, few will be able to save the money needed to pay for a nursing home stay. The obvious solution to this problem is long-term care insurance.

The baby boomers—who are currently between ages 35 and 50—are the youngest LTC market segment and, as such, will generally pay the lowest premiums. In fact, for the price of about two cups of coffee a day, a 40-year-old person can transfer the risk of long-term care costs to an insurer. Although this market segment may not collect benefits for many years, it will benefit from lower premiums. And with the passage of HIPAA in 1996, some of these premiums may be tax deductible. In addition to coverage for themselves, this group contains good prospects for LTC insurance for their parents who may still be healthy and able to qualify for coverage.

Ideally, the best prospects in this group will not have children living at home. It's difficult to sell the advantages of long-term care insurance to those whose primary concerns are caring for their families and financing their children's college education. Actually, in this market segment solid life, retirement and disability plans should be in place before a long-term care policy is even discussed. As you work the LTC market, and as you come across these baby boomers who are still raising families, take the opportunity to assess their need for life and disability insurance. If they buy their basic needs from you and you service them well, they'll likely be receptive to a discussion of long-term care coverage in the future.

## The Empty Nesters

The second LTC market segment is the mature market—people age 50 to 64. Often called "empty nesters," this segment controls more than 77 percent of the nation's wealth. This group also accounts for 42 percent of all after-tax income—which translates into one-half of the total domestic discretionary income—or around $160 billion annually. Nearly 75 percent of households falling into this category own their own homes—and almost 80 percent of these homeowners own their homes mortgage-free. Although it can be described generally as wealthy, the mature market is actually a diverse group of people, varying widely by income, family status, occupation and social class.

In the past, people who reached age 50 could look forward to 10 or 15 more years of employment, a short retirement and a relatively early death. But, because of advances in health care and the resulting increased longevity, the needs of those age 50 and older are shifting from providing financial protection for their families and preparing for death to preparing for a longer life and providing financial protection for their own personal needs.

The 50 and older age group is healthier, more active and better educated than were their parents or grandparents. As preretirees, many in this group are at the peak of their earnings potential and have high levels of discretionary income; as "empty nesters," with children no longer living at home and no longer needing financial support and assistance, they might actually find that their living expenses are reduced. These two factors greatly enhance their ability to pay for long-term care insurance.

Studies have shown that this group, as buyers of goods and services, are strongly influenced by quality and service—not just price. As a whole this group is interested in fully understanding a product and its benefits. They will appreciate an agent who can offer a first-class product, explain its provisions thoroughly, show how it will benefit them and then stay in contact with them to ensure that their coverage is meeting their needs and expectations.

Long-term health-care coverage is an important need for this group. It's likely that a married couple will have seen at least one parent or in-law decline and die, perhaps after a nursing home stay. They are concerned that their current insurance will not handle all their medical and long-term care needs in the future. Like the older baby boomers, these individuals are good prospects for long-term care insurance—for themselves and their parents.

## The "New" Retirees

The retiree group consists of approximately 20 million people who are over age 65. In many cases, they will have enjoyed their peak financial years just prior to retirement. Though most live on a fixed income—Social Security and pension benefits supplemented by investments and savings—the fact is, seniors have the highest net worth of any age group. Approximately 90 percent of those with household incomes of more than $30,000 own their own homes. Many have paid off their mortgages, have little or no installment debt and often have substantial sums of money to invest. Although they want to maximize return on their money, they are also risk-averse and prefer rather conservative investments. Their primary concern is safety. For example, most seniors maintain bank savings accounts or certificates of deposit rather than other higher yielding but riskier investments for their retirement funds.

In the early phases of retirement, seniors will be active and probably spend much of their disposable income on travel, recreation and leisure activities. They might belong to affinity groups and have strong feelings about remaining self-reliant. Many retirees enjoy second "careers" in the service sector in order to remain involved in their community, to make new social contacts, to continue their "going to work" routine and/or to supplement their income. During their retirement planning process, most retirees learn a great deal about their financial needs and the insurance options available to meet those needs. They know how much money they will require to maintain their standard of living and what their existing insurance policies do and do not cover. They understand their expenses and income and are able to budget better than others.

As an approach to this group, an agent can provide a valuable service by helping these individuals understand how their private insurance fits with the government's programs and how neither adequately addresses the long-term care need. The agent can point out that Medicare (even with supplemental Part B coverage and a Medigap policy) does not fully cover a retiree's exposure to all medical costs, treatments or services. The agent can stress that Medicare pays less than 10 percent of nursing home costs and has strict requirements for home health care. Once new retirees understand that this need is not currently filled, they are eager to do something about it.

All in all, these new retirees are good prospects for long-term care insurance. It's likely that they've seen friends who've needed care and had to spend down their assets on nursing home care. Moreover, they can budget to pay for the coverage. They remain active and healthy and can thus meet underwriting requirements. Once an agent demonstrates the inadequacies of their existing insurance program and the current government programs, these prospects will readily see that there is no other payor for the broad range of long-term care services available today. The new retiree will have to obtain insurance or use his or her own assets to get the care he or she

## ILL. 8.2　■　*Long Term Care Market*

### Baby Boomers

Age:　　35–50
Ability:　Healthy
Assets:　Growing
Outlook:　May have other financial
　　　　planning/insurance needs
　　　　that take priority over LTC
　　　　insurance.

### Empty Nesters

Age:　　50–65
Ability:　Healthy
Assets:　Income level at peak; final
　　　　stages of asset building.
Outlook:　Excellent LTC insurance
　　　　prospects.

### New Retirees

Age:　　65–75
Ability:　Varies; some chronic
　　　　conditions begin to appear.
Assets:　Peak asset level; income
　　　　level often remains good.
Outlook:　Excellent LTC insurance
　　　　prospects.

### Golden Retirees

Age:　　75+
Ability:　Varies; multiple chronic
　　　　conditions may appear.
Assets:　Income often stretched just
　　　　to meet living expenses.
Outlook:　Fair LTC prospects, though
　　　　careful selection is required.

may want. New retirees rate long-term care as the financial need that they're least prepared for but most anxious to do something about.

## The Golden Retirees

As the life expectancy of our population rises, golden retirees—those age 75 and older—will be the fastest growing group in the United States over the next 40 years. Medical advances have eliminated many of the acute conditions that once resulted in earlier death. People are living longer—but not always better.

Golden retirees are slowing down their lifestyles. Their activities outside the home are reduced; they are seeing friends enter nursing homes or become dependent on their children. They live on a limited fixed income and, perhaps for the first time, are beginning to experience chronic conditions associated with the aging process.

After age 75, two kinds of changes take place in the body that are clearly related to aging: functional loss and a reduction in homeostasis. As people age, their *functional ability* to perform certain voluntary tasks (such as lifting) and involuntary tasks (the pumping of the heart) is lessened. In addition, *homeostasis* (the body's ability to maintain normal operating levels) is greatly reduced. Therefore, the elderly are more susceptible to chills or heat exhaustion.

These individuals understand the need for long-term care insurance better than any other group. Unfortunately, they often cannot qualify for coverage because of health conditions or because they cannot afford the higher premiums for their advanced age. Many of these retirees live on a limited fixed income; the median income for those over age 75 is about $8,000. An adequate long-term care policy could easily cost 10 percent of that income. Though there will be exceptions, generally speaking, members of this group will not be quality LTC prospects.

Keep in mind that the above categories contain generalizations. Because your prospect is a certain age, don't assume they fit neatly into one of the above categories. There are people in their 60s and even 70s who still have children at home and the concerns that go along with supporting children. Others have few financial worries and are perfect prospects for long-term care insurance. Conversely, there are people in their 40s and 50s who didn't have children or whose children are independent. These people are most likely concerned about building and protecting a retirement nest egg. However, some in this age group are currently unable to care for themselves—11 percent of all nursing home residents are under age 65 years old.

The way to find out your prospect's concerns and overall situation is to talk with them. While you should be aware of broad trends that are present in the population, good communication skills will prove more valuable in your efforts to serve the long-term care market.

---

### ILL. 8.3 ■ *The Market for Employer-Sponsored Plans*

When propsecting for long-term plan sales, business should not be ignored. Although individual sales account for most of the market, more than 10 percent or 650,000 policies were sold through employer groups by the end of 1996. With only 1,532 employers offering group coverage, there is ample room for growth. The policyholders in these groups will include employees, family members and retirees who enrolled in a corporate-sponsored plan.

Both large and small employers are now sponsoring long-term care insurance programs as a natural complement to their existing benefits package. The passage of HIPAA should increase the number of employer-sponsored plans as employer-paid TQ premiums are now tax deductible for the employer (though not if the coverage is provided through a flexible spending or cafeteria plan). The ease of payroll deduction, higher policy persistency and decreased administration costs allow insurers to offer group-sponsored long-term care insurance at a lower cost to insureds. In addition to helping employees protect their retirement savings, the employer can also reduce productivity losses caused by employees who must leave work to care for disabled parents or grandparents.

---

## ■ SUCCESSFUL LONG-TERM CARE SELLING TECHNIQUES

While there are approximately 72 million Americans over the age of 50, only about 5 million long-term care policies have been sold since they were first offered for sale in 1965. Though as we've seen, a certain percentage would not qualify as prospects or buyers, the fact remains that consumers rate long-term care highest as a financial need that they have not yet addressed. Research shows that people have not prepared for this need because:

- they're not sure who to turn to for advice;

- they're not sure who sells coverage; or

- no one has discussed the problem with them.

Thus, it should be clear that the market is not only untapped but willing and receptive to a knowledgeable agent who can skillfully explain the long-term care need and show how his or her product can meet it.

### Where to Begin?

An agent new to the long-term care field may be concerned about where to begin his or her prospecting and marketing efforts. Chances are you already have the necessary sales skills; for example, you probably have a prospecting system that works well for you, such as referred leads, direct mail or seminar selling. It's no different in the long-term care market; you should continue to concentrate on those methods you find comfortable and, more importantly, that produce results. What you do want to do is to focus your prospecting efforts, carefully define your market and understand the traits and characteristics of the prospects you'll be calling on.

Especially when selling long-term care insurance, you will find that prospecting within a specific market segment—such as those between age 50 and 64—will allow you to increase your effectiveness, productivity and earnings. By analyzing what factors or characteristics the specific market segment you select shares, you can better address their needs. You'll find that although prospects for long-term care insurance are a large, diverse group of people, they tend to have the following traits in common:

- *They do not want to be thought of as "old."* People over age 50 tend to judge their age more by how they feel than the number of years they have lived. When viewing people their own age, individuals do not believe they look or act that old. If asked to identify someone as "old," they often will point to someone 15 years their senior. This difference usually grows wider as they age—few 85-year-old people feel they are 85 years old. They consider age more relevant with wine and antiques than with humans.

- *Their primary concern is maintaining both functional and financial independence.* This group is concerned that their health will deteriorate to the point where they will need someone to take care of them and that they will have to spend their nest egg to obtain that care. They are determined to remain self-reliant and contribute to society. They spend their money on things they truly need, not on things others tell them they need. This purchasing method helps to protect their financial independence.

- *They want personalized customer service from people they can trust.* Even if it has not happened to them personally, older people have seen reports in the news or have friends who, as consumers, have been taken advantage of or have been treated unfavorably. Therefore, they have become leery of salespeople who use a "hard" close. They prefer a careful, thorough explanation of the problem and the solution, then time to make an informed decision. They will develop trust for the salesperson who explains products well, answers questions honestly and openly and allows them time to make their informed decision. Prospects will purchase from the salesperson who shows that his or her primary motivation is meeting the prospect's needs and working for the prospect's interests.

- *They are drawn to products or services that result in a favorable experience.* Although it is true of most consumers, elderly individuals who have worked hard for many years now expect others to "work" for them. They want personalized attention when purchasing a quality product and a favorable experience when spending their money. If the salesperson does not make the experience enjoyable, this group will do business somewhere else.

Sometimes, they will simply not purchase a product though they may have a great need for it.

- *They seek value in every purchase.* Over their lifetime, the older population has purchased many products that have not stood the test of time. As a result, they have discovered it is better to purchase quality products that will serve their needs over a long period of time and will be there when they need it. In addition, the quality and reputation of the company offering the product is very important to this group. With long-term care insurance, the provider is often considered more important than the technical aspects of the policy. And the agent may be considered as important as, or more important than, the insurer.

- *Physical and financial security are key buying decision factors.* This group has worked a lifetime in order to save enough money to enjoy its retirement years. If this nest egg is lost, they do not have time to build another. Knowing their assets are safe and secure if their physical condition should deteriorate is essential.

## Handling Objections

As you know, prospects can voice a great variety of excuses for not buying. In the case of long-term care, prospects are often uninformed about the facts and may repeat erroneous information that they've seen in the media or heard from friends. If you have the facts to refute any objection the prospect offers, you will have the key to the barrier that blocks the sale. You can instantly recognize what is in the prospect's mind, expose it and dispose of it by giving the proper facts about long-term care and LTC insurance protection.

Let's look at some of the most common myths that surface as sales objections. These myths must be overcome with facts presented in the proper manner at the point of sale. You'll need to know the facts before you approach your prospects. The knowledge you gain in previous chapters can now be used to educate your prospects on why long-term care insurance is a wise decision for them to make.

*Myth #1: "I've never been sick a day in my life; I'll never need a nursing home."*

The thought of becoming infirm is particularly disturbing for someone who thinks that he or she is "strong as an ox." Such people tend to believe that illness or disability will "happen to the other guy." The truth is that the longer people live, the more likely they are to become chronically ill. Forty-three percent of those age 65 and older will spend time in a nursing home; others will need care in their homes or adult day centers. And most of the people receiving this care also thought it would never happen to them.

*Myth #2:* *"Nursing home care isn't that expensive. If we ever need it, we can afford it."*

Because many older Americans haven't been exposed to the expense recently, they have no idea how much long-term nursing home care actually costs. The average cost of a stay is over $45,000 annually and almost 50 percent of nursing home residents stay 2.5 years. That's over $100,000 just for long-term care and doesn't include other expenses such as clothing, transportation, life insurance or personal needs.

*Myth #3:* *"I'm already covered by Medicare or Medicaid."*

Medicare pays for short-term recuperative care, but it does not pay for custodial long-term care—the care most needed by nursing home residents. As for Medicaid, the applicant must be virtually impoverished in order to qualify. And, even if the prospect does qualify for Medicaid, it may not cover the cost of the nursing home he or she chooses. The choice of nursing home is based on how much Medicaid will pay and is limited to availability. Frequently, the resident is unhappy with the facility Medicaid chooses.

*Myth #4:* *"My children will take care of me."*

Adult children are usually sincere when they say, "Mom will never have to go to a nursing home; I'll take care of her." However, taking care of a parent is more difficult than most adult children can imagine. Care frequently involves heavy lifting, bathing, incontinence management or control of abusive behavior resulting from senile dementia. Also, few people have the patience or the ability to provide the necessary care 24 hours a day, seven days a week that people afflicted with Alzheimer's disease require. In a two-career family there is frequently no one home to do the caring unless one person leaves a career—which only compounds the family's financial burdens.

Elderly prospects should understand that discussing LTC does not necessarily mean that their children want to "put them in a home." Adult children, many of them elderly themselves, may simply be physically or emotionally unable to care for their parents. With long-term care insurance, the care recipient and caregivers have the financial ability to consider several options.

*Myth #5:* *"Long-term care insurance has a bad reputation for not paying claims."*

Long-term care insurance has received its share of bad publicity. In addition to documented agent abuse, there were stringent gatekeeping provisions designed to prevent excessive claims costs. However, companies today are providing better products and agents are better trained. Furthermore, the federal government and most state governments have moved to regulate the design and sale of long-term care products to provide greater consumer protection. To ease their minds, you may want to inform consumers about insurance companies' claims payment histories and their record of premium adjustments. Both cast a positive light on the LTC insurance industry.

### ILL. 8.4 ■ *Sample Long-Term Care Premiums*

Policy Specifications:
- Nursing home benefit $100 per day
- 90-day elimination period
- 4-year benefit maximum
- 5 percent compounded annually inflation protection

| Age | Company A | Company B | Company C | Company D |
|-----|-----------|-----------|-----------|-----------|
| 60 | $ 517.79 | $1,240 | $ 795.40 | $ 658 |
| 70 | $1,217.50 | $2,440 | $1,615.40 | $1,645 |
| 75 | $2,160.46 | $4,000 | $2,509.20 | $2,394 |

Source: Life Insurance Selling, December 1998

*Myth #6:* *"Long-term care insurance costs too much."*

Many people say they cannot afford something they don't want or don't understand why they need it just to get the salesman "off their back." A recent survey indicated that 40 percent of those surveyed did not know what long-term care insurance would cost. Those age 50 and younger overestimated the actual cost by a factor of three or four. This objection can often be handled by informing individuals of the actual cost (and the many benefits) of long-term care insurance.

While many people overestimate the cost of long-term care insurance, the high actuarial probability of a nursing home stay *does* make it relatively expensive. Some people simply will be unable to afford to purchase coverage. However, if coverage is purchased while the prospect is younger and healthier, the cost is substantially less. Currently, a 40-year-old prospect might pay an annual premium of $750 for LTC insurance; the cost of the same coverage might rise to $3,100 for a 70-year-old prospect.

Seniors, who at first glance found LTC premiums cost prohibitive, have discovered creative ways to finance the cost of coverage. Some use intergenerational contracts in which children pay for LTC insurance premiums in exchange for the promise of an inheritance. Other seniors who are "house rich, cash poor" have used home equity conversion through reverse annuity mortgages or a sale and leaseback with family members as other ways to generate financing for premiums. Still others found that a switch in the allocation of their investment assets could provide the additional income to cover the premium.

*Myth #7: "I want to wait to see what the government will cover."*

Politicians and advocacy groups have proposed a number of health-care plans, including universal health-care insurance, for nearly 50 years. Unfortunately, the government's current health-care programs are already underfunded and it is unlikely that taxpayers alone will be willing—or able—to support further health-care expansions. And, even if long-term care becomes part of a government health plan, it's probable that seniors will be expected to pay a large portion of the cost of care.

Furthermore, one can argue that the passage of the Health Insurance Portability and Accountability Act (HIPAA) makes it less likely that a new government plan to cover long-term care will be presented anytime soon. Congress may feel that they have addressed the long-term care cost problem by providing tax benefits to TQ buyers.

While waiting for any future governmental health plan, seniors are susceptible to unprotected illness or injury that would preclude them from future insurability. And, as they age, their premiums will also increase. Eligible prospects would be wise to purchase LTC coverage as soon as possible to protect against loss and higher premiums.

## The Organized Sales Presentation

In many cases, the entire LTC sales process can be accomplished in one interview or meeting. In other cases, prospects will want you to come back before making their decision. The prospect is often motivated to purchase LTC insurance by factors stronger than any agent can present. The prospect tends to purchase coverage because of love for a spouse or other family member. The financial burden of caring for the client's care is removed while the assets and family income are protected and the standard of living is maintained. Long-term care insurance also eases concerns regarding loss of independence and dignity while enhancing the freedom of choice that becomes increasingly important as people age.

There are two principles that form the foundation for a strong, effective LTC sales presentation. The first is that its purpose is to *uncover the needs of the prospect and eventually show how long-term care insurance satisfies those needs.* As with every insurance sale, everything you do and say during the presentation is part of the strategy to influence the prospect to make a decision that, prior to your presentation, he or she had no thought of making.

The second principle is that the function of the agent is to *help people solve financial problems.* It's likely that many of the people you talk to will not recognize the problems associated with long-term care, or, even if they do, they will be inclined to ignore them. Your role is to isolate these problems and present them to your prospects in such a way that they will want to do something about them. An agent does not create problems—he or she helps to identify problems and then present solutions to the problem.

The long-term care presentation, like other insurance sales presentations follows a pattern. The presentation usually follows six steps:

1. Build trust with the prospect.

2. Identify the prospect's particular needs by asking questions.

3. Educate the prospect about the need for long-term care insurance.

4. Offer a quality product backed with excellent service.

5. Allow time for the prospect to make an informed decision about purchasing long-term care insurance.

6. Close the sale.

When prospects are approached by enthusiastic agents who are able to help them understand the facts about long-term care, they generally cannot help but see the need for a quality long-term care insurance product. Those who have had a favorable educational and sales experience are also likely to tell their friends about your service and product. This benefits you because referrals that result from your successful sales will, in turn, reduce your future prospecting time. Remember that a referral is more likely than a cold call to secure another appointment (and LTC sale) for you.

### Seminar Selling

Seminar selling has a particular niche within the long-term care insurance market. Most prospects have heard about the need for long-term care insurance. Perhaps he or she knows someone who has bought the product. However, unlike auto or homeowner's insurance, these prospects may never have seen someone benefit from an LTC policy; they have no frame of reference to suggest they should buy a plan. Even with all these negatives, they're still interested in the product. They don't want to commit to a one-on-one meeting without additional information but they are willing to attend a seminar. This makes seminar selling an important part of the LTC marketing effort.

For the agent, his or her first seminar is always the hardest because there are so many unknowns. There are a few companies who sell long-term care seminars. The long-term care insurance company you represent may have a seminar available for your use. If not, many vendors market them. Most of these are professionally created and offer advice for each step of the process. However, you will still need to do a great deal of work. For an idea of the amount of work and planning involved in presenting an LTC seminar, see Ill. 8.5.

### ILL. 8.5 ■ *Preparing for an LTC Seminar*

It is beyond the scope of this text to provide you with the detailed, step-by-step information you'll need in order to give a successful LTC seminar. However, we will briefly describe the planning that must be undertaken so that you can see the amount and type of planning required.

**Eight or more weeks prior to the seminar**

- Talk with your manager about the options available and some practical advice.
- Set a time and date for the seminar.
- Obtain a long-term care seminar kit (including slides, etc.).

**Six weeks prior to the seminar**

- Determine an invitation method.
- Order promotional and invitation materials.
- Determine who will speak. If you plan to speak, do you want an "outside expert" such as an attorney or nursing home administrator to co-host the seminar?
- Secure a seminar site and necessary equipment.
- Plan for meals or refreshments.
- Place advertisements and public service notices.

**Five weeks prior to the seminar**

- Develop an invitation list.
- Print invitations.
- Address envelopes.

**Four weeks prior to the seminar**

- Mail invitations.
- Practice presenting the seminar.

**Three weeks prior to seminar**

- Order supplies for seminar participants.
- Confirm with site and equipment provider.
- Obtain local data on nursing facility costs, home care costs and Medicaid asset and income requirements.
- Develop a calling list from the invitation list.
- Practice presenting the seminar.

**Two weeks prior to the seminar**

- Call invitees.
- Practice presenting the seminar.
- Prepare opening and closing remarks.

**One week prior to the seminar**

- Prepare participant packets with handouts.
- Continue calling invitees.
- Confirm seminar site and equipment.
- Confirm meal or refreshment arrangement.
- Practice presenting the seminar.

*Continued*

---

**ILL. 8.5 ■ *Preparing for an LTC Seminar (Cont.)***

---

**Day before the seminar**

- Call attendees to confirm participation.

**Day of the seminar**

- Obtain necessary equipment.
- Organize room, handouts and equipment.
- Practice presenting the seminar in the room with the equipment.
- Greet guests.
- Conduct the seminar.

**Day after the seminar**

- Begin calling attendees.

**Week after the seminar**

- Complete calls to all attendees.
- Begin meeting with attendees.

**Two weeks after the seminar**

- Continue meeting with attendees.
- Send applications to the company.
- Arrange for underwriting requirements when appropriate.

---

As with any sales presentation, you want people to leave the seminar understanding the facts about long-term care. Generally, people who understand the financial risks presented by LTC will see the need for LTC insurance. However, the key to successful seminar selling is follow-up. You can host the best organized seminar, have great attendance and make the finest presentation in the world and still not have a successful seminar. The ultimate success of your seminar will be determined after the seminar is over: how many people were you able to motivate to protect their life savings from the costs of long-term care?

■ **SUMMARY**

Long-term care is a new product to most prospects and many will question its value. To build excitement and interest within your customer base, you should be well-informed about the product itself and the benefits it offers. Your enthusiasm about educating your prospects and clients about the need for long-term care insurance will generate sales for you and protection for them. Whatever market segment you choose to pursue, now is the time for you to get into the long-term care market.

■ **CHAPTER 8 QUESTIONS FOR REVIEW**

1. There are approximately 72 million Americans above the age of 50. Approximately how many of these individuals own long-term care insurance?

   A. Less than 1 million
   B. 4 million
   C. 24 million
   D. 36 million

2. Prospects for long-term care insurance share all of the following traits EXCEPT they

   A. tend to judge their age more by how they feel than by the number of years they have lived
   B. are concerned that they will be unable to remain financially independent
   C. are more concerned about a product's price than the quality and reputation of the company and agent offering the product
   D. tend to purchase additional products from salespeople who have been knowledgeable and patient

3. During the sales presentation, the agent should identify the prospect's needs by

   A. asking questions
   B. generalizing based on the prospect's age
   C. generalizing based on the prospect's income
   D. covering the technical details of the long-term care policy

4. In order to qualify for long-term care insurance, prospects must meet criteria in all of the following areas EXCEPT

   A. assets
   B. agility
   C. age
   D. ability

5. According to the text, which of the following LTC prospecting methods is least likely to result in sales?

   A. Seminar selling
   B. Referred leads
   C. Direct mail
   D. Cold calls

6. The market for long-term care insurance is

   A. stagnant
   B. declining
   C. growing
   D. none of the above

7. Which market segment provides the best prospects for long-term care insurance?

   A. Generation X
   B. Baby boomers
   C. Empty nesters
   D. Golden retirees

8. Buyers of long-term care insurance want

   A. the lowest initial price possible
   B. personalized service from people they trust
   C. to buy off the Internet
   D. to enter a nursing home

9. Seminar selling of long-term care insurance

   A. attracts prospects not willing to have a one-on-one meeting
   B. is best organized and presented in a couple weeks
   C. is a success if many people
   D. is all of the above

10. Long-term care insurance is

    A. well understood by most people over age 50
    B. likely to be replaced with a government program
    C. too expensive for most consumers
    D. a needs-based educational sale

# Understanding the LTC Environment

O nce you are armed with the product knowledge needed to sell long-term care insurance, you will have the challenge of motivating prospects to take action. You will draw on the skills you've used in earlier sales experiences, and the ones you've learned in this course, to find prospects, determine their needs and encourage them to buy long-term care insurance. In spite of the fact that LTC insurance is so essential, most people will need to be convinced that they need coverage. And you may encounter prospects who are suspicious of insurance agents in general and long-term care insurance in particular. In this chapter, we'll look at why the public is sometimes mistrustful of long-term care insurance companies and their products. We'll also suggest ways that you, as a knowledgeable LTC producer, can help to restore consumer confidence in the today's LTC industry and its products.

■ ■ ■ ■ ■

## ■ MAKING SENSE OF THE PUBLIC'S MISTRUST

You have probably heard the argument that the public interest would be better served if the federal government had more control over the insurance industry. Over the years, the public—especially elderly insurance buyers—has fallen victim to less than ethical marketing practices and less than desirable insurance policies. In many cases, seniors purchased duplicate coverage or policies that had so many restrictions and exclusions that they were virtually useless. Frankly, some of the early LTC policies and agents fit in this category.

Consumers and advocacy groups have expressed concern that insurers and agents who market long-term care insurance today will repeat the mistakes made by those who originally sold Medicare supplement (Medigap) coverage. When Medigap coverage was introduced in the 1980s, abuses by insurers and agents alike gave rise to some of the most outspoken criticism of the insurance industry in its history. Policy benefits or other provisions were misrepresented. Consumers were sold multiple policies that duplicated coverage they already had under retiree health benefits or another Medigap policy.

This negative publicity has sometimes created an unfriendly marketing environment for long-term care insurance among the elderly—and without justification. Medigap and LTC insurance policies cover completely different risks. Medigap insurance is designed to supplement Medicare's coverage by filling in some of the program's gaps; LTC has nothing to do with Medicare. The only similarity between Medicare supplement insurance and long-term care insurance is that the products are often sold to the same customers.

In a perfect world, you would be able to prospect among individuals who have the ability and desire to buy and retain LTC insurance. Most sales would be relatively easy and both you and your client would be happy with the experience. But we do not live in a perfect world and it is sometimes difficult to make a sale. There are currently four things that have affected—both positively and negatively—the ability of insurance companies and agents to sell long-term care insurance. They are state regulations, friends of the elderly, the media and consumers themselves. Let's look at each of these in more detail.

## ■ STATE REGULATION OF LONG-TERM CARE INSURANCE

As we discussed earlier, the federal government passed the Health Insurance Portability and Accountability Act (HIPAA) and it was signed into law in August 1996. This legislation created federal standards for qualified long-term care insurance. However, these standards for LTC policies merely determine whether a policy will qualify for favorable federal tax treatment. The general task of regulating long-term care insurance still rests with the state.

The National Association of Insurance Commissioners (NAIC) in its Long-Term Care Model Act and Model Regulation provides samples states are encouraged to adopt as their LTC regulations or as part of their LTC regulations. The model and regulations are updated regularly. Most states have adopted some portion of the act and may revise their regulations even before the NAIC advises insurance departments to do so. The models are designed to balance the need to protect the consumers from products providing only illusionary benefits and to help insurance companies offer meaningful products consumers are able to purchase. Most states' models of long-term care law and regulations follow the NAIC's definition of long-term care insurance. (See Ill. 9.1.)

### Insurer Regulations

In addition to following NAIC guidelines, most states also require that every insurer providing LTC coverage in that state adhere to certain state guidelines and

---

### ILL. 9.1 ■ *NAIC Definition of Long-Term Care*

"*L*ong-term care insurance means any insurance policy or rider advertised, marketed, offered or designed to provide coverage for not less than twelve (12) consecutive months for each covered person on an expense incurred, indemnity, prepaid or other basis; for one or more necessary or medically necessary diagnostic, preventive, therapeutic, rehabilitative, maintenance or personal care services, provided in a setting other than an acute care unit of a hospital. Such term includes group and individual annuities and life insurance policies or riders which provide directly or which supplement long-term care insurance. Such term also includes a policy or rider which provides for payment of benefits based upon cognitive impairments or the loss of functional capacity.

"Long-term care insurance may be issued by insurers; fraternal benefit societies; nonprofit health, hospital and medical service corporations; prepaid health plans; health maintenance organizations or any similar organization to the extent they are otherwise authorized to issue life or health insurance. Long-term care insurance shall not include any insurance policy which is offered primarily to provide basic Medicare supplement coverage, basic hospital expense coverage, basic medical-surgical expense coverage, hospital confinement indemnity coverage, major medical expense coverage, disability income or related asset-protection coverage, accident-only coverage, specified disease or specifed accident coverage, or limited benefit health coverage.

"With regard to life insurance, this term does not include life insurance policies which accelerate the death benefit specifically for one or more of the qualifying events of terminal illness, medical conditions requiring extraordinary medical intervention, or permanent institutional confinement, and which provide the option of a lump-sum payment for those benefits and in which neither the benefits nor the eligibility for the benefits is conditioned upon the receipt of long-term care. Notwithstanding any other provision contained herein, any product advertised, marketed or offered as long-term care insurance shall be subject to the provisions of this Act."

*Source: NAIC Model Regulation Service, July 1998.*

---

restrictions. These regulations vary by state but often include specific mention of the following:

- types of products and forms the insurer must offer;

- policy language and coverage that must be included;

- loss ratios the insurer must experience for those products;

- what may be included in advertising;

- commission structure that may be employed for agents;

- listing of all agents or other representatives authorized by the insurer to sell its LTC products;

- continuing education requirements for agents;

- the underwriting that must be done over certain ages; and

- penalties that may be imposed for failure to comply with these regulations.

To further complicate matters, states often interpret the NAIC regulations differently from one another and some states even interpret their own mandated LTC regulations differently from the way in which insurers interpret those regulations. When the NAIC Model is updated and a state convenes to adopt the updated material, the state's limited resources often slows the approval process to anywhere from a few weeks to a few years.

State insurance departments face a tremendous challenge in implementing adoption of the NAIC's mandated service, coverage and eligibility requirements. Most state insurance departments are understaffed and overburdened. Some states do not have regular access to actuarial data; few train their regulatory staff on long-term care issues; over half do not track the number of long-term care insurance filings; counseling programs are not available in some states. State legislatures do not meet on a year-round basis and, when they do meet, often consider other issues on their dockets more important than long-term care insurance regulations.[1]

Before an insurance company can sell its LTC product in a state, it must be approved by that state's insurance department. In most cases, the company must meet that state's LTC requirements and then seek and obtain approval from every other state, plus the District of Columbia, in which it wants to sell the policy. In order to do this, insurance companies must have employees who constantly:

- monitor the new NAIC and state requirements;

- determine how their products meet those requirements;

- develop and price the new products;

- submit the revised products to the state (or states) for approval;

- make changes as the state (or states) requires;

- design new marketing materials;

---

[1] American Association of Retired Persons, "State Variation in the Regulation of Long-Term Care Insurance Products," by Project Hope, January 1992.

- print, stock and distribute LTC materials; and

- communicate new information to agents.

All this work creates additional expense for the insurance company. Add to this the product variations by state and the resulting administration challenges. Some insurers have found their overhead costs exceed income expectations, and they are no longer selling long-term care insurance.

## Agent Licensing and Continuing Education

Most state insurance departments have enacted regulations that describe what licensing and/or continuing education requirements an agent must meet before he or she may market, sell or solicit long-term care insurance. These regulations provide important consumer protection standards for LTC policies and their sale. Typically, the state will regulate the following:

- type of license the agent must have in order to sell LTC;

- number and frequency of approved continuing education (CE) credits needed; and

- consequences imposed when an agent fails to comply with LTC licensing and/or CE requirements.

As an agent, you must be aware of the existing laws and proposed legislation for the states in which you sell LTC insurance. To assist you with this monumental task, the LTC companies you represent will be able to supply you with the information you need to legally market long-term care insurance.

## Professional Code of Ethics

Insurance agents are expected to conduct their business at a high ethical level and to develop a highly sensitive service-oriented attitude toward their prospects and clients. To protect the consumer and to support the ethics of the industry, most states have enacted certain laws and regulations to control and discourage unscrupulous or unwitting actions of agents who may not have these high standards.

There are three common violations of ethics condemned by all professional insurance organizations and considered illegal in virtually all states. These violations are *rebating, misrepresentation* and *twisting.*

### Rebating

Rebating occurs when an agent returns part of his or her commission to the applicant or policyowner (in effect reducing the policyowner's premium) in order to induce the purchase of insurance. For example, if the LTC premium is $1,250 and the agent returns $250 to the applicant, the agent is rebating no matter what the stated reason for the return.

Rebating is discriminatory because the agent is allowing one person to secure LTC insurance benefits at a lower price than another person. Aside from the penalties to be imposed by the state insurance commissioner, rebating is a punishable crime in most states.

### Misrepresentation

There are many forms of misrepresentation—any one of which can mean trouble for the insurance agent or consumer. Let's specifically consider two types of misrepresentation as they apply to the solicitation or sale of long-term care insurance.

1. *Misrepresentation of a policy or its provisions*—Never lead a prospect or policyowner to believe that the LTC policy will cover every expense related to long-term care. A prospect should always be presented with an outline of the policy coverages and the agent should clearly explain what is (and is not) covered under the policy. Many states also require the LTC applicant to sign a statement indicating that he or she has read the outline of coverage and understands its provisions.

2. *Misrepresentation to secure issuance of a contract*—Filling out an application with false information is a crime. Making a false statement to an applicant or prospect with the intent of securing his or her application for insurance is also misrepresentation.

All questions on the application should be asked of the applicant and the answers recorded on the application. It is not the agent's role to determine which medical conditions are important and which are not; that determination should be left to the company's underwriters.

There will be situations where the applicant is unaware of a medical condition or is aware of the condition but fails to disclose it. In such a situation, it is typically the applicant and not the agent who may be guilty of misrepresentation.

### Twisting

*Twisting* means attempting to replace, through misrepresentation, either an existing insurance plan or a newly proposed one. Because it is based on misrepresentation, twisting is never justified.

Some agents will attempt to justify twisting by calling the action "policy replacement." *Replacement* is the act of persuading a policyowner to discontinue or lapse an existing policy and to purchase a new policy. Unlike twisting, replacement is not necessarily illegal nor in all cases unwarranted because in some instances a policyowner might be better off with a different insurance plan. For example, if the insured has an older LTC plan without guaranteed renewability then that plan should be revised or replaced to include that essential provision.

Because replacement interrupts an existing plan and requires the policyowner to begin anew with a different plan at an older attained age, replacement is often suspect. Most states, recognizing the potential for abuse, have imposed strict guidelines on replacement, including limits on commissions paid to agents who sell replacement policies. The insurance industry itself considers it a questionable activity and discourages its practice. Replacement is, therefore, justified only if it is in the best interest of the policyowner.

## ■ FRIENDS OF THE ELDERLY

Over the past several years, many organizations have been formed that consider themselves "friends of the elderly." Typically, these organizations are formed by religious, political, ethnic or governmental groups and generally provide information and referral, support groups, case management, caregiver support, friendly visits, medical claims and billing assistance, Ombudsman services and so forth. These groups have become outspoken champions for what they perceive to be the best interests of people in retirement or nearing retirement.

Probably the largest and most vocal of these groups that speak for all the elderly is the *American Association of Retired Persons (AARP),* a nonprofit, nonpartisan organization with more than 32 million members age 50 and over. The Association, established in 1958 by Dr. Ethel Percy Andrus, strives to better the lives of older Americans through service, advocacy, education and volunteer efforts. There are currently more than 350,000 volunteers and 4,000 local chapters that seek to carry out AARP's mission in the areas of community service, legislation and education efforts, health care and quality of life issues (with an emphasis on older women and minorities), older workers' rights and retirement planning.

As an agent, you should be aware of the many organizations that are available to assist your elderly clients in making their decisions about whether to purchase everything from a new car to long-term care insurance. These groups often give well-intended, free advice; however, the issues are not always well researched. For example, the rising cost of nursing home care has led some advocates to the conclusion that LTC insurance is not worthwhile because insurance purchased today will not cover tomorrow's high costs. Obviously, when faced with this argument, you'll want to point out the options that are available to increase benefits automatically.

You'll want to acknowledge the good work of many of these advocacy groups, but you'll also want to stress that you are a licensed, trained professional who is dedicated to serving your clients. When you display a personal interest in your prospects and policyowners and make thoughtful recommendations on their insurance programs on a regular basis, you increase your chances of placing LTC insurance with those clients.

## ■ THE MEDIA

Some members of the media look for human interest stories and find that reporting victimization of elderly people by the insurance industry often makes good copy. There are some unscrupulous agents operating in the LTC market who have misrepresented the provisions of a policy or replaced policies just to earn additional commissions. Certainly, the media should be applauded for alerting the public about such practices. However, these situations portray only a very small segment of the long-term care insurance industry.

Claimants who receive long-term care insurance benefits in a timely manner do not make news; claimants who are denied benefits do. Some state insurance departments collect information about the ratio of paid claims to denied claims and make this information public. The numbers clearly show there are very few people filing LTC claims who have those claims denied. Yet there is still a public perception that collecting long-term care insurance benefits is difficult if not impossible.

Today, there are usually only two reasons for a claimant to be denied coverage: (1) the insured purchased an early LTC plan that was filled with restrictions and limitations; or (2) the insured purchased a policy from a company that practices post-claim underwriting. As discussed in Chapter 6, the older LTC policies had benefit triggers that mirrored Medicare's requirements. If insureds have one of these policies and cannot meet those requirements, their claims will be denied. And, if a company practices post-claim underwriting as discussed in Chapter 7, the consumer, the agent, the insurer and the insurance industry as a whole can suffer. Denying claims based on the insured's lack of knowledge about his or her condition or the insurer's underwriting guidelines creates a poor reputation for the insurer who practices this underwriting technique and also distrust of the industry in general. The agent, as a representative of both the insurer and the industry, suffers as well.

Many insurance industry "watchdogs" feel that agents should be able to explain every aspect of the LTC product they are representing. Although a knowledge of LTC is essential, you may not know everything about your product. For example, the prospect may ask an extremely technical question or may wish to purchase a specific type of coverage, for a specific amount, for a specific period of time. You may have never dealt with such a specific request in the past and the situation may not have been covered in your company's training materials. It is appropriate to tell the client that you'll need to speak with the insurance company to determine whether they will consider this coverage request. In addition to helping you to avoid misrepresentation, a call to the company gives your prospect an accurate answer. If you strive for excellence when selling long-term care insurance, you'll enhance both your own reputation and that of the insurance industry.

## ■ CONSUMER MISINFORMATION

Most Americans are concerned about the availability of affordable health insurance, particularly after they retire. Because of the inadequacies of earlier LTC policies, many consumers are leery of long-term care insurance. Although national studies indicate that the longer a person lives, the more likely he or she will need some kind of long-term care, few people want to discuss this reality with an insurance agent. Consumers would like to believe that they won't need long-term care or that, if they do need it, coverage will be provided by the government.

As an agent, you should help your prospects and clients understand the facts of long-term care and explain how current government programs are inadequate to meet most LTC needs. If your clients are currently employed, you should encourage them to obtain, review and retain all available documentation on their retiree health benefit entitlements so they will be aware of potential gaps in coverage. You should also help them understand that the LTC coverage that you are offering will cover long-term, ongoing assisted living and help protect their family from emotional and financial devastation.

You can improve consumer confidence in LTC products by encouraging your prospects to compare the benefits and limitations of coverage, exclusions and premiums of several companies and agents. You should provide the prospect with an outline of coverage and invite them to ask questions about the insurer and the policy. If the prospect decides to purchase an LTC policy, remind him or her that the policy may be canceled during the "free-look" period. Finally, advise the consumer that any questions about the agent, the insurance company or the LTC policy may be referred to the state insurance department, when the consumer is not getting satisfactory answers from the source of concern.

Service begins and ends with the agent. Make quality work your byword. Make it the base of your professional career by carefully selecting prospects, by selling to fit needs and by providing prompt and dedicated service. These are not easy accomplishments. They require constant attention. However, the rewards you will earn for a job well done will be tremendous and your future success in selling LTC products will be everything you want it to be.

## ■ SUMMARY

There are many critics of long-term care insurance. Much of the criticism results from a failure to understand the principles of insurance. Many people expect more from long-term care insurance than can be delivered or more than they are willing to pay for.

You can rise above all the criticism. You are providing a valuable service by selling LTC insurance. Think about the dollars you are providing people who might not otherwise be able to have the care they need. Think about the pride and dignity you are preserving. Remember you are providing your clients with the financial resources to choose the types of providers of care they'll need when they are not as independent as they are today. If you are an agent who can help your clients see that you want to protect and safeguard their future, you will be successful in the long-term care insurance market.

## ■ CHAPTER 9 QUESTIONS FOR REVIEW

1. Consumer confidence in long-term care insurance coverage has been damaged by all of the following EXCEPT

   A. the negative publicity generated by improperly marketed Medigap policies
   B. early LTC policies containing many coverage restrictions
   C. unscrupulous agents who mislead consumers regarding LTC coverage
   D. insurance regulations designed to protect the consumer

2. The National Association of Insurance Commissioners establishes long-term care regulations that

   A. the federal government reviews and enforces
   B. states are required to adopt without amendments
   C. are considered guidelines that states may choose to follow
   D. are considered part of each state's insurance code

3. Many states have regulations that require an individual who sells long-term care insurance to

   A. have a valid life or health insurance license
   B. complete a specified number of continuing education credits
   C. provide the prospect with an outline of LTC coverage
   D. all of the above

4. Which of the following is an example of misrepresentation?

   A. Telling a prospect that another LTC insurer is going out of business, even though it isn't
   B. Filling out an application with knowingly false information given to you by a prospect
   C. Telling prospects that an LTC policy will provide coverage even if they fail the company's medical exam
   D. All of the above

5. When an agent replaces one LTC plan with another of equal or less value in order to obtain additional commission, the agent is probably guilty of

   A. rebating
   B. twisting
   C. competition
   D. misrepresentation

6. The public's uneasiness with long-term care insurance results from

   A. early policies with many restrictions and exclusions
   B. the few agents who sold duplicate coverage to seniors
   C. less than ethical marketing practices
   D. all of the above

7. The National Association of Insurance Commissioners (NAIC)

   A. wrote the Health Insurance Portability and Accountability Act of 1996 (HIPAA)
   B. is part of the federal government
   C. develops model language for state insurance departments to adopt
   D. approves all long-term care insurance policies

8. Which of the following is appropriate for a long-term care insurance agent?

   A. licensing
   B. rebating
   C. misrepresenting
   D. twisting

9. Consumers are likely to

   A. ignore media shows that demonstrate the inadequacies of older long-term care policies
   B. believe an insurance agent who focuses on service
   C. thoroughly understand their retiree health benefit package
   D. have their long-term care insurance claim denied

# 10

# LTC Alternatives

W e live in a dynamic, ever-changing social and economic order. The continuous adaptation to changing circumstances and priorities requires the development of new methodology, new procedures, new relationships and new ideas. The aging of our population—and the corresponding increase in the need for long-term care services—has prompted many to reconsider how this kind of care can be financed and delivered. Throughout this text, we've looked at a number of ways in which health-care costs of the elderly can be covered—both private and government sponsored. In this chapter, we will discuss a growing trend in long-term care coverage that addresses this need through a combination of both private and social insurance.

■ ■ ■ ■ ■

## ■ SOCIAL INSURANCE VS. PRIVATE INSURANCE

There is no question that the need for long-term care is growing. However, there are different ideas about who should pay for the care and how the high costs of long-term care should be funded. Discussion about financing long-term care services and cost tends to divide people into two groups. One group would have the government take the lead in financing LTC services. Any gaps in coverage would be filled by an individual's savings or by a supplemental, private insurance policy. The other group tends to feel that the private sector—the individual and insurance companies—should be the primary payor, with the government providing supplemental coverage after personal resources are exhausted. Let's look at these two options more closely.

## Social Insurance

Those who favor government funding of long-term care point to Social Security and Medicare as prototypes. Social Security, the most important form of financial protection in the United States, pays benefits when a person's income is affected by three significant events—retirement, disability or death. Medicare, as you've learned, is a government insurance program instituted to provide a delivery and payment system of medical and hospital care for people age 65 or older and people with disabilities.

The Social Security system provides protection to virtually every working American. There is no risk selection or underwriting, and every individual covered has access to the benefits regardless of health status or income. Both the employer and the employee pay taxes for Social Security and Medicare—based on a percentage of the employee's income—but the employee gets all the benefits. Many people argue that this is probably the greatest social insurance program ever devised. Many retirees believe it is their economic salvation. Families appreciate the benefits paid to their children when a parent dies. Disabled people are assisted with needed income and rehabilitation. But does Social Security function well and will it be available in the future?

These questions have been debated for many years and the debate will probably continue. Because of the increased numbers of people collecting Social Security and Medicare, many people now believe that it is no longer a question of *if* Social Security will run out of money but *when*. Consider the changing demographics of the United States: people are living longer lives and thus receiving benefits for a longer period of time. Over the course of their retirement, people receive between three and four times more in benefits than they paid in as contributions. In addition, the ratio of workers (whose current taxes help to fund current benefits) to retirees is decreasing significantly as more people are retiring and fewer people are entering the work force. As the baby boomers begin to collect Social Security, a huge burden will be put on the remaining workers such as your children or grandchildren to fund the system.

The nation's experience with Social Security and changing demographics have led most lawmakers to realize that a social insurance program to pay for long-term care is not affordable. This also can be inferred from the passage of HIPAA—it will be harder to qualify for Medicaid and there are tax benefits when individuals purchase private long-term care insurance.

## Employment-Based Health Insurance

For many years, the health-care system of the United States has been inextricably linked to employment. Besides the obvious problems this causes when employees fear losing their jobs, employment-based health insurance also couples the ability of an employee to obtain health care with an employer's ability to purchase insurance.

Unfortunately, many small businesses are unable to afford insurance because of sky-rocketing health-care costs.

Many business people oppose a government-sponsored system because they fear increased federal bureaucracy. However, other groups insist that the success of other countries in controlling health-care costs through government involvement is a clear indication of the wisdom of this solution.

## Medical Savings Accounts

A medical savings account (MSA) is a trust created to pay the qualified medical expenses of the person for whom the trust was created. While a detailed discussion of MSAs is beyond the scope of this text, a brief overview of the topic is appropriate.

On a limited trial basis during the next several years, MSAs will be available to small business employees and self-employed individuals with a *high deductible health plan* (what constitutes a "high deductible health plan" varies according to whether the plan is an individual plan or a family plan). Eligible employees and their employers can then contribute certain amounts to the MSA and receive favorable tax treatment; account balances can be used to cover qualified medical expenses, including long-term care insurance premiums. In certain cases, the employee may be able to accumulate a sufficient sum of money to self-insure his or her LTC risk, or at least to extend the elimination period on an LTC policy.

Beginning in 1999, MSAs are also available on a trial basis to Medicare beneficiaries. See the section on Medicare+Choice in Chapter 3 for a discussion of Medicare Medical Savings Account plans.

## Single-Payor System

Some people advocate a national health-care system for the United States using the Canadian medical system as a model. Canadian health insurance is organized around a *single-payor* national health program based upon a tax-funded, government-mandated program that is administered on the local level. Advocates of a single-payor system feel that it controls costs, sets national health-care expenditures, eliminates financial barriers to health care, promotes planning and improves the status of health.

Those who oppose a single-payor system note that such reform would necessitate changes in the system of health care delivery, particularly in the expansion of primary-care and preventive medicine. Most physicians in Canada are primary-care physicians who identify and treat long-term problems before they become more costly. However, physicians in the United States tend to specialize and conduct highly specialized medical procedures at higher fees. It is unlikely that specialists would willingly become primary-care providers in an effort to reduce health-care costs. Furthermore, the Canadian and other single-payor systems do not cover expenses associated with nursing home or long-term care.

## Managed Competition

In 1993 President Clinton proposed the concept of *managed competition,* a plan to provide reliable, affordable health insurance to all people through a system of giant buying groups called *alliances.* These alliances would negotiate with health-care providers for medical services at the lowest possible prices. Under the proposed plan, physicians' and other health professionals fees, hospital services, preventative care, home health care, outpatient rehabilitation and a number of other coverages are provided. In order to reduce costs, long-term care and dental care were eliminated from the plan.

All alliances would be required to offer identical coverage, but individuals may choose from at least three plans to receive basic coverage. Under the proposal, individuals could retain their own doctors under a fee-for-services plan, join a *health maintenance organization (HMO)* with clinic-like operations or choose a combination of HMO and fee-for-service called a *preferred provider organization (PPO).* Individuals' out-of-pocket costs would vary depending on the type of plan they chose.

However, this proposed universal health coverage was neither approved nor passed by Congress. It does not appear that such a plan will be passed in the near future.

## The Cost of Designing a Program

Could a social insurance program similar to Social Security be designed to fund long-term care? Certainly—legislators and advocates for social insurance have designed a number of complete programs that offer everything from basic care to complete nursing home care, adult day services, home care and a variety of other coverages. However, every proposal has a price tag attached to it.

The difficulty is not getting legislators to design a program; the difficulty is funding the program in a way that taxpayers are willing to accept. A social insurance program administered by the government would pick up the private sector's current costs. Simply put, instead of a few insureds remitting premiums to insurers to pay for LTC, all taxpayers would pay additional taxes every year to fund coverage. Current projections are that the additional tax would add about $500 to each taxpayer's bill the first year and this initial amount would increase about 10 percent each year to fund the projected increases for nursing home costs.

Consider the government's current cost of providing nursing home care. By the end of 1996, the cost of nursing home care paid by Medicare was $8.9 billion. Medicaid, the fastest growing state program, paid another $37.5 billion; as it is, Medicaid has affected most states' ability to finance other discretionary programs, such as education and infrastructure repair. According to the Health Care Financing Administration's projections, by 2007 the federal government's cost will rise to $60 billion with state and local jurisdictions adding another $17.2 billion—a total of a whopping $87.2 billion—for the government's portion of nursing home care.

In theory, the beneficiaries of social insurance should be the population over age 65 who currently spend four times as much for health care as do younger people. However, the real beneficiaries of a government entitlement program are the heirs of the nursing home resident who would receive their full inheritance while the government pays the nursing home bills. This raises even more questions. Is a government program that protects inheritances the best use of tax dollars? Should the government pay the cost of long-term care only for those who cannot afford to pay it? Are taxpayers willing (or able) to pay extra taxes to finance an LTC social insurance program?

The public's answers to these questions will determine whether a social insurance program will be enacted. However, because all levels of government are slashing budgets and looking for ways to reduce expenses, it seems unlikely that the government will want to take on another health-care program. The trend in public policy seems to be on expanding health insurance coverage to those who are currently uninsured and underinsured. There is no way to extend benefits to these people without affecting those who are currently insured. Some measures under consideration are increased taxes for working Americans; increased Medicare premiums, coinsurance and deductibles; restricted access to care; implementation of managed care programs and so on.

A number of states are also considering the establishment of *public/private partnerships* that could be used to fund long-term care. Although the government takes the lead in establishing these partnerships, the private sector also contributes to this program. Let's take a closer look at these plans.

## ■ THE PARTNERSHIP PROGRAMS

As stated in Chapter 4, Medicaid programs tend to be the largest single budget item for most states and projections show this expense will continue to increase. In order to reduce their budget deficits, states are looking for ways to contain Medicaid expenses. One of the newest ways to address this problem is with a partnership program between state government and the insurance industry.

Experimental *partnership programs* were developed as a way for individuals to access Medicaid reimbursement without impoverishing themselves. These programs, supported with funds from the Robert Wood Johnson Foundation, provide a way for the elderly to retain more of their assets and yet qualify for Medicaid benefits—if they purchase long-term care insurance first. In essence, consumers contribute to the cost of their care through insurance, and insurers are able to "pool" long-term risks, limit the risks they assume and, therefore, offer more affordable long-term care coverage.

Under a partnership plan, insureds obtain a form of long-term "partnership" with insurers who will provide them with a certain amount of LTC protection. If they collect maximum benefits under this coverage, they will then qualify for Medicaid and still be permitted to retain assets equal to the amount of insurance benefits they received. These partnerships permit state governments (the public sector) and insurance companies (the private sector) to work as one unit in an effort to save tax dollars and to promote independence from government control by using insurance dollars to pay the nursing home bills.

In general, these partnerships have four key objectives:

1. stimulate the availability of private long-term care insurance;

2. remove the fear of impoverishment due to a need for health-care services;

3. contain the growth of public expenditures; and

4. improve the understanding of the financing of long-term care through state counseling services.

The plans were pioneered by California, Connecticut, Indiana and New York. The participating states designed insurance plans specifically for these partnerships and required interested insurers to report on their experience with the plans. Many additional states have now passed such legislation or have it pending; however, expansion has been limited by the Omnibus Budget Reconciliation Act of 1993. Under the Medicare-Medicaid Amendments of this act, states other than the four previously mentioned cannot design or implement these programs free of estate recovery outlined in Chapter 4. This stipulation will limit acceptance of them by consumers and the insurance industry outside the four original states.

## Partnership Plan Design

The primary plan design allows the owner of a partnership plan to receive insurance benefits before applying for Medicaid. Under the plan, the insurance company reimburses the insured for services that would have been covered by Medicaid if the insured had been an eligible Medicaid recipient. Those services include nursing home care, home health care, adult day services, respite care and supportive home care. The amount of benefits paid by the insurance company are excluded from the applicant's total assets when applying for Medicaid. In other words, the state Medicaid program does not count this amount as part of his or her assets. Once qualified for Medicaid, persons receiving these types of services must contribute their income toward their care in the same way as required for other Medicaid recipients.

Let's look at an example to illustrate how a partnership plan works. Assume that Bill, an insured under a partnership program, becomes disabled and must enter a nursing home. As an insured, Bill receives $50,000 of insurance benefits from the long-term care partnership plan to help cover his cost of care. When Bill applies for Medicaid, he may exclude the base $2,000 that every Medicaid applicant is allowed *plus* these insurance benefits from his total assets—or $52,000—and still qualify for Medicaid reimbursement. Any income Bill receives still goes toward the cost of care and Medicaid pays the nursing home the reimbursement rate less the amount that Bill paid.

A second model of asset protection is being tested in New York. People in this partnership plan are able to keep all their assets after receiving insurance benefits for three years of nursing home care or six years of home health care or a combination of the two (in which two days of home care equals one day of nursing home care). This design has been well received by both consumers and the insurance industry. States are considering switching to this design to gain wider acceptance.

## Partnership Insurance Design Requirements

Selected insurance companies have developed specific products to participate in these pilot programs. Because the partnership plans must receive state approval and, in some cases, the insurance department's approval, consumers should feel confident when purchasing a plan. The plans are designed to cover all possibilities of spending down one's own money.

The plan design must offer benefits for nursing home care, home health care, attendant care, adult day services and respite care. The amount payable for the cost of nursing home care must be at least 75 percent of the average local nursing home costs (as determined by the state each year) and one-half of the nursing home amount for the cost of home care and community services. Because the partnership plan must be "the payor of last resort," it will not pay benefits if Medicare, private health insurance or any other possible payor pays benefits.

## Reporting Requirements

In exchange for the state's approval, insurance companies must report their experience with the partnership plans. Depending on the state, these reports must provide actual plan experience on an annual, semiannual or quarterly basis. These reports are used by the state and participating insurers to monitor the success of the program. A report is required for each of the following:

- newly registered insureds

- insureds who have changed or dropped their policies

- insureds assessed for benefit eligibility

- insureds who received claim payments for the last three months

- insureds who received claim payments for the last six months

- insureds who met the elimination periods

- summary of all activity on all policies and applications

- applicants denied coverage

- sales of partnership policies under a group

## Benefits of the Partnership Programs

The partnership programs have benefits for insurers, agents, consumers, state governments and nursing homes. As insurers offer approved state plans, more publicity about the need for LTC insurance will be generated and consumers will have a renewed confidence in the products insurers are offering. In addition, more agents are likely to enter the long-term care insurance market to work for one of the companies participating in the partnership. Most states are beginning to require product-specific continuing education for producers who sell LTC partnership products, which benefits the insurance industry, the agent and the consumer.

Consumers can also obtain information about partnership programs from state counseling programs. These programs will also encourage consumers to plan for their possible long-term care needs. Under these partnership plans, consumers can protect at least a portion of their assets from being spent on long-term care and will not have to rely on Medicaid estate planning to retain their savings. They receive nursing home care first as a private pay patient and still have some financial independence if they must rely on the Medicaid program.

State governments are anticipating that these programs will reduce or at least slow the rapid growth in their Medicaid expenses. This goal will likely be obtained with the partnerships in combination with the elimination of many of the Medicaid estate planning options discussed in Chapter 4. This will also benefit taxpayers who will not have to finance the expanded Medicaid budgets.

Finally, fewer people will suffer the loss of financial independence if they have some long-term care insurance available. Nursing homes will receive more payments from their middle-class residents before they qualify for Medicaid. Because fewer residents will be financially destitute, nursing homes should be able to improve both the quality and quantity of care they provide.

It is far too early to know whether the new partnership programs are a success. Suggested alternatives to these programs tend to go to two extremes: a national health insurance that includes a long-term care payment system or elimination of government involvement with individuals paying for their own long-term care, either with or without insurance. At this point, neither of these alternatives seem likely. Because funds are limited, federal changes will probably come in stages and be limited to basic health care. Seniors, the poor and the disabled will probably continue to receive Medicare and Medicaid programs. Government programs will be stretched to the limit and the elderly may find themselves without the long-term care protection they need. Increasingly, private insurance will be used to a larger extent to fund the cost of long-term care.

## ■ SUMMARY

Eventually, everybody will make a choice about the level of responsibility they are willing to accept when paying for nursing home care: full, partial or none. Those who choose to accept full responsibility for their problems will either have saved a substantial amount to pay for the cost of nursing care or they will have an alternative source of income such as an insurance policy. Those who accept partial responsibility will look to government programs—such as partnership programs—to pay a portion of their care. Those who are either too poor to pay for their own care or to purchase an insurance policy will be unable to take responsibility for their own care. These people will rely on Medicaid.

Although advocates for social insurance will continue to push for a government-funded program, it seems likely that taxpayers will not be willing to fund the ever-growing cost of long-term care. The solution to the problem of long-term care is insurance—and the market is here to stay. As an agent who realizes the importance of long-term care insurance, you will have the opportunity to provide a variety of high-quality LTC products.

## ■ CHAPTER 10 QUESTIONS FOR REVIEW

1. In an effort to reduce Medicaid expenditures, partnership programs have been developed between

   A. state and federal governments
   B. Medicaid and local community programs
   C. individuals and state governments
   D. state governments and insurers

2. In 1996, the cost of long-term care paid by Medicaid was

   A. $1.5 billion
   B. $9 billion
   C. $37.5 billion
   D. $100 billion

3. All of the following are objectives of partnership programs, EXCEPT

    A. removing the elderly's fear of impoverishment
    B. containing the growth of government expenditures
    C. reducing the average cost of nursing home care
    D. stimulating the availability of private LTC insurance

4. Which of the following statements about a social insurance program to fund LTC is correct?

    A. A social insurance program would pick up the private sector's current costs.
    B. The elderly are willing to pay extra taxes to fund the program.
    C. Benefits could be extended to all elderly people at little cost.
    D. A social insurance program would reduce the cost of long-term care.

5. Insurance companies must report their experience with the partnership plans to the state and include information about all of the following EXCEPT

    A. newly registered insureds
    B. agents who have replaced coverage
    C. applicants denied coverage
    D. activity on all policies and applications

6. A social insurance program for long-term care

    A. provides the most cost-effective solution to solving the long-term care challenge
    B. would likely replace Medicare or Social Security
    C. adds to the tax burden of younger, working Americans
    D. is the result of HIPAA

7. Medical savings accounts (MSAs) can be used

    A. to pay long-term care insurance premiums
    B. the same way as a cafeteria plan for employee benefits
    C. in conjunction with a low deductible health insurance plan
    D. for all of the above

8. The long-term care insurance partnership programs are

    A. designed to replace long-term care insurance
    B. available in all states and Washington D.C.
    C. helping to reduce Medicare's budget
    D. helping insurers work with state governments

9. The partnership program design helps consumers

    A. qualify for Medicare Part B
    B. retain some of their assets and still qualify for Medicaid
    C. report their assets to the Medicaid case workers
    D. pay for long-term care using Medicare's budget

# ..... Answer Key to Questions for Review

**CHAPTER 1**

1. B
2. C
3. C
4. C
5. B
6. A
7. C
8. B

**CHAPTER 2**

1. B
2. D
3. D
4. C
5. B
6. A
7. C
8. B
9. A
10. C

**CHAPTER 3**

1. A
2. D
3. B
4. B
5. A
6. B
7. C
8. A

**CHAPTER 4**

1. B
2. C
3. D
4. C
5. A
6. D
7. A
8. C

**CHAPTER 5**

1. D
2. A
3. A
4. D
5. C
6. A
7. B
8. C

**CHAPTER 6**

1. C
2. B
3. D
4. D
5. A
6. B
7. C
8. D
9. B

## CHAPTER 7

1. B
2. C
3. C
4. C
5. C
6. C
7. A
8. D
9. A
10. C

## CHAPTER 8

1. B
2. C
3. A
4. B
5. D
6. C
7. C
8. B
9. A
10. D

## CHAPTER 9

1. D
2. C
3. D
4. D
5. B
6. D
7. C
8. A
9. B

## CHAPTER 10

1. D
2. C
3. C
4. A
5. B
6. C
7. A
8. D
9. B

# ····· Appendix A

# Web Sites Listing

his appendix contains a list of Web sites that are of interest for insurance agents.

**www.aarp.org**

American Association of Retired Persons
*The leading advocacy and information source for people over age 50*

**www. aahsa.org**

American Association of Homes and Services for the Aging
*A national organization of 5,000 not-for-profit care providers*

**www.ahca.org**

American Health Care Association
*A federation of 50 affiliated associations of care providers*

**www.ahcpr.gov**

Agency for Health Care Policy and Research
*Current research and studies on long-term care*

**www.alz.org**

Alzheimer's Association
*Information on research, caregiving, and publications*

**www.aoa.dhhs.gov**

Administration on Aging
*A central source for information on the health, economic and social status of older Americans*

**www.centerltc.com**

Center for Long Term Care Financing
*News and insights on Medicaid and its impact on the sale of long-term care insurance*

**www.gao.gov**

General Accounting Office
*Many reports regarding long-term care providers, programs and insurance*

**www.gpo.ucop.edu**

Part of the General Accounting Office
*The motherlode of government reports from multiple agencies*

**www.hcfa.gov**

Health Care Financing Administration
*The most current and objective statistics regarding long-term care*

**www.medicare.gov**

Medicare
*Provides information on Medicare programs and providers*

**www.mr-longtermcare.com**

Mr. Long-Term Care
*Expert interviews, articles and reports from an insurance agent's perspective*

**www.ncoa.org**

The National Council of the Aging
*A group of organizations providing research, education and advocacy*

**www.ncoa.org/nadsa/index.htm**

National Adult Day Services Association
*The adult day services branch of the National Council on the Aging*

# Appendix B

# Sample Long-Term Care Policy

T his appendix contains a sample long-term care health policy that represents a typical policy issued by long-term care insurers in the United States. It reflects the standard language and provisions found in actual policies.

# XYZ Insurance Company

**THIS POLICY IS INTENDED TO BE A QUALIFIED LONG-TERM CARE INSURANCE CONTRACT UNDER THE FEDERAL TAX CODE.**

We are pleased to issue this Long-Term Care Insurance Policy to you. It was issued in consideration of Your application and payment of the required premium. We suggest You carefully read it.

### GUARANTEED RENEWABLE FOR LIFE
### PREMIUMS SUBJECT TO CHANGE

Your policy will remain in effect during Your lifetime as long as each premium is paid on time. We cannot cancel or refuse to renew Your policy. We cannot change Your policy without Your consent. However, We may change the premium rates. Any change will apply to all policies in the same class as Yours in the state where the policy was issued. We will notify You in writing 31 days before Your premium changes. Coverage begins and ends at 12:01 a.m. Standard Time at Your residence. Your policy provides a refund of unearned premium when We are notified of Your death. A refund of unearned premium will not be made for any other reason.

### 30-DAY REVIEW PERIOD

If You feel this policy does not meet Your insurance needs, return it to Us or Your agent within 30 days after You have received it. We will return Your premium and consider the policy never to have been issued.

### CHECK YOUR APPLICATION

**Caution: The issuance of this long-term insurance policy is based upon Your responses to the questions on Your application. A copy of Your application Is attached. If Your answers are Incorrect or untrue, We have the right to deny benefits or rescind Your policy. The best time to clear up any questions Is now, before a claim arises! If, for any reason, any of Your answers are incorrect, contact XYZ at (800) 555-2525 or write to us at 4321 North Nonesuch Road, Fauxville, MO 94519-1001.**

### NOTICE TO BUYER

**This policy may not cover all of the costs associated with long-term care incurred by You during the period of coverage. You are advised to review carefully all policy limitations.**

SIGNED FOR THE XYZ INSURANCE COMPANY

Signature of
Senior Operations Officer

COUNTERSIGNED BY_____
Licensed Resident Agent (where required by law)

# POLICY SCHEDULE

This policy schedule provides You with specific information about the product You selected. It tells You which benefits You choose and how much they will cost. General policy information is also provided.

## BENEFITS

| | |
|---|---|
| Elimination Period per Lifetime................................................ | 30 Days |
| Maximum Daily Home and Adult Day Care Benefit .......................... | $     50 |
| Maximum Daily Facility Benefit ................................................ | $    100 |
| Maximum Lifetime Benefit....................................................... | $146,000 |

This Policy Does Not Include a Nonforfeiture Benefit

## OPTIONAL BENEFITS

| | |
|---|---|
| Compound Automatic Increase Benefit Rider............................................ | Included |

## PREMIUM SUMMARY

| | |
|---|---|
| Total Annual Premium Before Discounts................................................ | $1,346.80 |
| Total Annual Premium Less Spouse and/or Group Discounts ................................. | $1,212.12 |
| Mode of Payment ................................................................................ | Annual |
| Renewal Premium Based on Mode of Payment................................................ | $1,212.12 |

## GENERAL POLICY INFORMATION

| | |
|---|---|
| Policy Number ................................................................................ | 1234567 |
| Effective Date of Coverage ................................................................ | July 1, 1997 |
| First Renewal Date............................................................................ | July 1, 1998 |
| Name of Insured................................................................................ | John A. Doe |

## GUIDE TO YOUR LONG-TERM CARE POLICY

**The following is a Guide to Your Long-Term Care Policy. It tells You what is included in Your policy and on what page(s) You can find it.**

6

## SECTION 1: DEFINITIONS OF IMPORTANT TERMS

**This section provides the meaning of special terms used throughout this policy. The first letter of each word or words in a phrase is capitalized to help You easily recognize them wherever they appear in the policy.**

### THE FOLLOWING DEFINITIONS REFER TO THOSE INVOLVED IN THE CONTRACT

**WE, OUR, US**

The XYZ Insurance Company,
4231 North Nonesuch Road,
Fauxville, MO 94519-1001

**YOU, YOUR, YOURSELF**

The insured named in the Policy Schedule.

### THE FOLLOWING DEFINITIONS RELATE TO THE ELIGIBILITY FOR BENEFITS

**HOME AND COMMUNITY-BASED CARE**

Qualified Long-Term Care which is provided:

1. in a Home Convalescent Unit by a Home Health Care Agency; or

2. in an Alternate Care Facility; or

3. in an Adult Day Care facility.

**QUALIFIED LONG-TERM CARE**

Necessary diagnostic, preventive, therapeutic, curing, treating, mitigating, and rehabilitative services, and Maintenance or Personal Services, which:

1. are required by a Chronically ill individual, and

2. are provided pursuant to a Plan of Care prescribed by a Licensed Health Care Practitioner.

**HOME CONVALESCENT UNIT**

1. Your home;

2. a private home;

3. a home for the retired or aged;

4. a place which provides residential care; or

5. a section of a nursing facility providing only residential care.

It does not mean a hospital.

**HOME HEALTH CARE AGENCY**

An entity that provides home health care or hospice services and:

1. has an agreement as a provider of home health care services or hospice care under the Medicare program; or

2. is licensed or accredited by state law as a Home Health Care Agency or hospice, if such licensing or accreditation is required by the state in which the care is received.

For purposes of this policy, a licensed therapist, a registered nurse, a licensed practical nurse, or a licensed vocational nurse operating within the scope of his or her license will be considered a Home Health Care Agency.

**ALTERNATE CARE FACILITY**

A facility that is engaged primarily in providing ongoing care and related services to inpatients in one location and meets all of the following criteria:

1. provides 24 hour a day care and services sufficient to support needs resulting from inability to perform Activities of Daily Living or Cognitive Impairment; and

2. has a trained and ready to respond employee on duty at all times to provide that care; and

3. provides 3 meals a day and accommodates dates special dietary needs; and

4. is licensed or accredited by the appropriate agency to provide such care, if such licensing or accreditation is required by the state in which the care is received; and

5. has formal arrangements for the services of a physician or nurse to furnish medical care in case of emergency; and

6. has appropriate methods and procedures for handling and administering drugs and biologicals.

These requirements are typically met by hospice care facilities or assisted living facilities that are either free standing facilities or part of a life-care

9

community. They may also be met by some personal care and adult congregate care facilities. They are generally NOT met by individual residences or independent living units.

An Alternate Care Facility does not mean a Long-Term Care Facility, hospital or clinic, boarding home, or a place which operates primarily for the treatment of alcoholics or drug addicts. However, care or services provided in these facilities may be covered subject to the conditions of the Alternate Plan of Care Benefit provision.

**ADULT DAY CARE**

A community-based group program that provides health, social, and related support services in a facility which is licensed or certified by the state as an Adult Day Care Center to impaired adults. It does not mean 24-hour care.

**MAINTENANCE OR PERSONAL SERVICES**

Any care the primary purpose of which is the provision of needed assistance with any of the disabilities as a result of which You are Chronically ill (including the protection from threats to health and safety due to severe Cognitive Impairment).

**CHRONICALLY ILL**

Certified by a Licensed Health Care Practitioner as:

1. being unable to perform (without substantial assistance from another individual) at least 2 Activities of Daily Living for a period of at least 90 days due to a loss of functional capacity, or

2. requiring substantial supervision to protect Yourself from threats to health and safety due to severe Cognitive Impairment.

You will not be considered Chronically ill for any period unless within the 12 months prior to such period a Licensed Health Care Practitioner has certified that You meet the above requirements.

**PLAN OF CARE**

A program of care and treatment:

1. initiated by and approved in writing by a Licensed Health Care Practitioner before the start of such care and treatment; and

2. confirmed in writing at least once every 60 days.

**LICENSED HEALTH CARE PRACTITIONER**

Any physician, registered professional nurse, or licensed social worker.

**ACTIVITIES OF DAILY LIVING (ADLS)**

The Activities of Daily Living are:

1. Eating. Feeding Yourself by getting food into Your body from a receptacle (such as a plate, cup or table) or by a feeding tube or intravenously.

2. Dressing. Putting on and taking off all items of clothing and any necessary braces, fasteners, or artificial limbs.

3. Bathing. Washing Yourself by sponge bath; or in either a tub or shower, including the task of getting in or out of the tub or shower.

4. Toileting. Getting to and from the toilet, getting on and off the toilet, and performing associated personal hygiene.

5. Transferring. Moving into or out of a bed, chair, or wheelchair.

6. Continence. The ability to maintain control of bowel and bladder function; or, when unable to maintain control of bowel or bladder function, the ability to perform associated personal hygiene, including caring for a catheter or colostomy bag.

**COGNITIVE IMPAIRMENT**

A deficiency in Your short- or long-term memory, orientation as to person, place and time, deductive or abstract reasoning, or judgment as it relates to safety awareness.

**MEDICAL HELP SYSTEM**

A communication system, located in your home, used to summon medical attention in case of a medical emergency.

**INFORMAL CAREGIVER**

The person who has the primary responsibility of caring for You in Your Home Convalescent Unit. A person who is paid for caring for You cannot be an Informal Caregiver.

**CAREGIVER TRAINING**

Training provided by a Home Health Care Agency, Long-Term Care Facility, or hospital and received by the Informal Caregiver to care for You in Your residence.

**RESPITE CARE**

Qualified Long-Term Care, provided by or through a Long-Term Care Facility, Alternate Care Facility, or Home Health Care Agency, to temporarily relieve the Informal Caregiver.

**LONG TERM CARE FACILITY**

A place which:

1. is licensed by the state where it is located; and

2. provides skilled, intermediate, or custodial nursing care on an inpatient basis under the supervision of a physician; and

3. has 24-hour-a-day nursing services provided by or under the supervision of a registered nurse (R.N.), licensed vocational nurse (L.V.N.), or licensed practical nurse (L.P.N.), and

4. keeps a daily medical record of each patient; and

5. may be either a freestanding facility or a distinct part of a facility such as a ward, wing, unit, or swing-bed of a hospital or other institution.

A Long-Term Care Facility does not mean a hospital or clinic, boarding home, a place which operates primarily for the treatment of alcoholics or drug addicts, or a hospice. However, care or services provided in these facilities may be covered subject to the conditions of the Alternate Plan of Care Benefit provision.

**PREEXISTING CONDITION**

A health condition for which You received medical advice or treatment within the 6 months before Your Effective Date of Coverage.

**EFFECTIVE DATE OF COVERAGE**

The date when coverage starts under Your policy. It is shown on the Policy Schedule.

**ELIMINATION PERIOD**

The number of days in which covered Qualified Long-Term Care services are provided to You before this policy begins to pay benefits. It is shown on the Policy Schedule and can be satisfied by any combination of days of a Long-Term Care Facility stay or days of Home and Community-Based Care. These days of care or services need not be continuous but must be accumulated within a continuous period of 730 days. This Elimination Period has to be satisfied only once while Your policy is in effect.

**MAXIMUM LIFETIME BENEFIT**

The total amount We will pay in Your lifetime for all benefits provided by Your policy. Your Maximum Lifetime Benefit is shown on the Policy Schedule.

## SECTION 2: BENEFITS

**This section provides the following information about Your policy:**

1. **Your Benefits under this policy;**

2. **The conditions under which You will receive benefits;**

3. **How long You can receive benefits.**

## GENERAL BENEFIT INFORMATION

**WHAT IS IN THE POLICY SCHEDULE**

The Policy Schedule shows You the Elimination Period, the Maximum Daily Home and Adult Day Care Benefit, the Maximum Daily Facility Benefit, and the Maximum Lifetime Benefit. It also includes optional benefit information, if applicable, and premium and general policy information.

**LIMITATIONS OR CONDITIONS ON ELIGIBILITY BENEFITS**

Except where otherwise stated, no benefits under Your policy will be paid:

1. for any services You receive or expenses You incur unless:

   (a) such services are required because You are Chronically ill; and

   (b) You satisfy the Elimination Period; and

2. in excess of the Maximum Lifetime Benefit

**WHAT HAPPENS IF YOU TERMINATE YOUR POLICY**

If you terminate Your policy, it will not affect any claim beginning before such termination. We will continue to provide benefits, subject to all of the provisions of Your policy, until You have not received Qualified Long-Term Care for at least 180 consecutive days.

**COVERAGE FOR ALZHEIMER'S DISEASE**

Your policy provides benefits, subject to all of its provisions, for nervous or mental disorders of organic origin, including Alzheimer's Disease or senile dementia, which are determined by clinical diagnosis or tests.

**NO NEED FOR HOSPITALIZATION**

You are not required to be hospitalized before receiving benefits under Your policy.

## HOME AND COMMUNITY-BASED CARE BENEFITS

**WHAT IS THE HOME AND COMMUNITY BASED CARE BENEFIT AND HOW DOES IT WORK**

Each day You require Home and Community Based Care, We will pay benefits as follows:

A. For Qualified Long-Term Care received in a Home Convalescent Unit or Adult Day Care center, the lesser of:

1. The Maximum Daily Home and Adult Day Care Benefit; or

2. The total of:

   a. The expenses incurred for occupational, physical, respiratory, or speech therapy; or nursing care services provided by a registered nurse (R.N.) or a licensed practical or vocational nurse (L.P.N. or L.V.N.), and

   b. The expenses incurred for services provided by a medical social worker, home health aide, homemaker and similar services; and

   c. The expenses incurred for Adult Day Care.

B. For Qualified Long-Term Care received in an Alternate Care Facility, including room and board, the lesser of:

1. The Maximum Daily Facility Benefit shown in the Schedule, or

2. The expenses incurred for such care.

We will pay for up to 21 days of Respite Care per calendar year as follows:

A. For Respite Care provided by a Long-Term Care Facility or Alternate Care Facility, the lesser of:

1. The Maximum Daily Facility Benefit shown in the Schedule, or

2. The expenses incurred for each day of such care.

B. For Respite Care received in a Home Convalescent Unit or Adult Day Care facility, the lesser of:

1. The Maximum Daily Home and Adult Day Care Benefit, or

2. The expenses incurred for each day of such care.

The Elimination Period does not apply to this benefit and days of Respite Care will not be used to satisfy the Elimination Period. Unused days cannot be carried over into the next calendar year. The total We will pay for Home and Community-Based Care, including Respite Care services, received in a day will not exceed the Maximum Daily Home and Adult Day Care Benefit.

**MEDICAL HELP BENEFIT**

We will pay the actual expense You incur each month, up to 25 percent of the Maximum Daily Home and Adult Day Care Benefit, for up to 12 months in Your lifetime, for the rental or lease of a Medical Help System for Your home during a Plan of Care. We will only pay the Medical Help Benefit for a system installed in Your home while Your policy is in effect.

We will not pay for any charges for normal telephone service while the system is installed or for a home security system.

**CAREGIVER TRAINING BENEFIT**

If You require Qualified Long-Term Care, We will pay 100 percent of the expenses incurred for Caregiver Training, not to exceed 5 times the Maximum Daily Home and Adult Day Care Benefit during a Plan of Care. The Elimination Period does not apply to this benefit.

If You require a stay in a Long-Term Care Facility or are hospitalized, the Caregiver Training Benefit will only be payable if the training will make it possible for You to return to or remain in a Home Convalescent Unit where You can be cared for by the Informal Caregiver.

## LONG TERM CARE FACILITY BENEFIT

**WHAT IS THE LONG-TERM CARE FACILITY BENEFIT AND HOW DOES IT WORK**

If You require Qualified Long-Term Care in a Long-Term Care Facility, for each day of Your stay We will pay the lesser of:

1. The Maximum Daily Facility Benefit, or

2. The charges made by the Long-Term Care Facility for Your Qualified Long-Term Care, including room and board.

**BED RESERVATION BENEFIT**

We will continue to pay the Long-Term Care Facility Benefit when You are charged for Your room in a Long-Term Care Facility while You are temporarily absent during the course of Your Long Term Care Facility stay. This Bed Reservation Benefit will be limited to 21 days per calendar year. Unused days cannot be carried over into the next calendar year. Such days may be used to satisfy the Elimination Period.

## WAIVER OF PREMIUM BENEFIT

**WHEN WILL PREMIUM BE WAIVED**

After You receive 12 days of covered Qualified Long-Term Care, We will waive or refund premium on a quarterly basis. Such waiver or refund will:

1. begin on the next day that coincides with the same day of the month as Your Effective Date of Coverage; and

2. continue for each subsequent 3-month period as long as You receive at least 12 days of covered care or services in the prior 3-month period. The initial 12 days of covered care or services need not be consecutive, but they must be incurred within a 3-month period.

Days You are hospitalized or days used to satisfy the Elimination Period can be used to satisfy the qualifications for this benefit.

**WHEN WILL PREMIUM NOT BE WAIVED**

You must pay the premium for any 3-month period that follows a 3-month period in which You received less than 12 days of covered care or services. We will notify You of the amount due and the date it is due.

When You have not received covered care or services for 180 consecutive days, Your premiums will become due and payable on the same premium mode that was in effect prior to the start of this benefit. We will notify You of the amount due and the date it is due.

## ALTERNATE PLAN OF CARE BENEFIT

**WHAT IS THE ALTERNATE PLAN OF CARE BENEFIT AND HOW DOES IT WORK**

If You would otherwise require a Long-Term Care Facility stay under a Plan of Care, We may pay for alternate services, devices or types of care under a written Alternate Plan of Care, if such plan is medically acceptable. This Alternate Plan of Care:

1. must be agreed to by You, Your physician, and Us; and

2. will be developed by or with Licensed Health Care Professionals.

Any plan, including the benefit levels to be payable, may be adopted, as long as it is mutually agreeable to You, Your physician and Us. The Company is not obligated to provide benefits for services received prior to such agreement.

Agreement to participate in an Alternate Plan of Care will not waive any of Your or Our rights under the policy.

Any benefits payable under this provision will count against the Maximum Lifetime Benefit.

This plan may specify special treatments or different sites or levels of care. Some of the services You may receive may differ from those otherwise covered by Your policy. In this case, benefits will be paid at the levels specified and agreed to in the Alternate Plan of Care.

## SECTION 3: EXCLUSIONS AND LIMITATIONS

**This section tells You under what circumstances benefits are not payable even if You would otherwise qualify for benefits under another section of this policy.**

**WHEN THIS POLICY WILL NOT PROVIDE BENEFITS**

This policy will not pay benefits for any care or services which are:

1. provided without charge in the absence of insurance; or

2. due to a condition for which You can receive benefits under Workers' Compensation or the Occupational Disease Act or Law; or

3. due to mental, psychoneurotic, or personality disorders without evidence of organic disease (Alzheimer's Disease and senile dementia are not excluded from coverage); or

4. the result of war or any act of war; or

5. a. reimbursable under title XVIII of the Social Security Act (Medicare) or would be so reimbursable but for the application of a deductible or coinsurance amount; or

   b. reimbursable under any other federal, or state health care plan or law, except Medicaid.

We will reduce Our benefits payable by the dollar amount paid from the government health care plan or law to the extent that the combination of Our coverage and governmental coverage exceeds 100 percent of the actual charge for the covered services.

**PREEXISTING CONDITION LIMITATION**

We will not pay for a loss due to a Preexisting Condition which You did not disclose in the application unless the loss begins more than 6 months after the Effective Date of Coverage. However, providing incorrect information may cause Your policy to be voided.

If this policy replaces another long-term care insurance policy, the 6-month time period above is waived to the extent it was satisfied under the replaced policy.

Losses due to Preexisting Conditions shown on the application are covered immediately.

## SECTION 4: CLAIMS

**This section tells You:**

1. **How to notify Us of a claim;**

2. **How to file a claim;**

3. **When to file a claim;**

4. **When and how claims are paid;**

5. **Our rights in investigating a claim;**

6. **What happens to a claim if Your age is stated incorrectly on the application; and**

7. **Your legal rights regarding claims.**

**NOTIFYING US OF A CLAIM**

You must notify Us in writing of a claim within 30 days after a covered loss begins, or as soon as reasonably possible.

The notice must identify You and be sent to Us at Our Home Office, XYZ Insurance Company, 4321 Nonesuch Road, Fauxville, MO 94519-1001 or Your agent.

**HOW TO FILE A CLAIM**

We will send You a claim form within 15 days after We receive notice of Your claim. If We do not, You can meet the requirements of providing Us with a written proof of loss by sending Us a written statement describing the type and nature of Your loss.

**WHEN TO FILE A CLAIM**

You must send Us written proof of loss within 90 days after the end of the period for which You are claiming benefits.

If this is not possible, Your claim will not be affected. However, unless You are legally incapable, You must notify Us within one year from the time proof is otherwise required.

**CARE MANAGEMENT SERVICES**

During Your claim, We can, with Your agreement, provide You with access to care management professionals who can work with You, Your family, and Your doctor to determine and monitor the appropriate plan of care, including assessments of Your situations and investigation of available care resources. This service will be provided with no cost to You and will not count against your benefit limits.

**WHEN YOUR CLAIM IS PAID**

We will pay Your claim immediately after We receive due written proof of loss.

**HOW CLAIMS ARE PAID**

We will pay benefits to You, or Your estate, unless You have requested in writing that payment be made otherwise.

If benefits are payable to Your estate, We may pay up to $1,000 to any relative of Yours We feel is entitled to the benefits. Any payments made in good faith will discharge Us to the extent of the payment.

**OUR RIGHTS TO OBTAIN INFORMATION**

At Our expense, We have the right to have a physician or, other qualified medical personnel examine You or obtain an assessment of Your impairment as often as reasonably necessary while You are receiving benefits.

**MISSTATEMENT OF YOUR AGE**

If Your age has been misstated on the application, Your policy benefits will be based on the amount Your premium would have purchased at Your correct age. If We would not have issued a policy, We will refund the premium You paid.

**LIMITATIONS ON LEGAL ACTIONS**

You cannot sue or bring legal action against Us:

1. before 60 days after We receive written proof of loss; or

2. more than three years after written proof of loss is required.

## SECTION 5: PREMIUM PAYMENT AND REINSTATEMENT OF YOUR POLICY

**This section tells you:**

**1. When Your premium should be paid;**

**2. What happens if Your premium is not paid within a certain time period;**

**3. What happens to Your premium at Your death; and**

**4. How to reinstate Your policy if it is terminated.**

**PAYING PREMIUMS**

Premiums are to be paid with United States currency. They are due at the beginning of each policy term. Payment may be made to Us at Our Home Office at XYZ Insurance Company, 4321 North Nonesuch Road, Fauxville, MO 94519-1001, or to Your agent. You can change the policy term if You notify Us in writing.

**WHAT HAPPENS WHEN PREMIUMS ARE NOT PAID**

Except as provided under the Unintentional Lapse Protection below, You are allowed a 31 day grace period for late payment of each premium due after the first premium. Your policy will remain in force during this period.

If You do not pay Your premium by the end of the grace period, the policy will terminate.

**UNINTENTIONAL LAPSE PROTECTION**

You have the right to designate an individual in addition to Yourself to receive notification when Your policy will terminate because of non-payment of premium.

We will give the person You designate notification of the impending termination at least 30 days before the date such termination will occur. The notice will be given to the designated person no earlier than 30 days after the premium due date.

On every renewal of Your policy, You will be given the right to change the designated person.

**WHAT HAPPENS TO YOUR PREMIUMS IF YOU DIE**

When We are notified of Your death, We will make a refund of any unearned premium paid for the period beyond Your death.

**PUTTING THE POLICY BACK IN FORCE**

If Your policy is terminated, a subsequent acceptance of premium by Us or by Our agent without requiring an application for reinstatement will reinstate Your policy.

If We do require an application for reinstatement and accept Your premium, We may issue a conditional premium receipt. If We approve Your application, Your policy will be reinstated as of the date of Our approval. If We do not approve Your application, We will notify You in writing within 45 days after the date of Your application.

If We do not notify You within 45 days, the policy will be reinstated on the 45th day after the date of the conditional premium receipt.

The reinstated policy will cover only losses due to conditions that begin after the date of reinstatement. In all other aspects, Your rights and Ours will be the same as before the policy terminated, unless there are new provisions added due to the reinstatement. The premium We accept for reinstatement may be used for the period for which premiums had not been paid. We can apply the premium back for as many as 60 days before the date of reinstatement.

**PUTTING THE POLICY BACK IN FORCE AFTER NONPAYMENT OF PREMIUM DUE TO COGNITIVE IMPAIRMENT OR FUNCTIONAL INCAPACITY**

Also, within 6 months following termination of Your policy for non-payment of premium, You, or any person authorized to act on Your behalf, may request reinstatement of Your policy on the basis that You suffered from Cognitive Impairment or functional incapacity, or if You would otherwise qualify for benefits under the policy, at the time of policy termination.

We will require evidence of clinical diagnosis or tests demonstrating that You suffered from Cognitive Impairment or functional incapacity at the time of policy termination. If such demonstration substantiates, to our satisfaction, the existence of Cognitive Impairment or functional incapacity at the time of policy termination, We will reinstate Your policy. The clinical diagnosis and tests will be at Your expense. Functional incapacity means the Inability to Perform at least Two Activities of Daily Living.

If We reinstate Your policy after nonpayment of premium due to Cognitive Impairment, or functional incapacity:

1. This reinstatement shall not require any evidence of insurability.

2. The reinstated policy shall cover loss occurring from the date of policy cancellation. There shall be no gaps in coverage. Coverage will be at the level provided prior to reinstatement.

3. Premium shall be paid from the date of the last premium payment at the rate which would have been in effect had the policy remained in force. Payment must be made within 15 days following Our request.

## SECTION 6: THE CONTRACT

**This section tells You:**

**1. What makes up the contract;**

**2. Situations where time limits apply to claims**

**WHAT MAKES UP THE CONTRACT**

This policy is a legal, binding contract between You and Us. The contract is made up of:

1. the policy;

2. the application; and

3. any attached papers.

No one can change any part of this policy or waive any of its provisions unless the change is approved in writing on the policy by one of Our officers.

**IMPORTANCE OF INFORMATION ON THE APPLICATION/TIME LIMIT ON CERTAIN DEFENSES**

We issued this policy based on information You provided. Any incorrect or omitted information known to You at the time of application may cause Your policy to be voided or a claim to be denied.

If Your policy has been in force for less than six (6) months, We may rescind it or deny any otherwise valid claim upon a showing of misrepresentation that is material to the acceptance of coverage.

If Your policy has been in force for at least six (6) months but less than two (2) years, We may rescind it or deny any otherwise valid claim upon a showing of misrepresentation that is both material to the acceptance of coverage and which pertains to the conditions for which benefits are sought.

After Your policy has been in force for 2 years, only fraudulent misstatements in the application can be used to void the policy or deny a claim for loss incurred after the 2-year period.

If We have paid benefits under this policy, such benefit payments may not be recovered by Us in the event that Your policy is rescinded.

# XYZ Insurance Company

## SIMPLE AUTOMATIC INCREASE BENEFIT RIDER

In consideration of the additional premium of _____, it is agreed that the following benefit is added to Your policy.

## SIMPLE AUTOMATIC INCREASE BENEFIT

**WHAT IS THE SIMPLE AUTOMATIC INCREASE BENEFIT**

On each anniversary of Your policy Effective Date of Coverage, the benefits provided in Your policy will be increased as follows:

1. Maximum Daily Facility Benefit

   This benefit amount will be increased by a fixed amount of 5 percent of the Maximum Daily Facility Benefit shown in the Policy Schedule.

2. Maximum Daily Home and Adult Day Care Benefit

   This benefit limit will be increased by a fixed amount of 5 percent of the Maximum Daily Home and Adult Day Care Benefit shown in the Policy Schedule.

3. Maximum Lifetime Benefit

   The Maximum Lifetime Benefit defined in Your policy is replaced by the following:

   The Maximum Lifetime Benefit on the current anniversary date is the Maximum Lifetime Benefit on the previous anniversary date, increased by an amount equal to the Remaining Maximum Lifetime Benefit multiplied by the Increase Factor.

   The Remaining Maximum Lifetime Benefit is the Maximum Lifetime Benefit on the previous anniversary date less the total of all claims paid to the current anniversary date.

**THIS OPTION IS NOT AVAILABLE IN ALL STATES.**

The Increase Factor is the proportionate increase in Your daily benefit amount from the previous anniversary date to the current anniversary date.

Annual increases will occur even if benefits are being paid.

This rider takes effect _____ and ends at the same time as the policy to which it is attached. It is subject to the definitions, limitations, and provisions of the policy which are consistent with the rider.

**SIGNED FOR THE XYZ INSURANCE COMPANY**

_____          _____
        Chairman of the Board                                          Secretary